I Just Made the Tea

Tales from 30 years inside Formula 1

Di Spires

with Bernard Ferguson

**Forewords by Murray Walker OBE
and Michael Schumacher**

Haynes Publishing

© Diana Spires and Bernard Ferguson 2012

Published in June 2012
This paperback edition published in June 2013

A catalogue record for this book is available from the British Library

ISBN 978 0 85733 392 6

Library of Congress control card no 2013932264

Published by Haynes Publishing,
Sparkford, Yeovil, Somerset BA22 7JJ, UK
Tel: 01963 442030 Fax: 01963 440001
Int. tel: +44 1963 442030 Int. fax: +44 1963 440001
E-mail: sales@haynes.co.uk
Website: www.haynes.co.uk

Haynes North America Inc.,
861 Lawrence Drive, Newbury Park, California 91320, USA

Designed and typeset by Dominic Stickland

Printed and bound in the USA by Odcombe Press LP,
1299 Bridgestone Parkway, La Vergne, TN 37086

Cover illustrations
Front Artwork by Julian Kirk.
Back Di Spires celebrating her birthday with her two favourite drivers – Ayrton Senna and Elio de Angelis.

CONTENTS

FOREWORD BY MURRAY WALKER OBE

Motorsport is a wonderful world of achievers – drivers, team owners, race officials, sponsors, engineers, mechanics and media people, to list but a few. If you are fortunate enough to have one of Bernie Ecclestone's magic passes which give you access to the paddock, you very soon come to realise how privileged you are, because it makes you part of a world where everyone is fiercely competitive but, at the same time, very friendly. There's a warm feeling of belonging and being at the centre of it all, which is cemented by the time happily spent in the various teams' motorhomes, luxuriating in their hospitality and savouring the gossip!

If you did the job I was lucky enough to do you were welcome in all of them, but the one that everyone wanted to go to most of all was the one run by Stuart and Di Spires. In Formula 1 and at the World Rally Championship that meant Benetton and Ford (and latterly at Bridgestone test sessions). You knew that you'd be greeted by two of the nicest and most human people in the paddock, and that there'd be a wonderful breakfast, an equally enjoyable lunch, a cup of tea, a juicy bit of information – or all four! Stuart and Di are very special people, and I regard myself as honoured to be able to call them my friends, as do Michael Schumacher, Johnny Herbert, Nelson Piquet, Bernie himself and so many more.

So it's good to know that Di has finally written her book.

There have been plenty of books by drivers and various other Formula 1 people but, unless I'm very much mistaken, none by one of those warm, friendly people from the motorhomes who keep us all going. No one knew the Formula 1 and World Rally scenes better than Di, but if she is really going to tell us everything she knows about us I hope she's got a good lawyer!

Murray Walker OBE

FOREWORD BY MICHAEL SCHUMACHER

My first encounter with Di was somewhat embarrassing. I had just entered Formula 1, 20 years ago, and after a long day of driving and briefings I was hungry and searching for something to eat, so I knocked at the kitchen door of the Benetton hospitality. I was told to just ask for 'Mum', which I did, feeling stupid that very moment. Hey, I had never seen that woman before, so I expected a rather unpleasant reaction. Instead, what I got was a warm smile – and I very quickly got used to calling Di 'Mum' without any feeling of embarrassment. Not only because I understood that nearly everybody in the paddock called her this, but more so because she and Stuart were caring for me so much during my Benetton time that I really saw them as parents, somehow.

I like to look back to those early years, even if I am sometimes shocked about how time has passed so quickly. I remember us sitting together in the motorhome, or even once in the house where they stay in the south of France where Mum and Dad had invited Corinna and me for dinner. I am still convinced their nicknames were the perfect match for them.

I am sure this book is as enjoyable to read as were the evenings we were having fun together.

Michael Schumacher

PROLOGUE

It was Thursday, 5 September 1991, at Italy's Monza race circuit. I was in the kitchen of the Benetton motorhome, making flasks of tea for the mechanics working hard to set up the garage for that weekend's Formula 1 Grand Prix, when there was a knock at the door. I looked out and saw a chubby-cheeked, curly-haired chap standing there, looking in.

As I opened the door he said, 'Are you Mum?'

'I could be. Why, who told you to say that?'

'Johnny Herbert.'

'I'm Mum, then,' I said, still feeling a little puzzled.

'Well, here I am,' the young man said, smiling nervously and shifting his weight from foot to foot expectantly. Still confused I asked him, 'What's your name? Have you come to see someone?'

Amused, he looked at me and said, 'I'm Michael Schumacher, your new driver.'

Fast forward to Valencia, at the first official test of the 2010 Formula 1 season. I was outside the Bridgestone motorhome talking to a photographer when a silver Mercedes pulled up nearby. I was still talking and hadn't taken much notice when I heard a familiar voice shouting to me, 'Mum! Mum! Di!' When I looked up it was Michael. Getting out of his car, he came straight over and hugged me; it was wonderful because he was coming back to Formula 1 after three years in retirement.

'You're back then, Michael,' was all I could say, and he replied enigmatically, 'I have opened the second chapter which will round up everything.'

I'm not quite sure who first referred to Stuart and me as 'Mum' and 'Dad', but it wasn't long after we started in motorsport. By that time we had decided we didn't want to have any children, so it's amazing to think that after all these years we have now become 'Mum' and 'Dad' to hundreds.

Our story is their story.

Chapter 1

WE'RE OFF AND RUNNING — SOMETIMES!

I could tell by the look on his face that it was bad news. 'That's it, then,' Stuart said, as he put the phone down. 'They don't want us; they've given it to another couple.'

We avoided making eye contact, knowing that our hopes had been dashed for the second time.

'Did he say why?' I asked.

'He said the other couple spoke some European languages and that just gave them the edge.' It had been a nail-biting time waiting for the outcome of an interview and now we were gutted, as this had been our second attempt at getting into Formula 1 and we had missed out again.

My mother died when I was quite young so my brother Garry had to keep an eye on me while Dad was at work, which meant I had to tag along wherever he and his friends went. Garry and his mates enjoyed any kind of racing, so my trips out with them included sporting events like scrambling (now motocross), or if someone in the group could lay his hands on a car it would involve a visit to a motor racing event, generally at Silverstone as that was the closest circuit to home.

When Stuart and I met some time later we found we both had an interest in motorsport – in fact Stu had probably been visiting the same events as we had a few years previously. Stu's family were 'better off' than mine as they actually had a car, which made it easier for him to take in more events. By the time we met Stuart had his own car, and one of our first outings together was inevitably to Silverstone with a group of his friends. We all used to camp, whatever the weather, and we thoroughly enjoyed ourselves, but we were always peering longingly through the fence into the paddock area.

The next step was to buy a VW van and convert it into a camper, as this allowed us to travel further afield to such places as Zolder, Zandvoort, Dijon and the Nürburgring. We loved the racing environment and we had a growing determination to turn our interest into a job; by the mid-1970s we were convinced that we would make it happen, whatever it took. We weren't sure what we were actually going to do, but we were definitely going to do it!

In 1976 'hospitality' in Formula 1 had only just started and it certainly wasn't what it is now. Fundamentally, the job was to provide barbecued meals out of the back of a van. The concept of Formula 1 hospitality had first come to our attention at the Belgian Grand Prix in Zolder in May of that year. We were fans of Hesketh Racing and became friends with someone working for the team who was kind enough to get us into the paddock, which was much easier then than it is now. We saw this couple cooking on a little round barbecue outside the Lotus motorhome, and when we asked our friend who they were and whether they were members of the team, he said, 'Yes, but their job is to drive the motorhome and do the cooking.'

We decided there and then that we'd found what we were looking for: our route into Formula 1. The only problem was that neither Stu nor I had ever done any catering before! Still, that was only a minor problem with a career at stake. From then on we took every opportunity we could to get into the paddock to try to understand what was required and to decide how to set ourselves up.

We didn't have any real contacts and no clue as to how to set about getting involved in the business, but we placed an advert in the premier motorsport weekly magazine, *Autosport*. No one was more surprised than us when we were lucky enough to get an interview with a man called Rod Campbell, in the front room of his house near Oxford. At that time Rod was PR and marketing supremo for Chesterfield cigarettes and he was working with a driver called Brett Lunger. The idea was that Brett would come into Formula 1 with a team to be called Chesterfield Racing. We were offered the job, but our euphoria was to be short lived as the team never materialised, a huge disappointment at the time. Incidentally, Rod went on to form Campbell and Company, which was the main PR agency for the Ford Motor Company. He became a millionaire and we didn't. Still, life's like that.

Undeterred, and now fully experienced at advertising in *Autosport*, we tried again in 1977 and were amazed to get a response once more, this time from Peter Warr, inviting us to an interview for Walter Wolf Racing where he was team manager. We went along for the interview in Reading and got down to the shortlist. The offer was £175 per week for the two of us and although, at that time, we were both earning good salaries compared with most people, we thought that it wouldn't be too bad because we'd have our expenses paid and our food provided as part of the deal when we were away. Peter had told us that he would be in touch in a couple of weeks as he had other couples to see.

The time dragged on and we thought we had been forgotten, but this had been the call we were waiting for – so now it was back to the day jobs.

I was a civil servant and Stuart was working for a company called Chloride Alcad, testing batteries. I worked for the Department of Employment, which also had links with the Advisory, Conciliation and Arbitration Service (better known as ACAS), established to mediate during industrial disputes.

As part of my role I had an office at British Leyland in their Longbridge factory, so I have always been involved with cars in a way. The reason we had a permanent office in the factory was because of the number of labour relations problems the company was experiencing. The main protagonists were the company and an influential communist trades union spokesman called Derek Robinson, or 'Red Robbo' as the tabloids loved to refer to him. 'Red Robbo' was the chief convenor of the Transport and General Workers' Union and had quite a reputation as a troublemaker. Actually, he and I got on very well. If he was in a good mood he called me 'Diana' and if we were in for a row he called me 'Mrs Spires', so I always had a pretty good idea how any meeting was going to go before it started. I used to sit in on the convenors' meetings, and other important activities, so it was a pretty interesting job. However, neither Stuart nor I were doing what we really wanted to do.

Two days after that disappointing phone call we received, as promised, a letter confirming that we hadn't got the job. Needless to say it had included the phrase 'we will keep your details on file in case any suitable opportunity arises' which, being in the employment service, I knew meant nothing at all.

How wrong can you be?

We must have made some kind of impression as, a short while later, Peter Warr went to a meeting that was also attended by John Surtees, and apparently they were talking about various things when the subject of hospitality came up. It seemed that John was looking for a new couple to take care of his hospitality motorhome as one of the people he employed at the time had become ill and couldn't travel. We found out later that Peter had told him he knew a really nice couple but he hadn't hired them as they didn't speak any other languages. He had hired an older pair who had travelled a lot and spoke French and German.

Following their meeting John got his team manager, Peter Briggs, to phone us, and he told us we had been recommended by Peter Warr and asked if we could go down to the Surtees

Racing factory in Kent for an interview. This was in April 1978, just before the season started, so naturally we jumped at the chance to go off to Edenbridge for the meeting, although by this time we were beginning to wonder if our Formula 1 dream would ever materialise. We were really focused after not getting the Walter Wolf job and I was so determined that, for some reason, I can even remember what Peter was wearing on the day: a bright green V-necked cableknit sweater and brown corduroy trousers. I suspect he doesn't really want to be reminded of that now.

The interview seemed to go quite well and Peter said he would let us know the following day. When Stuart was asked if he had ever driven any large vehicles he said, 'Well, I have driven vans, but nothing larger.' Laughing, Peter replied, 'That's no problem as the motorhome isn't much bigger than a van. Oh, and one other thing. You'll be living in it!' We had expected that, of course, and our travels in the converted VW had given us a bit of practice.

We asked if he could show us the motorhome before we left Edenbridge. 'Sorry, I can't,' he replied. 'It's at Silverstone. It's been there since the last race of last season because someone borrowed it and it broke down; it's been there for five months. By the way, the other thing is that the wage is £35 per week for the two of you.' On the way home we decided that, even if we got the job, there was no way we could accept as it wouldn't even pay the mortgage on the house we had moved into only six months earlier.

Peter phoned us the next day. 'I have been speaking to John and what we've decided is that we'd like you to start, and if Stuart is prepared to do the tyres and a bit of lap timing as well then we'll offer you £45 a week between you.'

We said that we would have to think about it and get back to him. We put the phone down and we did think about it, for about five seconds, then we just looked at each other and said, 'Well, we've got to do it, haven't we?' So we took the job and a cut of about £18,000 a year in our joint salary. We had to borrow money from Stuart's mum to pay the mortgage while we were away because there was no way we could afford it on £45 a week. For that amount Stuart was to be tyre man, pit-board signaller and general dogsbody on top of helping me out with the motorhome duties and doing the driving; his mum thought we were mad, but she supported us at the beginning and that allowed us to get started.

By that time it was late April and the first Grand Prix we were scheduled to attend was in Monaco, in May; to compound matters we were told we had to leave the UK on 1 May as there was a test at Circuit Paul Ricard at Le Castellet in the south of France before the Monaco Grand Prix. The next big issue was how to get around the problem of our existing jobs. Stuart just gave a week's notice and left, but not without featuring in the company's monthly magazine under the heading 'Hitting the road for a new challenge'.

I was supposed to give a month's notice as, at the time, I was in quite a senior position with 70 staff working for me. I went in on the Monday after the offer and told my area manager – who fortunately loved motorsport – that I was leaving.

'When?' he asked.

'Friday,' I replied, to which he said words to the effect of 'You can't', although expressed slightly more colourfully than that.

I explained that I could, as I had already worked out that I had three weeks' annual leave due and if I worked through that current week I could go on Friday. Having delivered that *fait accompli* I disappeared quickly, before he could argue. In fairness he didn't complain, but he did say, 'Just think, you are going to lose your pension and all your benefits.'

I didn't care. Our dream was about to become reality.

Chapter 2

REALITY BITES – OR AT LEAST NIBBLES

The dream turned into reality pretty quickly when we went to Silverstone to pick up the hospitality vehicle. To the technically minded it was a 23ft American Dodge Superior motorhome with a roll-out canopy. To the more practically minded it was far from superior; it was a mess. Stuart had never driven anything so big before, which didn't matter much because it wouldn't move. The dirty washing up was still in the sink from the year before and the place was overrun with mice. It had been sitting there for months in that condition.

'What have we done?' we thought. 'This is where we have to live while we travel round Europe catering for a race team and its guests.' A vehicle 23ft long may seem pretty large when you are driving it, but for living purposes it's minute. It had a tiny bedroom in the back, where we had to make up our bed, and a little kitchenette where we had to prepare the food for the team – and that was it. We had a roll-out awning for people to sit under to eat and we had to transport all the tables and chairs inside the truck; consequently, when we were on the road, it was loaded to the gunwales which made it almost impossible to get into our bed. This was apparent immediately, but what was slightly less clear was that we would break down on our way to or from every Grand Prix except one, which surprisingly was the furthest trip, distance-wise, between Jarama in Spain and Anderstorp in Sweden. It took us some time to realise that the cause of these breakdowns was the fact that the mice had sustained themselves over the previous winter by slowly chewing through the electric wiring. It wasn't clear which colour they liked best; they had tried them all.

Once we were part of the crew we realised that Team Surtees had what could be euphemistically called 'budget restrictions'. There was no money to refurbish the vehicle so we cleaned it up, got rid of most of the mice and we were ready to go. Or so we thought. We'd taken the motorhome to our house to load it up and when we parked on the street it still looked big – but when we tried to put our clothes in the wardrobe, which was about one foot wide, it seemed to have shrunk. It was a little like Doctor Who's Tardis, only in reverse: big on the outside and small inside. But finally we were ready to set off for Paul Ricard – our first experience of racing as insiders – and we were as excited as schoolkids on their first trip to the seaside.

The Surtees mechanics had given the motorhome a service of sorts before we set off, but bearing in mind these were British race mechanics and it was an American motorhome it wasn't the most thorough job ever because, as usual, everybody was in a rush. Consequently, having set off for Paul Ricard, we then broke down on a French motorway and never made it to the test. Being new, we didn't know how many days the test went on for, and back then there were no mobile phones so we couldn't contact the team to find out when they would be leaving for Monaco. By the time we got our reluctant Dodge going again, and eventually found the Paul Ricard circuit, everyone else had already left for the Grand Prix.

I remember we were going up the steep hill leading to the back of Monaco and we came upon the Lotus motorhome, which had broken down by the side of the road. Although we had never met these people before we thought that we should stop and see if we could help. They looked at us in a fairly suspicious fashion, obviously wondering who on earth we were. Lotus people thought themselves a little bit superior in those days. Mike and Ann Murphy were running the outfit at the time and Mike said to Ann, 'Look, I'll stay here. Will you go with them into Monaco and find the team manager and tell him we've broken down?' We took Ann aboard and when we got into town she jumped out as if we didn't exist, met up with Joe Ramirez, who was the Lotus team manager at the time, and left us to get on with it.

'What do we do now? We don't even know where to go or where to park!' I said to Stuart, never being one to avoid stating the obvious. There we were, completely overwhelmed, heading for our first working Grand Prix: we'd missed the test, we were in Monaco in the pitch dark, it was after midnight and we were completely shattered.

We'd been told by Peter Briggs that we would have to park on the harbour wall and we had followed the signs to the port. As we approached in the darkness we could just make out the other motorhomes lined up. It was pretty late by then and nobody seemed to be around; as we sat there assessing the situation and wondering where to park a voice from the gloom said, 'You're new, aren't you?'

'Yes, we've missed the test and broken down en route.'

'Oh well, you won't know where to park then, will you? Just put it over there and if anyone asks tell them that Bernie Ecclestone said it was all right!'

Bernie was with Brabham then, but he was still checking on things at midnight on the Tuesday before the Grand Prix. He'd obviously spotted that we were bemused by it all and stepped in. Even in 1978 he was on the case. Bernie has always been all right with us ever since – not exactly big buddies, but Stuart has always got on with him.

Starting our career in Monaco couldn't have been a bigger challenge. It was 10 May 1978, a date which will always be imprinted on my mind. I had always been a huge fan of the

Beatles so to find one of the first guests we ever had was George Harrison was absolutely mind blowing. As he came into the awning I tried to compose myself. 'What can I get you?' I asked, trying not to act like a stupid schoolgirl.

'I'd love a cup of tea, and you wouldn't have any Mr Kipling's Country Slices, would you?' To this day, whenever I see a Mr Kipling's Country Slice, I think of George Harrison. We met him a number of times after that but, like they say, 'You always remember the first time.'

That first Grand Prix was certainly a steep learning curve, but an amazing experience nevertheless.

After Monaco we slowly tried to get into the swing of things and learned as we went along. We were pretty naïve, really. We had never been out on a limb like that before, and we didn't speak any languages apart from a bit of school French, which wasn't much use in Germany or Spain (otherwise we might have earned £175 a week), but we quickly learnt the value of travelling with other people. Those of us motorhomers who had started at the same time got together and, as we were in the same situation and it was all brand new to all of us, we shared the good times and the bad times. Sometimes, sitting at the side of the road, we even shared the thought that we had made the biggest mistake of our lives.

In theory, we had a budget of around £300 per race weekend to buy food, look after the team and guests, and buy fuel, which wasn't exactly a king's ransom. However, there were times when Team Surtees didn't even have that. Consequently, we never had a big float of travelling money and we were often on a wing and a prayer with a few coppers in our pockets. Unlike today, when we broke down we had to find a phone box by the side of the road; otherwise we just had to ring the factory once a week to say we were alive and well. We had a garage service card, which Peter Briggs had been very quick to give us: the team's race trucks were sponsored by Van Hool of Belgium and Pete just told us to ring their number if we had any breakdowns.

Unfortunately that wasn't very helpful when we broke down in Spain or Portugal, but at least it got him off the hook when we had a problem. We broke down with monotonous regularity and we used to ring up saying, 'Pete, we've broken down again.'

'Oh well, you will sort it, won't you?' he'd say, and we did. Somehow we turned up at every Grand Prix, but I have no idea how we managed it.

The food we offered was a bit limited – nothing like today, or even 20 years ago. The guys had a cooked breakfast, but it took a while because we only had a little cooker that was smaller than a domestic hob, and a tiny oven, so we gave them bacon and egg sandwiches and tea out of a flask. Sometimes they may have had a bought-in pizza or something similar. It was all down to what we were able to serve, really. Often it was just sandwiches, but even trying to prepare those in the little kitchenette was pretty difficult. Fortunately the number of people travelling to races then was a fraction of what it is now. I have a photo showing the entire Surtees team: 14 of us, including the person who took the picture. However, those were the people who supported the fly-away or non-European races; for the European races the head count rocketed up to 20.

We carried a barbecue so that when the weather was good we could prepare the food outside among the fuel drums and all the other equipment, which was a relief because we could usually buy provisions to put on it. Some countries were a bit of a challenge for us, though, because I didn't know what exotic stuff like mozzarella cheese was then – not many people outside Italy did. We did have pasta over in England, but it was always spaghetti; we didn't know about all this other odd-shaped floppy stuff in bags. It would be easier if we had been starting now because everybody eats pasta, but back then the lads had never even seen it, they had no idea what it was and they definitely didn't want to eat it. For most of us at that time a prawn cocktail, Berni Inn steak and a schooner of sherry was the height of sophistication.

I was able to cook baked potatoes, but I could only fit six in the oven at once so the lads had to eat in relays in the evening, huddled in their coats. The awning sides had long since disintegrated, and with no cash available to replace them they stayed in tatters. When we could, we parked near the race trucks to get a bit of shelter. In those days the paddock was one big family and the motorhomers lent and borrowed between themselves. Sometimes, if the home next door wasn't doing an evening meal, I would borrow their oven so I could do 12 baked potatoes, which was a real breakthrough. They would do the same another evening.

Although it wasn't quite so regimented, the paddock layout was pretty similar in some respects to what it is now. The teams lined up based on their championship position from the previous season, which meant the successful teams were at one end while the less successful teams were right down at the other end. We were down the wrong end, as the Surtees team hadn't done very well; our little orange and white Dodge didn't look too superior and certainly didn't stand comparison with the best of the motorhomes, belonging to McLaren, way up at the top end of the paddock. Some things never change. I remember pulling up at Zolder that first season and we were still a bit in awe – we had watched all these Grands Prix and to think we were now actually part of it was very intimidating. Just like today, when we arrived at the circuit we had to park in the corner of the paddock until someone told us where to go. We'd parked in front of the McLaren hospitality truck and Bob McMurray, who is now a close friend, came rushing out and shouted, 'You can't park that there.'

'Why not?'

'Because you're in my way!'

Even then the team had an eye for perfection and didn't want anything to spoil it, but to be fair they have done as much as anyone to raise the bar on presentation at race circuits.

We began to get used to this new life and we started to make friends with people from the other teams. We came across drivers like Mario Andretti, and all those others we'd been watching from the paying side of the racetrack, and they used to come into the motorhome and speak to us. We still didn't believe it was happening! Then, as quickly as it started, it looked like it was all over. We had only been hired for the European season, which was nine races, and that finished in September, but we had a reprieve when we were asked to go to the United States and Canada. That had never been part of the plan, but we found out later that John Surtees quite liked us and he said that the team really needed Stuart to do the tyres and that I could do things as well. They hired a little motorhome for us locally and there we were. 'The problem is that the team can't really pay you any wages for the trip as it's outside the budget,' John said. So we went to Watkins Glen and Canada without any pay, just expenses and a bit of pocket money.

One day while we were at Watkins Glen I was alone in the hired motorhome when Mario's Andretti's wife, who was not a small lady, knocked on the door. Mario was driving for Lotus and the Lotus motorhome was locked. We were the nearest facility so she asked if she could use our washroom. I said that was no problem, but when she got into the cubicle the door wouldn't shut – I remember to this day that she was actually wedged in this tiny space. She wouldn't use the public facilities at the track (which we called the 'sentry boxes') as they were so awful and stank to high heaven. Now she couldn't get out of our toilet, so, as Stuart was doing something on the pit wall, I had to go to the Lotus garage and get somebody to ask Mario to come to our motorhome to retrieve his wife because she was stuck fast! That was a bit of an experience for all concerned.

She kept saying 'Go and fetch Mario!' and I kept saying 'Well, he's busy; it's qualifying.' When he finally arrived I left them to it because I was trying to make the lads' tea, but it just shows that anyone could go into any other motorhome then (even if they couldn't always leave!) and no one was bothered.

The Montréal GP was the first race on the island circuit, where it is held now, but the motorhomes were at the end of the rowing canal and all I can remember is that it was October, snowing, and we were freezing. John Surtees said that we could have his hotel room until he arrived, because of the weather, which was kind of him. When we moved back to the motorhome we kept the oven on all night in an effort to keep warm.

All too quickly the season was over and the team closed down. We'd had a wonderful time working at Surtees – it was the biggest and best year's experience we'd ever had; not the most successful, but it was the first. We admired John Surtees because he was still, after all that time, suffering the painful after-effects of a major accident he'd had racing sports cars in Canada. Peter Briggs had warned us that we would have to allow for some of John's outbursts. 'He can be very fiery due to the pain, so just back off a bit because he is a very genuine person.' And he was both of those things.

In that close environment I sometimes heard things I wished I hadn't. I'd often be working at the sink while the team were having their meetings at the back of the motorhome, and John was regularly pretty hard on his drivers; he was a driver himself and the only man who will ever win both two-wheel and four-wheel world championships, so he was entitled to be a bit demanding. We often thought that, although John knew we were there, he didn't really notice us as we were just around all the time doing the food. He used to speak to us but we didn't have what you could call deep conversations, although towards the end of the season, when it became apparent that the team would not have the money to continue in Formula 1 for the following year, he asked us what we were planning to do.

We told him not to worry about it as we had enjoyed the year and it had been a great experience. We would either go back to our jobs or try something else, but we wouldn't have missed the opportunity he had provided us with for anything.

'I have an idea,' he said. 'Would you like to move down to one of my cottages and run my motorbike museum for me?'

I thought, 'All year he's been distant, but to find that he was concerned for our future is really nice.' Whatever is said about John Surtees, he was brilliant and he still is. It was so sad that his son Henry was killed in a Formula 2 crash in 2009, destroying John's dream that he would become a top driver like himself.

We have worked for good people and some who were not so good in the business, and I think we were fortunate to start with 'Briggsy'. Peter was a perfect foil for John Surtees, because John used to just 'go off on one' at any time and, even in those days, Peter wanted to do it all properly but was hamstrung by a lack of budget.

Peter became a good friend, and he always will be. Sadly, he and his wife Theresa have now split up, but we are still close to them both and even became legal guardians to their son Tom, until he reached 18, just in case they were wiped out in a plane crash or something. Just like everything else he did, Briggsy made sure it was all done legally, to the extent that we had to sign a document that effectively stated that if anything happened to them, and we were still involved in motorsport, then motorsport could actually take precedence. I don't know what we would have done in those circumstances. Anyway, all was well, and Tom now works for McLaren.

The season was over but I was fortunate and the civil service re-employed me for the winter. My old job had been filled and I had to go back at a lower grade, but that was to be expected. Stuart was lucky too, as he was able to go back to his old job as well. It was very good of the civil service to have me back, but I hated it. 'I just can't do this anymore,' I thought. 'What am I doing back here?' Stuart and I had experienced something totally different and realised just how big the world was and what alternatives were out there. But, despite my misgivings, I returned to my old job for the next three winters.

Chapter 3

SAUSAGE AND SMASH

Our first year in the job had introduced us to all manner of different people, places and experiences, but one of the most interesting was the chance to get close to our drivers. This would happen regularly throughout our careers, but Team Surtees was our first experience and it blew us away because the team had a total of five drivers that season.

Rupert Keegan was one of the nominated drivers and he had quite an entourage: his father, who was the owner of British Air Ferries at the time, came along, as did Rupert's two brothers. They had their own converted coach, which saw plenty of action as they entertained a lot of ladies in there, and it was parked next to our motorhome, which often led to sleepless nights for us as well as them. Rupert was a nice guy, as well as being a bit of a ladies' man, but he was the youngest of the family and Dad, who had put a lot of money into his son's racing, paid John for Rupert's drive that season.

The other driver to start the season was Vittorio Brambilla, who was in his second year with the team. His nickname was the Gorilla, Brambilla the Gorilla, and he had a disturbing habit of coming up behind me while I was at the sink and hitting the back of my knees, which always left me collapsed on the floor. He didn't know his own strength, and it hurt, but he was such a nice guy I couldn't get angry with him.

Unfortunately both drivers were injured during the season. Rupert had a big accident at Zandvoort: a post went through the back of his hand when he crashed into the catch fencing. He had to stay in Zandvoort hospital when all the team went home, so the team manager Peter Briggs asked us to stay around the area and visit him. 'By the way,' he said, 'have you got any sausages left? That's all he will eat.' So we ended up visiting Rupert every afternoon for the next four days with a packet of sausage sandwiches.

Rupert was lying in bed with his arm held up in a plastic bag. There were pegs through his hand and the plastic bag kept filling up with blood. One day we took Tom and Irene Morton from the Shadow team to see him, but unfortunately Tom took one look at Rupert's arm and fainted, which wasn't the most reassuring visit Rupert ever had. It's actually a good job Tom didn't take a look at Rupert's neighbour in the next-door bed. Rupert had crashed a Formula 1 car into the catch fence at high speed and had a sore hand; the guy in the next bed had only fallen off his pushbike but he was in a terrible state.

At Monza Rupert was replaced by a paying Italian driver called 'Gimax', which was a pseudonym he raced under. He was quite well known in Italy, apparently. He turned up on the first day of the Monza event with a suitcase and went into the back of the motorhome with our team management. When he flipped open the case it was absolutely full of US dollars.

We thought we should leave them to it. As we stepped out of the motorhome Stu said to me, 'He's got a rug on, hasn't he,' and I have to admit that I'd noticed it as well. Anyway, all the financial transactions seemed to be in order and our new fully paid-up driver went out for the first practice session. Afterwards the group all came together to debrief on how the session had gone. 'Gimax' sat there with his fireproof balaclava on throughout the whole meeting, despite the fact it was so hot and stuffy everyone else was wilting in that small room. In the end John Surtees said, 'Look, will you take that thing off, as I can't stand looking at you in it for one minute longer.' 'Gimax' reluctantly agreed, but as he took off his balaclava his wig came off as well. You can imagine the scene. His drive was short lived and he didn't qualify for the race, probably because the team over-fuelled his car so it was too heavy to make the grid, but he had paid and that was that.

In the actual Monza race Brambilla was tangled up in Lotus driver Ronnie Peterson's fatal accident, which was awful. There were ten cars involved in the crash on the first lap of the race, after Riccardo Patrese's Arrows had hit James Hunt's McLaren, which in turn hit Ronnie's Lotus, spinning it into the fence. Vittorio had tried to avoid the main crash scene but had hit Peterson's car, suffered a serious head injury and been taken to intensive care. It seemed as though Peterson, who had severe leg injuries but was conscious and talking, was in better shape than Vittorio, but complications set in and Ronnie subsequently died at the Ospedale Maggiore at Niguardia, where he shared the intensive care ward with Brambilla.

Initially we had to hang around again. However, we were later told we had to leave because of the Italian attitude to accidents. In Italy, if anyone dies at a sporting event there has to be an investigation, which can mean that anyone remotely involved is unable to leave the country for some considerable time, until the investigation is complete. The Lotus team had already departed in a hurry, and while the Surtees team were only involved on the periphery it seemed appropriate for us to leave too. We went to see Vittorio before we left, but his family were by his bedside and he was unconscious for a long time. He eventually recovered and made a racing comeback, but without too much success. He later drove the medical car at Monza Formula 1 races, ferrying Professor Sid Watkins behind the first race lap for a number of years. Sadly, Vittorio passed away in 2001.

For the last two races of the season, in the USA and Canada, we had two new paying drivers, René Arnoux and Beppe Gabbiani.

René was there with his delightful wife Nellie, and as there was no money for more than one set of fireproof clothes she washed them overnight in the hotel bath. Unfortunately they were still wet the next day, so she brought them into the motorhome and asked me to put them in the oven, as he couldn't drive in wet kit. Straight after the lads had had breakfast I had to take all the racks out of the oven, turn it up as high as it would go to make it as hot as possible, then turn it off. I rolled his fireproofs up and put them in. He failed to finish the race and I only hope this wasn't due to being overcome with the bacon fumes from his clothes.

Our five drivers managed to take just one point between them all season, which was Vittorio's sixth place in Austria. The team ended 13th in the standings.

Chapter 4

MOVING BILLBOARD – WAS MY FACE RED?

Sponsorship had become vital to racing and, as a consequence, in addition to all the other equipment we had to squeeze into the small Surtees motorhome, it was necessary to carry all the sponsors' promotional goods and sample products around from country to country. We were also required to wear the team uniform at all times, except when we were off duty. Usually this is not onerous in any way, but there are times when it can be a bit, shall we say, embarrassing.

The Surtees situation was a bit delicate. The team's main sponsor was Durex and the logo was plastered on the motorhome, while our uniforms had 'Durex' prominently displayed all over the back (the name, not the product). At the racetrack that wasn't such an issue, but I remember going into Sainsbury's in Swanley when we were racing at Brands Hatch; it was raining and I had my uniform jacket on. I was with Irene Morton from Shadow and Megs Smalley from Walter Wolf Racing, who also had their team gear on. I hadn't really thought about it until I overheard two ladies saying, 'Look at that girl with Durex written all over her back. What a disgrace.' Was my face red?

At that time people were crazy for stickers of any kind and I remember that John had one made picturing a racing car with 'Durex' written all over it and a tag line which read 'The small family car!' The Durex management people regularly came to the track and left boxes of condoms and Durex stickers for us to distribute. I used to complain that it wasn't really appropriate for me to be giving out things like that, but of course it was just another unanticipated part of the job. The Americans were quite surprised and a bit confused when we went to Watkins Glen, because we were giving out our stickers and packets of Durex, and at that time the name was connected to a brand of sticky tape! The problem was made worse in Catholic countries like Italy where we used to have to give out stickers with a packet of Durex attached (not pinned!). Fortunately, I wasn't put in that situation too often, but we did have to carry stacks of the things around all the time in the motorhome as publicity material.

One of the downsides of travelling internationally in a motorhome was that we were constantly being stopped by the police, as they recognised that race teams would probably be carrying T-shirts or give-aways of some kind. At that time there was a great deal more paperwork involved in crossing borders and when we were stopped the authorities went through everything we had on board and 'confiscated' what they could. It's amazing how many boxes of Durex were arrested in this fashion when we were in Italy. In those unenlightened times we used to do a deal with Ferrari, as the guys couldn't readily buy contraceptives over the counter at home – we used to swap our product for Ferrari shirts, hats and other items.

If anyone in the pit lane was on a promise they knew where to come, as it were. This got a bit embarrassing sometimes, and maybe the lads didn't like having to ask me either, because they did a lot of humming and hawing. I remember a well-known driver of the day came around one evening and Stuart gave him some packets, and the next day he came back and threatened to sue us because his sample had burst. We were a bit put out until we realised he was joking.

'Your risk,' we told him, and then one of our friends said, 'They were all right when they were in the packet!'

Chapter 5

EATING, SLEEPING AND ROLLING IN THE HAY

We were determined that the racing lifestyle we had briefly experienced with Team Surtees was what we wanted to do. The winter spent back in our old jobs had convinced us we couldn't stand doing them any more, so just before Easter we resigned in the hope we could get back into racing. We turned up to a Formula 1 non-championship motor race held at Brands Hatch in April 1979, then entitled the 'Race of Champions', but we still didn't have anything fixed up for the year. The Race of Champions was an odd blend, with the field made up of seven cars that competed in the Formula 1 World Championship while the rest usually took part in the Aurora series, which was the British Formula 1 Championship.

The Surtees team was still racing, but they had moved over to the Aurora series. We were talking to Peter Briggs, who had remained as team manager, when up walked Ken Tyrrell and asked us what we were doing. 'Nothing really,' we said. 'We've gone back to our old jobs as we haven't managed to fix up anything in Formula 1.'

'Well, you'd better come and do our hospitality, then,' he said, and that was that.

Previously, Ken had decided to manage without any hospitality due to budget restrictions. He had his own motorhome, with a driver, and he'd managed by getting his wife Nora to do a lot of the catering work; if she was not on her perch on the pit wall she was making the meals. I'm sure she was pleased to see us!

When we turned up at Tyrrell we felt we had stepped up a notch. With Surtees there had been absolutely no budget and we were scratching around just to turn up by the time it was all coming to an end. Surtees weren't the only ones – teams like Shadow were in the same boat – but Tyrrell had been racing in Formula 1 since 1968, had won two World Championships with Jackie Stewart, and had worked with some other fantastic drivers. There was an aura about the team; there was an aura about John Surtees too, of course, but his team's results never matched those of Tyrrell.

With our new role at Tyrrell we had a significant pay rise to £80 a week. When we say we got £80 a week, it wasn't every week, of course; it was just the weeks during the season, and the European season at that, because we didn't do many fly-away races. We were still living, eating and sleeping in the motorhome, but we had a slightly better budget. It had gone up to £450, which was an increase of £150 per race. Stuart was doing the tyres again, along with the pit board and lots of other stuff too.

When we arrived, our drivers were Didier Pironi and Jean-Pierre Jarier, who was a real character. Being French, Jean-Pierre liked his food. In those days the drivers didn't have the nutritionists that they have today, but Ken had his own views on the subject. Basically, he wouldn't let the drivers eat before a race in case they had an accident. His opinion was simply that if they needed an operation, the longer it was since they had eaten, the better off they would be.

Jean-Pierre took a different view. What he wanted was food, specifically meat; either a steak or a chop or something similar. I found myself stuck in the middle of the pair of them, Ken not wanting his drivers to eat and Jean-Pierre begging for food, claiming that if he didn't eat properly he would flake out during the race. In the end I used to cook his chop or steak and he would sneak back after the pre-race briefing and gobble it down while Ken was in the garage.

'I don't really think you should be doing this,' I'd say. Smiling, he'd just reply, 'Don't worry, I'll take the blame.'

Then one day I got caught. Ken had one of his well-known outbursts and shouted, 'I told you not to feed him!' To which I could only splutter, 'Well, he was adamant.' Ken wasn't impressed.

At one race in France, Jean-Pierre's friend turned up with a cooler box in which he'd brought his weekend ration of meat, and he gave it to me to cook for him without Ken knowing. When I didn't do it straight away it became a bit difficult, as Jean-Pierre used to stand there with the meat and say, 'Well, if you don't cook it, I will.' One time I called his bluff, gave him the frying pan and told him to get on with it – so he did. When Ken found out it was another one of his 'froth jobs', which were so called because he got so excited he used to spit over anyone within range!

It wasn't only on the food front that Jean-Pierre defied convention, because he liked a drop of red wine. He even liked a drop of red wine immediately before a race. He never got it from me, but he knew where the bottles and the glasses were. In addition, he had friends driving for the French teams who were competing that year and shared his attitude towards diet and refreshment, so he used to nip off now and again to see one of them. At that time it was common for the French and Italian teams to drop everything around midday, unless the cars were on track, and set up their tables with the food and wine they required for a two-hour lunch break. That's something that would never happen now.

Despite all this, the season went along relatively calmly because Didier Pironi was a nice guy too. I remember one time in Zeltweg, a wonderful part of Austria, we were having our lunch break and this beautiful Austrian lady, to whom Didier had taken a shine, turned up and they disappeared. When he came back I asked, 'Have you had any lunch?'

'Oh yes,' he replied.

'Turn around,' I suggested, and when he did the white shorts and T-shirt he had on were covered in very green grass marks. I asked him where he had been and he smiled, saying, 'Up there!' and pointing to the grassy slopes above the circuit.

'Have you really had lunch?' I repeated, and he finally admitted that he 'hadn't had time!' We knew what he'd had for 'lunch', but before the banter started Ken walked up. We expected an explosion, but all he said was 'Been rolling in the hay again, Didier?' and walked off with a smile on his face. I can still picture it. Presumably he was happy that at least Didier hadn't been eating as well!

When he was actually eating Didier really liked gravy, or 'brown sauce', as he described it, on just about everything. Bisto was his favourite. When he first started asking for brown sauce I thought he meant HP or something similar, but he said, 'No, I like that brown sauce that you make' so the 'brown sauce' went on everything except his salad.

Sometimes, at tests, Stuart would be sent out around the track to work the speed-trap equipment to help with the lap timing. What Ken didn't realise was that then, like now, if it was hot Stu had a tendency to fall asleep. On one occasion Didier had been on track during a test and came back laughing his head off. 'I've just woken him up,' he said. I wondered what he meant at first, and then it dawned on me: 'Oh God, I hope nobody's noticed!' Apparently on one lap Didier had spotted that Stu was asleep and not recording the times, so when he came around again he stopped right alongside him and revved the car like mad to wake him up. It's astonishing that Stu could sleep like that, just on the other side of the Armco fence, without any ear defenders. Mind you, Stuart could sleep anywhere, including on the pit wall during testing.

Sadly, Didier was killed along with his two crewmen in an

offshore powerboat racing accident near the Isle of Wight in 1987. The boat rode over a rough wave, causing it to flip over. Some weeks after his death Didier's girlfriend gave birth to twin boys. She named them Didier and Gilles.

On one occasion we went to Imola to test the track but Jean-Pierre was not available as he was ill. It was widely reported that he had food poisoning and we took a bit of stick about that from all our neighbours and friends who were following the racing. When the truth came out it seemed the poor guy had hepatitis, which was definitely nothing to do with us. JP missed the German and Austrian Grands Prix, so Geoff Lees, and then Derek Daly, stood in. Ken ran a third car for Derek Daly in the final two races of the year in Canada and the USA.

Ken Tyrrell was a bit of a legend, and although he was a kind person he used to frighten me sometimes with his booming voice; I could hear him from one end of the motorhome to the other. But it was just his way. When we were in France we always had to bring wine back for him. We managed the best we could, but the motorhome was difficult to manoeuvre around some of the little lanes near the vineyards he sent us to. At that time there were very draconian restrictions on the number of bottles of wine one could legally bring into the country, so it took a long time to stow all our contraband under the seats and in other inaccessible places in the motorhome, particularly as there were boxes and boxes of it. Then we had to drive, very carefully, all the way to the Tyrrell home near Guildford. Ken liked a nice drop of red. Dijon was a particular favourite because he had winemaking 'friends' in the area. They would come to the race and in return Stuart would collect Ken's wine on the way home.

At the end of the European season, in September, we were once again kicking our heels. I went back to my old job, but Chloride were fed up with Stuart by then and wouldn't have him back. We didn't realise it at the time, but that was the end for us with the team.

We had become quite friendly with the Tyrrell family and were due to do the next year with them. Ken said he would be in touch about the details for the following season, and sure enough he was. However, what he had to say was that Italian white goods manufacturer Candy, who had started to sponsor the team during the 1979 season, had agreed to sponsor them in 1980, but this time they were going to pay for all the hospitality on the understanding that they brought their own chef. Working for Ken had been brilliant and we got on well with Nora, who was a lovely woman; dizzy but lovely. We'd been lucky again, in so far as the Tyrrell team had a fine bunch of lads, just like the ones at Surtees, and quite a few of them are still in the business, grown old just like us.

So we were without a team once more, back to thinking, 'Here we go again. We can't keep going on like this.' But by now it was in our blood. We couldn't stand the thought that we wouldn't be going away again as part of the circus, even if all we did was make the tea.

Chapter 6

ALL AT SEA – NEARLY

There was nothing on the horizon for us in Formula 1 for 1980 so there was no alternative but to go back to our old standby, the advert. I think we were in danger of becoming the *Autosport* classified department's best customers.

Amazingly, though, we got another call and this time it was from Ted Toleman, who was currently competing in both Formula 2 and offshore powerboat racing but had long-term aspirations towards Formula 1. Initially it appeared to be a backward step for us, but over the four seasons we were associated with the team I can honestly say we learned an amazing amount. In addition to winning the European Formula 2 Championship in our first year, as well as setting the standards for hospitality in Formula 1 offshore powerboat racing, we went drag racing, bought our own motorhome, got back into Formula 1, worked with future Formula 1 technical legends and laid the foundation of a friendship with Ayrton Senna and his family which would last until that fateful day at Imola in 1994.

Due to the job we do, one of the most important introductions we ever have is our first meeting with the motorhome where we are going to be living and working for the foreseeable future. Once again this was something of an experience. Ted Toleman had been racing powerboats in the States and had shipped back a luxurious American fifth-wheel trailer with a pop-out side, towed by a big Ford pick-up truck. Stuart and I had to go and collect it from Cougar Marine in Hamble on the River Solent. When we saw it we were astonished by the sheer size of it – each new motorhome seemed to present a bigger challenge. The first tentative miles involved nothing more serious than taking it back to our house in Alcester to load it up with all our stuff, ready to set off the very next day for our first event. It pretty well filled up the whole street and, as usual, stretched the tolerance of our neighbours. Stuart was, and still is, a brilliant driver and he can drive anything, but he had his work cut out with that thing.

The day after we collected it, our first overseas trip was to Pau in France for a Formula 2 race. Stu was a bit apprehensive, as he had never driven anything quite that long before, but undeterred we got to Southampton without any major problems and joined the queue for the ferry. Suddenly, to Stuart's horror, the trucks getting on in front of us were all turning in a big circle and then reversing on to the boat. Eventually it came to our turn and the man in charge of loading said, 'OK mate, you're next.'

Stu's face fell and he muttered something unrepeatable, before admitting to the startled loader that he had 'only picked the trailer up the day before and only driven it in a straight line'. He said, 'There is no way I am going to be able to reverse it on there.' He attempted it, however, and thought he was going reasonably well until one of the watching truckers said: 'You haven't done this before, have you?' It was a bit of a statement of the obvious really, but he was kind enough to walk alongside the trailer as Stu reversed it, and it went into a space between two large trucks as if it was made for the job (which of course it was). Stuart was really grateful and started to learn a bit about the truckers' code. Not wanting to be embarrassed on the return journey he got us to the port several hours too early so we were at the front of the queue in order that, when it was our turn to board, he could drive on to the boat, turn around at the far end and come back to face the right way to drive off. He was the first aboard by some considerable margin.

The Formula 1 Offshore Powerboat Championship and the European Formula 2 Championship couldn't really have provided us with a greater contrast in working environments. We supported some of the European powerboat races, which took us to places like Poole and the Isle of Wight, and we went to all the World Championship events, two rounds of which were in Britain, some in Italy and then a series of meetings in Key West, Florida.

Between these glamorous outings we supported Formula 2 races with our monster trailer at some of the old, traditional European race circuits, which on the one hand might have seemed a little less attractive, but at least had the benefit of allowing us to park the trailer and leave it for the weekend without having to worry about it. We also supported some races in the lower powerboat formulae, but it wasn't exactly a spectator sport: once they had gone they had, well, gone. The noise when they were starting up was terrific; they were fabulous boats. Stuart often used to go up in the helicopter and follow the race, which was the only way to see anything unless they happened to race past a headland. From my viewpoint it was quite peaceful once they had all gone; I just had to sit there and wait for them to come back.

After the Pau fiasco, the first powerboat event we had to attend with our giant rig was on the Isle of Wight. We got on the ferry without too much difficulty in Southampton, but when we reached the other end the unloading arrangements meant we had to drive down a ramp for some way before the next part of the ramp angled back upwards to get on the quayside. When we drove down the ramp the pick-up made it, but when it started the incline the metal skids on the back of the trailer dug into the ramp surface and the wheels lifted off the ground; naturally we weren't going anywhere then. Everyone panicked so the next step was to give it as many revs as possible and reverse the whole thing back on to the boat. As nobody had a better idea we sailed back to Southampton while everyone gave it some thought. We stayed aboard in Southampton, feeling pretty fed up, and then set off back to the Isle of Wight, where a plan had been hatched in our absence. On the next attempt at disembarking we had to stay on board until everything else was off the boat, which was then higher in the water. By employing various Heath Robinson blocks of wood and a great deal of blasphemy we finally made it on to the Isle of Wight. Having arrived, we had to park the monstrosity in the middle of Cowes, where we blocked up the entire place.

The next event after that was Brixham and we blocked that as well. The police had to come and divert the traffic because we got stuck trying to get down on to the seafront. We had some real experiences with that thing.

The Formula 2 races, as I've already mentioned, were a bit of a relief. The team, Toleman Motorsport, had been founded by Ted Toleman and Alex Hawkridge and first competed in Formula 2 in 1978. By 1980, their last year in the competition, the team were successfully running their own car which had been designed by Rory Byrne. Brian Henton and Derek Warwick were driving and they were both terrific people as well as being extremely quick; we got on really well with them and the whole team. As a bit of a novelty we were in the unusual position of being one of the wealthier teams in the series, rather than the poor relations; our motorhome was at least as big as most of the Formula 1 rigs, and the only one of that size in Formula 2, although it was, of course, shared with the offshore activities.

The Formula 2 season went well for us and Stuart continued to help the team out during the races. There was one chilling incident at Pau, however, which showed that Stu's quick reactions weren't restricted to driving, despite his tendency to fall asleep at a moment's notice. Stuart was standing in the garage alongside Derek Warwick, who had retired from the race, when Patrick Gaillard from Team Maurer came in for a pit stop in the pit next door. He accelerated to leave the pits before all the pit crew were clear and one of them, Ian Harrison, was pulled under one of the car's rear wheels, with the tyre rotating on his leg. Stu rushed to help and tried to keep the unfortunate Ian calm and still; he could see that Ian's foot was facing the wrong way in relation to his leg. Jim Vale and Micky Cowlishaw also arrived to help. Ian suffered a badly broken leg but, to this day, whenever we see him, he says: 'You saved my life in Pau.' Stuart always reacts in the same way – 'I didn't save your life; I may have saved your leg, but that's all.'

The defining race of that Formula 2 season was at Silverstone, and the Toleman team were set to finish first and second in the championship, with Brian Henton just edging out Derek Warwick. It should have been Toleman's glory day, except that on the Sunday morning the *News of the World* published some unsubstantiated allegations of misdemeanours by the team's managing director, Alex Hawkridge. Needless to say we all turned up for work expecting to have a special celebration only to find the *News of the World* being handed out to everyone in the paddock and the motorhome besieged by journalists. Nothing was ever proved and no charges were brought, but it ruined the weekend and took the edge off the championship. Ted warned us not to speak to anyone, and Alex sat in the motorhome all day and told us not to let any journalists anywhere near him. He asked Stuart to go and get him a newspaper and he just sat there staring at it. It's amazing that all those years later, in 2009, the same newspaper printed an awful lot of detailed bad press about Max Mosley, then head of the Fédération Internationale de l'Automobile (FIA), the ruling body of world motorsport. There weren't too many people in the paddock who shed a tear when the *News of the World* closed in 2011. They had published too many stories about Formula 1 personalities to get any sympathy from that quarter.

The powerboat season ended on a personal high note. Ted seemed to have taken a shine to us and so we went to Key West in Florida for the six weeks of the World Championships; that was the first time we started to really 'live the life'. We now had a decent salary, a reasonable budget for hospitality – and we were living in Florida for six weeks! We couldn't believe it. Unlike other offshore events, everything at Key West is going on around you and there's no respite. Ted had his massive trailer shipped back out there for the duration, which seemed a bit odd as they were available everywhere in the States. It was parked in Key West harbour all the time and we did the catering from there. Most of the teams had small motorhomes and just fed their team with sandwiches and American food 'to go', but Ted invited guests and ran it more in the style of a Formula 1 hospitality facility. There was a party atmosphere as all the drivers knew each other and mixed together happily. Quite a few of them were Italian, and everyone competing was very rich, most of them a lot richer than Ted. Maybe one or two of them had a bit of a 'past' – we were not too sure how some of them had earned their money...

As well as being owner of both the race teams Ted was the pilot of the powerboat entry; his partner 'Big' Clive Curtis was the throttle man. They ran the team from a facility in Hamble. Clive brought his son Steve, who was about 15 at the time, along to the races and Stu and I looked after him while the boats were on the water, little knowing that Steve would eventually become eight-times Offshore Powerboat World Champion and be given an MBE.

The upside of living in Florida for six weeks suddenly became a downside because Ted decided that he would leave the motorhome over in the USA for his sons to use during the winter. It was never to come back, as far as we knew.

Having been so successful in Formula 2, Ted finally took the big step of announcing he was entering Formula 1 for the 1981 season. The cars stayed in Formula 2 as customer cars with Alan Docking Racing. Derek and Brian stayed with the team too, as did the main engineering strength of Rory Byrne, Pat Symonds and John Gentry; the whole team package just moved up into Formula 1 – except for us. Unfortunately, due to the team's lack of a hospitality budget, our only full-time involvement was to arrange a motorhome which was driven there by a team member and used as an office and a place for drivers to sit. There was no permanent hospitality and the race team had their meals in a central catering facility organised by a company called MSL. They supplied most of the small teams in the paddock.

We had become extremely friendly with the drivers and the team, particularly Derek, his wife Rhonda and their family, and not being able to follow this big new adventure through was a bit of a blow. Once more we were ending the season with no prospects for the following year. This time, though, rather than letting it get us down, it was the catalyst for a major strategic rethink. We decided that we needed to take some bold steps if we were to get more control over our lives and not live from year to year based on the whims and financial strategies of other people. We decided that the way forward was to provide a hospitality package deal for an all-inclusive charge for the season. In that way we would own our own vehicle, provide the total catering facility and be fully self-contained. This was a bit of a bold move as we didn't really have any openings for the 1981 season, but we were determined not to let practical matters stand in our way – so we bought our own American motorhome.

Before we knew it, then, there we were in 1981, self-employed entrepreneurs with our own business called 'Plus 1' which signified we were the couple plus the vehicle (which was the '1'). We were the first people to do this, as most teams had their own vehicle. It was definitely a major step for us at the time, but we reasoned that the teams didn't want the bother of looking after their own facility and would rather just get a quote for the season, agree it, forget about it and leave all the practical difficulties to someone else. (Stuart couldn't forget about it, however, and ended up in hospital with a stomach ulcer from worrying about everything).

We contracted some work for Toleman at the odd Grand Prix, but the team was having trouble qualifying for races in that first year. We lined up one or two races with Tyrrell, and some powerboat races, but we certainly didn't have enough work to keep the business solvent. Off to the *Autosport* classified section again...

Hot-rod racer Barry Lee got in touch with us; Barry was sponsored by Total so the company paid for us to support him at some events. It was a bit of a culture shock, turning out at Ipswich stadium in the mud for these hot-rod races after we'd experienced Formula 1, even though we'd been at the 'impoverished' end of the paddock. There was a very different group of people at the hot-rod events. Barry himself was the personification of the likeable rogue and he was a big star in his field. He seemed a bit of an Essex 'wide boy' to us provincials, speaking in a really strong London accent and with the curly perm, the 'bling' bracelets, the medallions and all the accoutrements of a real down-to-earth Jack the Lad. I suppose he was a bit of a prototype Jeremy Clarkson.

Despite our very different backgrounds we became friendly with Barry. He knew what else we had been doing, and one day he said, 'I would love to meet Ted Toleman. I really admire what he's achieved, combining powerboating and motor racing.' As it happened, we had an upcoming powerboat event booked to do for Ted down on the south coast, and as Barry lived in Dagenham we thought that was a good opportunity to fix a meeting for them. Barry turned up at the event, we introduced them, and they became really big mates, with Barry becoming a regular guest at races. He also went out in the powerboat with Ted, and then became part of the Toleman Group, working on marketing the Formula 1 team. Who would have thought that it had been us that had introduced them in the first place? We just made the tea.

Barry's career went on to encompass such diverse areas as being Hot Rod World Champion, a rally driver and a television presenter. Our career during that early period, though, was somewhat more sluggish.

We worked hard through 1981 and 1982 to establish our business and managed to keep enough work coming in to justify our decision to go it alone. Toleman won increased sponsorship for 1983 with Iveco and Candy, and Chris Witty, Ted's marketing/PR guy, got in touch with us to organise a meeting with the then marketing director of Iveco to show him our motorhome. The meeting was arranged for that most glamorous of locations, Knutsford service station on the M6. Fortunately, he liked the motorhome (and us) and after we had done our sales pitch about the value of entertaining customers at Grands Prix we were back in Formula 1.

We were delighted to be back in the paddock, particularly because we were reunited with Derek Warwick, and we were introduced to Bruno Giacomelli, the second driver. Bruno was a crazy, charming Italian who owned a kitchen-fitting business in Brescia; I believe this helped him to get the drive, as it allowed him to bring funds to the team. Bruno and Derek got on well and were always fooling around. Unfortunately the car was initially not very successful; there was a whole spate of retirements from races and the odd failure to qualify. It did wear the drivers down, but there was still a family atmosphere within the team. With the likes of Rory Byrne, Gordon Message, Pat Symonds, ex-GP driver Peter Gethin, Chris Witty and engine man Brian Hart, as well as Ted and Alex around, there couldn't fail to be.

A highlight of that year was when Rick Parfitt of Status Quo and Roger Taylor of Queen came to the Monaco Grand Prix. They made a video to the Queen track 'Another One Bites the Dust', which was a bit unfortunate for Bruno as he had failed to qualify for the race and was beside himself. The team had a much better second half of the season and finished ninth in the championship. This gave Derek Warwick the chance to move on to the much better funded Renault team, which in turn paved the way for Toleman's greatest coup: the signing of Ayrton Senna. The season had its highs and lows, but at least we were back in the fastest lane of them all – or so we thought.

However, as usual, there was a dark cloud on the horizon. Ted liked to do things properly, but both offshore powerboat racing and Formula 1 were pretty expensive, and there were the first signs that he was slowly running out of funds.

Chapter 7

EARLY MOTORHOMERS – THE BAND OF GYPSIES

After a couple of years in the job we found ourselves thinking back to the time we put our original advert in *Autosport*. We thought we knew what a motorhomer did: they drove the vehicle, did some cooking and coped with whatever else came up – a bit like housekeepers on wheels. We learned very quickly that there was much more to it than that, and by the end of 1983 we had a fairly good idea of the kind of things that would 'come up'! We certainly weren't just the caterers. After sewing on badges, tending the sick, lap timing, acting as a psychotherapist, multilingual shopper, moving billboard and mixer of drivers' drinks, I found out that the job was somewhat different from what I'd imagined. Stuart, in the meantime, was driver, cook, tyre man and father confessor, trader in promotional knick-knacks, pit-board operative and motorhome mechanic, as well as being a major force in keeping down the European birth rate. He hadn't quite bargained for that either.

We took on the small task of keeping wives and girlfriends separated and acquiring certain creams in Brazil for tending to, shall we say, social diseases. Bailing people out of jail was one of our specialities. A team member who shall remain nameless was arrested following a dispute that got a bit physical and the police told us he could be released on receipt of a given amount of money. He was quite an important character for the next day's action, so we had to have a bit of a 'whip-round' and my catering budget ended up 1,000DM short in order to get him released. Stuart had to pay the money over and bring the chastened individual back in time for the race.

We thought we would be on the fringes of everything, but it was a real pleasure being integrated into the team to the extent we were. We'd imagined the team members would be doing their bit and we would be doing our bit, and although neither Stu nor I were professionally trained, we were pretty sure we could handle the kind of household cooking the teams originally said they wanted. Later we had to step up a bit, when some of the more well-funded teams wanted to look after their sponsors a little better. They moved on to trout and fine wine, but the lads still had their traditional stuff – cooked breakfast, sandwiches for lunch and jacket potatoes, or whatever we could get into the oven in the evening.

When we first started out in 1978 the need for hospitality facilities was just being recognised; as we have already mentioned, Mike and Ann Murphy were one of the first couples to be involved. As the teams became more organised and found extra sponsorship they decided that a bit of dry bread was all well and good if you were a prisoner, but a professional race team needed to be treated a little better. It started to become the norm for all the teams to have hospitality people to entertain their guests, as well as feeding the team and drivers, so they started looking for people like ourselves. When we finally got our chance we were one of about ten couples in the job, four of whom had started when we did. We were all a bit naïve; some of us knew a bit about racing and were interested in it, others didn't know anything. We were getting an inkling that there was more to it than met the eye, but we had no idea in the early stages just how much more.

The motorhomes didn't have much storage space and

conditions were very cramped. When drivers used to turn up with all their kit it was a bit of a problem – they used our shower tray for helmet storage during the day…

When we were washing up the waste from the sink used to go into a holding tank that regularly needed flushing out into a drain, which was fine if we were anywhere near a drain in the paddock, but at that time they were few and far between. We used to drain the tank wherever we could; it wasn't very nice but we had no option. However, at Monaco, running the water off during the day wasn't allowed in case it went into the harbour. (That is where it did end up, of course, but we had to do it when everyone was watching practice or qualifying.) It got a bit too busy one particular day after Stuart had gone off to do something or other. I was washing up when I suddenly caught wind of a pretty horrible smell. I thought, 'Oh God, it's the shower!' The quirk of the holding tank was that when it became over-full the water used to flow back into the shower basin. When I rushed over to see what was happening two crash helmets were floating in this stinking waste water – they were the helmets the drivers would be using the next day. Fortunately it was quite late in the afternoon, and when the drivers had finished their debrief they went straight off without coming back for their helmets. Stuart and I then had to sit up all night drying the crash helmets with my hairdryer.

One of the worst jobs I had to do was after one driver found it necessary to 'go' in his race suit. He just came over to me and said 'Di, I have got a problem', and stepped out of the suit. All I could think of saying was 'Thanks' and then I thought, 'I don't remember reading this in the job description.'

We have also had drivers being sick in their helmets and down the front of their suits and then sheepishly asking, 'Can you do anything with this?' I hadn't seen that written down anywhere either.

We have been babysitters and chauffeurs and, unfortunately, a bank – many of the drivers are like the royal family and turn up without any money, or alternatively turn up with their own money and without any of the local cash. This problem has reduced considerably since most of Europe adopted the Euro. However, we wouldn't have been very successful as a bank because none of them ever remembered to pay us back.

Quite often we were used by the team personnel as someone to talk over their problems with. Racing was quite a stressful occupation, particularly as everyone spent so much time away from home, and this often caused marital upsets. The guys would come along and talk about it to us rather than with their mates, who were not always sympathetic. Oddly, the drivers did the same, and occasionally so did the team bosses, or team principals as they are now described. Sometimes these discussions centred on things that, given the option, we would have preferred not to know. However, it was our job to act as some kind of touchstone; if there was anyone left at the track the motorhome was open and we were there, a port in a storm.

In those first years we met a lot of people who have become firm friends. We learned together through adversity and had loads of laughs. One of the couples we became really friendly with were Meg and Ken Smalley, the very people who could speak more languages than us and had actually got the 'Walter Wolf' job, so the first thing we said to them was: 'Look, I hope you don't mind, but we know what you are earning!' They looked surprised until we explained that we were the other couple who had got down to the shortlist in the interview process.

Relieved, they said, 'Yes, we heard about you. We are sorry we got the job.'

'So are we,' we joked. 'You are earning four times as much as us!' They were a strange couple, and although we are talking about more than 30 years ago he seemed to be about 80 then and she looked about 20. I don't think the gap was quite that much; in reality he was about 65 and she was probably about 25. I can picture him now – he looked a bit like Father Christmas, with white hair and a white beard, smoking a pipe and wearing

Dutch-style clogs. He hadn't a clue about racing and what it was all about and, in fairness, he wasn't particularly interested. He just sat on his chair outside the motorhome door, smoked his pipe and watched the world go by. I can't imagine anyone getting away with that now.

Meg used to do all the cooking, cleaning and everything else at the circuit. Ken did the driving and considered that his job was over when they arrived, at least until it was time to go again. They had travelled quite a bit and had previously lived in France. After a bottle of wine or two they admitted that they had told Peter Warr they spoke more languages than they did; they only actually spoke a little French, nothing else. I guess we would have been a bit better off if we had been more economical with the truth, but it never occurred to us. We travelled with Meg and Ken quite a lot, and it was a good thing we did because either their truck or ours would break down with monotonous regularity. We helped each other out – and we always got there in the end!

Tom and Irene Morton were another couple with whom we became friendly. They had only been married a year when they started working for Shadow Formula 1, and they found spending all those hours travelling and working together a bit difficult. Stuart and I had been married a while when we started in racing, so it was a lot easier for us. In any case, I had a bit of respite because Stuart was often working with the team, which gave me some time on my own. Although we shared the same environment all the time we both had our 'jobs within a job'. Tom and Irene had a large Chevy pick-up truck that towed an American-style caravan with a pop-out lounge. Tom had never driven anything like that before, and they were both only 21, but they had spotted the job advertised in a London paper. They applied and were successful, presumably on the basis that they were a nice couple. At the end of the working day we used to compare notes and swap stories.

These were the six of us who travelled together in that first year. When we arrived at the circuit we would park in our allotted slots and then try to go about our business. At that time we didn't have to arrive until the Thursday of a race weekend, so we turned up outside the circuit on Wednesday nights, set up on Thursday and were all prepared for when the team arrived on Friday. Well, that was the idea, but there was always something unexpected happening.

One of the major issues was shopping, once we'd arrived at the circuit, because we had driven the motorhome to the racetrack and so obviously didn't have a car. Tom was towing a trailer so he could unhitch the Chevy and we would all use that in rotation. Then it was a case of trying to buy what we could with whatever money was left from the previous race weekend's budget – by doing that, and a bit of scrounging here and there, we managed to get enough food together to see us through the first day. When we were paid that weekend's money we used to borrow a hire car to do the rest of the food shopping. Arriving at the shops we'd find all the other motorhomers lined up, doing the same as us – except for Brabham who didn't have a motorhome, just a little office in the truck and sometimes a small trailer for the drivers to sit in.

The other teams had a variety of types of vehicle. By today's standards it was all a bit ragged. McLaren, who were sponsored by Marlboro, had the biggest motorhome, and that didn't really change until recently when all the others started to catch up. At that time Lotus was the second biggest team, but for the first part of the season the top teams didn't really speak to us newcomers at the other end of the paddock; it meant we all stuck together and 'muddled through'.

By the time they got to Formula 1 the motorhomes had usually endured a tough life in other environments: they were sometimes unreliable and often turned up late. On one occasion the American motorhome that was the Fittipaldi hospitality unit didn't arrive until the Saturday night before the race so Emerson, who was driving for his own team in those days, just had to sit on the steps of his truck when he wasn't out on the track. I took food and drinks round for him and the boys as I couldn't bear to see them go hungry.

The team sizes were very different when we started, with a maximum of around 20 personnel, unlike the huge numbers that travel now. Fortunately that meant we didn't have to buy a massive amount of provisions for the weekend, although quite often we ended up doing lots of shopping for the boys, and sometimes the drivers would forget things like shampoo and toothpaste and we had to sort them out too. It's amazing the sort of things we've had to buy for people over the years – and everyone would promise to pay us back, but they rarely did. Then there was always the possibility the team would get a local sponsor for the weekend, and if they did we had to sew new logos on the fire suits overnight.

When the race weekend was over everybody left and it was down to us to break everything down and pack it away before leaving for the next stop along the way. It wasn't cost effective for the team to let us return home between races, as we were usually in Europe, and although it was better to travel with other motorhomers there was often a problem finding somewhere safe to park more than one unit. If the team's drivers had experienced a really bad day and failed to get a decent time, or in the older days not qualified for the race at all because there were more teams than race slots, they would be absolutely beside themselves. On some occasions it wasn't even worth us staying in the paddock and we pulled out early and told our friends that we would meet them down the road. We've spent hours in parking areas at the sides of major roads, trying to get to sleep with traffic whizzing by; sometimes we'd just managed it when a massive refrigerated truck would pull up alongside us and rattle away throughout the night.

We have also had many occasions when we've been stuck in lay-bys for days on end, waiting for Thursday so we could get into the next circuit. The major problem was that we had to feed ourselves between race weekends. A lot of motorhomers would buy extra on their last shopping trip at any location, to make sure they'd stocked up their fridges. They told us to do the same because, as they said, 'We have to live from now until the next race.' But I couldn't do that because I had never wasted anyone else's money and didn't intend to start. It was actually pretty academic anyway, as there usually wasn't enough money in the budget to do it. Sometimes we didn't have any food because it was a simple choice of buying the fuel or eating. Our three groups spent days together, sharing food, sharing money sometimes, and above all sharing experiences. We never divulged any secrets, though; well, none of us knew any really, but what we did know stayed confidential. Although the Shadow team were very Americanised, and had the poshest motorhome of our group, we were all aware that the team didn't have any more money than the rest of us.

Slowly we got to know some of the other people, particularly the Marlboro couple who were in the 'posh big red motorhome at the other end of the paddock'. They finally decided that the people 'up the other end' were probably quite civilised after all, and perhaps they could start talking to them. Bob McMurray had worked for Ron Dennis in the lower formulae for many years and his sister-in-law had married a Kiwi who was working in the UK for Nicholson McLaren Engines. Eventually they had both gone back to live in New Zealand, so Bob and Shaune used to spend the off-season staying with them. Then, at the end of 1976, they decided to move there permanently. They hadn't been there long, though, before Ron called Bob and told him that the team had Marlboro sponsorship and asked if they would come back and operate the hospitality vehicle for the season, returning to New Zealand in between – and that's what happened. Even in those days McLaren were probably the best-equipped team in the paddock, as they often are now. Bob and Shaune continued to run that hospitality facility for many years before moving to look after Ron Dennis's personal motorhome. They were the couple who probably helped us the most, but Bob was always Ron Dennis and McLaren through and through; the team could do no wrong in his eyes, and the rest of us were also fans. We all took it in good part. The motorhomers became a family within the big Formula 1 family. There were some strange couples doing the job, but then again they probably thought that we were strange too.

There was one team called Theodore Racing that was owned by millionaire businessman Teddy Yip from Hong Kong. His motorhome was a bright red converted horsebox run by an Irish family headed by Big Sid, with a son imaginatively called Little Sid and a wife whose name we never knew; we always assumed it was Mrs Sid. They were as Irish as anyone could be, and to this day I have no idea how they became involved with Teddy Yip. They were at the 'wrong' end of the paddock, with us, and they were very friendly, but I don't think the team managed to complete their first season.

A chap called Chris Leese operated the Goodyear motorhome. He had previously been a tyre fitter but had suffered a car accident that left him with a limp, and he was given the role of motorhomer, which was very unusual for a single person. Chris was fastidious about the carpets and curtains in the motorhome and cleaned them religiously after every GP, so if ever we were parked together Chrissy (or Glory, as he became known after a brand of carpet cleaner of the day) often had his curtains draped everywhere and foam tumbling down the motorhome steps from his carpet-cleaning activities. He also became famous for his open sandwiches, which he thought were very *cordon bleu*. He was a very likeable chap who managed well on his own; he took some stick from the other lads, but he gave plenty back in return.

Tim and Maureen Hargreaves were at Williams when it was Saudi-sponsored and they had a big American motorhome emblazoned in green and white Saudi colours. They didn't have a very big team, as Frank was only running one car that season.

Tim doubled up by working on the team as a fabricator while Maureen did most of the cooking herself and would scrounge a lift with one of us if we were going shopping. Tim's team job meant that Maureen was alone at the motorhome a good deal of the time so she was often unable to provide the same service, but she certainly did her best. Washing clothes was a big problem, as we were on the road a great deal, so when we were in the paddock with running water we would all rush to wash items before the team arrived. Maureen was one up on the rest of us because she had her little spinning hand-wash gadget, which did the job admirably. Clothes would then adorn the canopy on a makeshift line. But on occasions I did have to remind her that the team would arrive soon – Frank caught out Maureen once or twice by arriving early, but no doubt he'd seen it all before!

ATS were there with a German guy with bleached blonde hair who drove the truck and just cooked sausages for the whole weekend. Then there was Warsteiner Arrows, who had a motorhome run by Manfred and Charlotte Oettinger. They were very popular in the paddock as they were sponsored by Warsteiner beer. Warsteiner used to host a beer evening on Saturday nights, with a huge amount of beer on tap; that would no doubt be frowned upon now. Anyone could go along and there was always a number of drunken journalists, and quite a few mechanics who turned up when they had finished getting their car ready. We must have acquired a taste for the brand because we still find it tastes quite pleasant, even when it's not free. Manfred was one of the few of us who had actually been involved in catering before, as he'd had a nightclub in Germany before he joined the team.

We first met Manfred on the harbour wall at Monaco, where he had just started at the same time as us. There was a knock on our motorhome door and I opened it to find a chap in Warsteiner gear gesticulating with two fingers. It was obvious he didn't speak any English. After some moments I realised he wanted to borrow something which, after more two-fingered signalling, we realised was a pair of scissors followed by a tin opener. We became firm friends with him and Charlotte; she was initially left at home to run the nightclub. We had a strange experience with Manny on a visit to a famous museum in Speyer, near the Hockenheim circuit. There was a group of us and we were visiting the war section. Manfred introduced us to a guide who was standing by one of the cars on show. He proudly told us he'd been Hitler's driver and that we were looking at the car he drove him around in. It was one of those moments when none of us knew quite what to say – except Stuart, of course, who said, 'Well, it's in good nick; shame there's no bullet holes in it.' Stu's comment went right over the guide's head, and Manfred often made his own jokes about the war so he took it in good part, fortunately.

Manny's sense of humour was well known in the paddock. He's one of the few people to have left Bernie Ecclestone and his staff speechless with his repartee, the occasion being so unusual that it made the motoring press. The background to the story was that in 1987 Arrows were flying the US and British flags on separate poles at the races in honour of their drivers, Eddie Cheever and Derek Warwick. The Stars and Stripes was flying a little higher than the Union Jack, which upset Bernie, and he sent his man Alan Woollard along to the Arrows motorhome to investigate. When asked why the US flag was flying higher than the British one Manny responded simply, 'Because the pole is longer!'

Gilles Villeneuve and his wife Joann had their own motorhome where they stayed with their two children, Jacques and Melanie. They were a terrific family. Jacques's sister was older than him and I can remember Jacques pedalling his tricycle around the paddock between the motorhomes. Joann did their washing in the sink and used to hang it out to dry on a line tied to the fence and run to the outside ladder on their unit. I can't imagine Bernie allowing anything like that now; he wasn't too keen on it then, either. When Bernie was still at Brabham he was always inspecting the motorhomes, which was a bit odd as he didn't have one himself.

Those early seasons were a massive training ground for what was to come in subsequent years. We all slept in the motorhomes in those days, and we were locked in the paddock overnight, so we used to take turns to host all the other motorhomers in the evening. Then, on a Sunday night, we would all take our leftover food to one of the motorhomes and cook the whole lot up rather than throw it away. In the past motorhomers were generally couples, husband and wife or boyfriend and girlfriend, although quite a lot of them have since split up due to the strain of spending so much time together. In years gone by motorhomers would meet up at the end of the day and have a drink in each others' awnings, recounting what had happened to them during the day – not secrets or technical information, but the human stories and the anecdotes.

I always remember Maureen and Tim Hargreaves from Williams telling a story relating to when Carlos Reutemann was driving for the team. Apparently there was a debrief going on in their small motorhome and one of the guys, either Frank Williams or Patrick Head, had a particular liking for Twiglets, so she always put some out on the debrief table for everyone. On this particular occasion Carlos had turned up first for the session and had spotted the snack on the table. Maureen was working at the sink and as she half turned around she saw he'd taken out his earplugs and proceeded to clean his ears out with a Twiglet; really digging in with a vengeance. As she looked at him he was putting the offending item back in the bowl, whereupon Neil Oatley, Carlos's engineer, came in and with a shout of 'Great, Twiglets!' put that very one in his mouth and ate it. Maureen told us that she was gagging at the sink. She just couldn't tell Neil and hasn't to this day – so if you're reading this Neil, enjoy the memory!

We never went to bed while the lads were still working and quite often it was because our bedroom doubled as the office. People would be having a meeting at three in the morning and we would be standing around, waiting to go to bed. Some of the other motorhomers were different. I remember that Tim and Maureen used to tap Frank Williams and Patrick Head on the shoulder and point to the front of the truck and say, 'That's your bit, we're going to bed!' They just went to bed at the back and left the others to it. We could never do that. We have seen the sun come up at quite a lot of racing circuits, thinking: 'God, we've got another day's work to do tomorrow.'

We were real members of the team and basically saw it as our job to look after everyone – not only their food, but just about everything else they needed. We were definitely Mum and Dad to the team, the sponsors and the guests.

Chapter 8

THE LOTUS POSITION

Towards the end of the 1983 season we were in conversation with Mike and Ann Murphy, the Lotus motorhomers, who were originally from Vancouver. We had previously considered them to be a bit snooty, and I think they always thought of themselves as a cut above the rest of us – although they were perhaps entitled to feel that way as they were the first of the 'modern' motorhomers – but they actually became friends of ours. I am not sure how they became involved in Formula 1 in the first place; perhaps it was through Mario Andretti. Anyway, they had been with Lotus for quite a few years and on this occasion they mentioned to us that they were thinking of leaving and asked us if we would be interested in taking over their role with the team. At the time they knew we had an on/off relationship with Toleman, with no specific contract. To make matters worse, Toleman hadn't got much of a budget for the following season and it looked as though they would struggle, despite their new driver line-up. Mike and Ann were leaving because the team was not the same, in their opinion, without Colin Chapman. Colin, the Lotus founder and major driving force, had died in December 1982 and Peter Warr had been brought in by the family to take over the day-to-day running of the business.

We had our concerns, of course, because we really liked the

Toleman environment. Mike recommended us for an interview with Peter in his office in Ketteringham Hall in Hethel, which was quite daunting. Fortunately, Peter remembered us from the previous occasion when he had interviewed us for the Walter Wolf position, and he had seen us around the paddock. He was very pleasant and showed us around the facility, even Colin's old office, which seemed a bit creepy as it was exactly like it had been when he'd left it for the final time. Colin's pen was still balanced on its stand, his blotter was still there and his diary was open as if he had just popped out for lunch. It was eerie; the whole place was. We continued the tour and saw all the trophies. It was clear that Peter was proud of being part of it, and that certainly rubbed off on us. He was quite overpowering, and spoke so quickly and enthusiastically that it was plain he was totally absorbed in the whole enterprise.

John Player Limited sponsored the Lotus team in those days, under the banner of their John Player Special brand. It was made clear at our interview that Lotus was a team on the same level as McLaren and extremely well presented. The John Player Special black and gold livery gave the team an aura of achievement and tradition, backed up by the big names that had driven for them over the years and the success they had achieved. It had been two years since they had won a race, but being at JPS Lotus would be a very different proposition from what we had experienced up to then. The team's sponsors provided a good budget but they had high expectations, and they were very protective of the iconic black and gold livery.

'By the way, do you smoke?' Peter asked. When we said that we didn't, he just responded, 'Well, I don't blame you, but you do realise you will be handling an awful lot of cigarettes?'

'That's OK by us,' we said, not bothering to bring up our Durex-handling experience.

The interview seemed to go quite well but we were told that there were other applicants and we would be informed of the outcome in a couple of weeks. As these things do, it dragged on and as we hadn't heard anything we just thought we hadn't got the job. After what seemed an age, Peter called us and said, 'The job's yours! Would you like to come and pick up the motorhome?' We had seen it in the paddock and it was longer than anything else Stuart had driven, except for the Toleman American affair that had caused us so much aggravation. The black and gold monster was sometimes affectionately known as the 'Black Pig' (and at other times not so affectionately). It had a history of regularly breaking down, as all the big American motorhomes of the day tended to do. When we went to pick it up it had been in for repair and seemed to be running pretty well. We set off confidently to take it back to our house in Alcester, trying not to anticipate what the neighbours would think of this one. Needless to say, it broke down on the way home. Fortunately it wasn't a major problem and we got it fixed, brought it home, loaded it up and two days later we were gone.

It was a huge wrench to leave Toleman because we had spent so much time with the boys there. Ted was still in Formula 1, but he was running out of money and couldn't afford our motorhome and the full service he was used to. However, Lotus didn't need our motorhome either and we wanted to keep it employed. In the end we came to an arrangement to supply Ted with the motorhome cheaply, together with a driver and a girl to provide a low-level catering facility just serving sandwiches. In effect we went to work for Lotus to support this. It seems crazy now, but we have always been a bit soft.

The difference driving the Lotus unit was amazing; people passing by on the road used to hoot their horns and wave. The drivers' names and the championship-winning emblems were emblazoned on the side of the motorhome and we became relatively well known by association. The other difference was that we went up several rungs in the paddock pecking order.

Despite Peter's warning, we were astounded by the number of cigarettes we were expected to carry. We handed them out liberally at every opportunity, stashing the stock away as tightly as possible, but we could hardly move in the motorhome. The one thing we never resorted to was smoking them ourselves! In fairness, after our experiences with the Durex stock, it all seemed pretty straightforward.

Before we actually met up with the boys in the Lotus team Peter Warr said to us, 'Some of these lads go a bit over the top. They really enjoy themselves, but they get up to quite a few tricks. I'll give you one warning, though. If ever you are with Bob Dance in the evening and you see him leaving somewhere I suggest you leave as well because that means he is up to something.' We found out over the years that he had given us some very good advice.

There were some excellent people with the team, people like Nigel Stepney, and various others who have now dispersed around the paddock or stayed with Classic Team Lotus. One character was Kenny Szymanski, a steward with American Airlines who had previously been with Lotus. He arranged all his holidays and flight schedules to come to work at Grands Prix. He just got a flight to the nearest AA destination (that's American Airlines, not Alcoholics Anonymous) and would either arrange to be collected or hire a car and arrive at the circuit in his AA uniform. He would then change into team gear and suddenly emerge as assistant tyre man with Clive Hicks. The two of them became a famous double act; they had a really good relationship and got up to all sorts of pranks, most typically dressing up at the post-Monaco party at the Tip Top club where everyone went to drink expensive, warm beer into the early hours of the morning. Clive and Kenny would always make a grand entrance at midnight, dressed in whatever they felt fitted the bill at the time, whether it was as women, or animals, or whatever. They would come tottering down the hill from the hotel in their high heels and everyone would form an arch and clap them in. Whenever Kenny was at a race it brightened the weekend.

When Peter Warr was in the right mood, or at least not up to his neck in sponsors, he would join in. There were all the usual high jinks of people having water fights that went a bit too far, with curtains being pulled down in hotels and so on. I don't think any TVs went through the windows, so it wasn't really up to rock 'n' roll standards. The problem for us was that, even if we were not actually taking part, we usually got involved through 'friendly fire'!

We went to all the races with Lotus, including the 'fly-aways', as they were known. Fly-aways were logically the races to which we couldn't drive the motorhome, so we just hired whatever was available at the circuit. This was when we started being called Mum and Dad in a big way; I think the person who really started it all may have been Nigel Stepney, and it just went on from there.

Nigel Mansell was driving for the team then. We had known him and his wife Roseanne for a number of years and followed his fortunes as he climbed the ladder to Formula 1. The two of them lived on the southern outskirts of Birmingham in his early racing days, but as his career built up he moved to a spot about ten minutes from where we live. There was always coverage of Nigel's driving achievements in our local paper, and he also opened a small kart production factory in the area. When we joined Nigel at Lotus he seemed quite comfortable with the fact that we were from his own part of the world, and Roseanne seemed to enjoy the sense of familiarity, often sitting chatting over a cuppa.

We got to know Nigel's father as he often visited Grands Prix, although sadly not Nigel's mum who died during the time we worked together. Nigel's dad became friendly with a neighbour who had helped him to care for his wife during her illness, allowing him to visit some races. Nigel was quite distressed about their relationship and often talked to us about it. I used to say to him, 'Nigel, at least your dad's finding comfort with someone; he is probably lonely. I wish my dad had found a companion. He was alone for over 35 years.'

Nigel was often classed as a whinger by a lot of people, but he was an excellent and very determined driver. At Ferrari he had the nickname 'the Lion' and it suited him, although sometimes he tried too hard for the sympathy vote; it was a pity he sometimes felt the need to exaggerate his aches and pains. Whenever I noticed him limping I used to say, 'Isn't that a different foot from an hour ago?' I could get away with teasing him, and we all laughed about it. We remained friends with them both when he changed teams and Roseanne continued to come to our motorhome for tea and a chat; years later we even met up with them in Florida when they were living there. Roseanne was very down to earth and supported her husband throughout his career, and to us Nigel was just a bloke from down the road who drank loads of tea.

We went to Dallas with the team, which was the only race we ever did there. As usual we arrived at the hotel, which was called the Loews Anatole, a bit earlier than the team, and noticed that the car park was full of motorhomes. There was obviously some sort of filming going on. It transpired that the hotel was being used to film the nightclub scenes for the big hit television series of the time, *Dallas* – and the hotel pool was being used to film scenes at the Southfork pool area (Southfork being the house that the somewhat dysfunctional Ewing family shared in the series).

Nigel Mansell had got himself a 'fixer' in Dallas, as he did in most places. By coincidence the fixer, who was a man named Charles, was the insurance agent for the whole film set. After we had been introduced, Stu and I struck up a conversation with him, and I told Charles that I was a huge fan of the series. Straight away he said, 'We're starting the next episode tomorrow, come along.' So we did, and watched the whole thing being made. Afterwards Stuart and I were invited to dinner with almost the entire cast. It felt incredible – just the two of us and all those famous TV stars. We ended the evening back at Charles's house. What a day that was.

Lotus, unusually for them, invited the stars of the show to the Grand Prix. We only had a little hired motorhome and a Portakabin, but Bobby Ewing, JR and Sue Ellen all came to sit around and enjoy the afternoon. I had my photo taken with them, and particularly Ray Krebbs, played by Steve Kanaly, who was my favourite. We were taken to Southfork, which was actually quite small and was closed that day, but we were shown around anyway. Every time we saw an episode afterwards we could tell which shots were taken at the hotel and which at the house.

Charles loved Formula 1, and Nigel always loved anyone who loved him, so they got on well together. Charles invited Nigel and Roseanne for a buffet meal and to hang out at his somewhat palatial house over the weekend. He then asked us if we would like to go along as well, and bring some friends, so we invited Bob and Shaune, and when we arrived there were some 'stars' around as well. It was a splendid evening and I ended up having my photo taken with Nigel in Charles's jacuzzi. I always joked with Nigel that I would sell it to the press when he won the World Championship, but I have reserved it for this book!

In contrast with our brush with the TV stars, the boys in the team decided to use the rather opulent hotel reception for a bit of light exercise. There were two huge stone elephants in the foyer and I watched Bob Dance getting on top of one of them with a bottle of beer in his hand. Nigel Stepney was underneath him, shoving him up. Then Greg Field, a well-known prankster from the Toleman team, who were staying in the same hotel, helped another Lotus character nicknamed Woody up on to the other, and they started throwing beer at each other. As these things invariably do, it finally all went wrong when one of them tried to stand up. Predictably, he fell off and was on the point of being whisked to hospital when he finally convinced everyone he was OK – well, as OK as he ever was. The hotel management failed to see the funny side and called the police. It was a bit messy.

We have been back recently. We were on our way to Mexico

and over-nighted in Dallas. When we walked into the foyer there was just one elephant there; we never asked what happened to the other one. Sometimes it's better not to know. The hotel got their own back, though, because on the night we stayed there, there was a Jehovah's Witness convention taking place and we were the only ones not of that persuasion. It wasn't the same, and it wasn't the same at Southfork either. That's now just a big tourist attraction.

With Lotus we mainly had sponsors as guests, primarily John Player Special senior management. Marketing manager Peter Dyke and his wife as well as managing director Geoffrey Kent were regulars. Geoffrey usually fell asleep in the back of the motorhome, so I don't think he was an avid fan, although it might have been down to the previous night's refreshments. Lotus guests drank lots of wine, something we had not been used to with our previous teams. Peter Warr was a self-professed wine buff, though, so he made sure we learned a bit about it. He wanted us to buy decent wine for his guests and never blinked at paying £30 for a bottle, which in 1984 was quite a lot of money. He pampered JPS because they were very important to the team; perhaps he was just a bit too respectful sometimes, but he certainly looked after them. They were nice people, though, and I think they would have still appreciated it if he had been a bit more relaxed with them.

Oddly, when the sponsors came and sat in the motorhome, and only Stuart and I were present, they were very ordinary and down to earth – not in the least daunting. We always treated our guests with respect, whether we liked them or not, but these were really friendly people. I suppose some would have thought they were on a bit of a 'jolly', really. They used to drink quite a lot in the evening and come to the circuit a bit heavy headed next day, but they were sponsors and at that time companies often sponsored motor racing if the chief executive was interested. That black and gold liveried JPS Lotus will always be remembered by people of a certain age, so it obviously worked.

We met a number of other JPS people, who were also all very pleasant. Colin Chapman's wife Hazel used to come to quite a few of the races, along with her son Clive and his two sisters. It was still a family affair, despite the fact that Colin had been dead for a couple of years by then. It was a really odd environment because, despite the fact everyone was getting on with their jobs at the Grands Prix, it was almost as though Colin was still there. In fairness, the rest of the paddock seemed to act in the same way and that, in itself, kept an aura about the team. It was as if no one could accept that he wasn't around and they still referred to him all the time.

We worked our way through the season reasonably successfully, but there were some strange happenings in the motorhome. I have never believed in ghosts or the supernatural, but odd things did happen. Items used to disappear – things I knew I had in my kitchen suddenly weren't there – and there was neither rhyme nor reason for it. Sometimes the motorhome would start shaking in the middle of the night, as though there was some force in there that no one could explain. One night Nigel Stepney and Bob Dance were sitting chatting with us and the whole vehicle started shaking. Engineers being engineers, they thought it might be the jacks, or perhaps the electrics, but we never found out what was causing it.

We became quite friendly with some of the other sponsors. There was this guy called Theo from Tissot watches, who had been sponsors while Colin was alive, and he had stayed with the team. One day he suddenly said to us, 'Have you seen Colin's grave?' When we said we hadn't, he responded: 'Well, I keep trying to go and see it, but for some reason they won't let me.'

'We've seen the chapel and often seen flowers there,' we said, and left it at that. However, he decided to take himself off to Ketteringham Hall after the British Grand Prix, and when he arrived there he was met by one of the Lotus PR guys. Theo said who he was and mentioned that he wanted to see where Colin was buried. The Lotus guy, recognising his importance as a sponsor, took him to the little chapel in the grounds of the Hall.

Theo said, 'Well, where's his grave?'

The Lotus guy got flustered and pointed vaguely past the chapel. 'Here somewhere,' he said.

At the following Grand Prix, Theo came to see us and told us what had happened. Then he looked me in the eye and said: 'He's not dead, is he?'

I was really shocked. 'I'm sure he is,' I said, 'I don't think there is any way he would leave his family.' A lot of conspiracy theorists believed Colin was still alive, and in hiding from the authorities in the UK following his link with the DeLorean business, but we were never among them.

John DeLorean had been the chief executive of Chevrolet in the USA and was tipped to become the top man in General Motors worldwide; however, he decided to start his own sports car manufacturing operation and was drawn to West Belfast by the offer of massive subsidies from the British government. The Labour government of the day sank almost £100 million of British taxpayers' money into the project in the hope of reducing the chronic unemployment problem in the area with the provision of 2,000 jobs. DeLorean had signed an agreement with Lotus to design the car, and the government footed the bill for this design work by paying over £10 million into a company called General Product Development Services registered in Panama. The money disappeared and the Serious Fraud Office took a keen interest in the affairs of both DeLorean and Lotus after the DeLorean operation collapsed in 1982.

Despite the fact we were confident that Colin had passed away, we used to get some extremely odd phone calls. The phone was in the toilet area at the end of the motorhome, which I suppose was strange in itself, and I used to have to answer it. We kept hearing one particular man's voice, always asking the same question, which was 'Is Mrs Chapman there?' Sometimes she was and sometimes she wasn't. If she wasn't there, the voice would ask: 'Is Mr Bushell there, then?' and if he wasn't available either the voice would say, 'Can you tell him or her…?' and there was always some kind of cryptic message, totally unconnected with anything that was going on at the track.

I would go off and find Fred Bushell, who was the chief executive of Team Lotus, and repeat the message word for word. Fred always came back to the motorhome and took the phone into the toilet; the door would then slam shut and we could hear it being locked. It all seemed very odd, but I never tried to listen and never would. We have the kind of job where, very often, people spoke absolutely freely in front of us, because frankly if they couldn't then we shouldn't have been there. The rumours continued as to whether Colin was still alive, and there were always reporters coming around to speak to our PR people. It probably wasn't helped by everyone in the team acting as though he was still running the operation; this went on for the whole of the two years we were with the company.

Years later, in 1992, Fred Bushell pleaded guilty to the charge of conspiracy to defraud the DeLorean Motor Company and was jailed for three years. The money was never recovered.

Chapter 9

THE CARING SIDE OF FORMULA 1 – YES, REALLY!

Over the years Formula 1 has developed a reputation for being a dog-eat-dog, cut-throat world where everybody involved is just out for number one and doesn't give a damn about anyone else in the sport – unless, of course, they could be called on for a favour, in which case they would be your closest friend. Fortunately we have had a huge number of experiences which proved to us that Formula 1 had a heart and that even the toughest people in the sport would rally round when there was a real need. I just want to write about one or two occasions when the paddock pulled together to help out 'one of their own'.

I have already mentioned our friends Tim and Maureen Hargreaves from Williams and Bob and Shaune McMurray from McLaren, with whom we got into untold scrapes and laughed our way backwards and forwards across Europe and beyond. One particular set of circumstances, though, brought the six of us closer than ever, and united a disparate bunch of people from around the paddock.

Tim worked as a fabricator in the Williams factory during the week and also drove the team's large American motorhome to all the European races and tests. It was common during the 1970s and 1980s for the motorhomers to have roles in the team as well as being responsible for motorhome activities, and so in the same way that Stuart looked after the pit board at the circuit, Tim had a job in the Williams garage. It was in 1983, while Tim was pushing Keke Rosberg's car back from the pit lane into the garage in Hockenheim, that he suffered a heart attack and was rushed to Schwetzingen hospital. The other motorhomers all rallied around and we managed to help the Williams guys through the weekend, but after the race the whole circus was on the move again, except for Maureen, who stayed behind in Germany with Tim.

We remained with Maureen for as long as we could, together with Bob and Shaune, but eventually we had to leave for the next Grand Prix in Austria. Ron Dennis kindly agreed that Shaune could stay in Germany to support Maureen, and Williams managed to organise for the motorhome to be taken away and delivered to the next race, but what they couldn't arrange was for someone to provide the catering service. With the full approval of our team manager, Gordon Message, and a bit of help from the other motorhomers, we managed to feed the Williams team as well as our own. When the Grand Prix was over we travelled back to see Tim; fortunately he was on the mend. In fact he and Maureen had made some new friends. Maureen and Shaune had been found accommodation near the hospital at Hotel Zum Ritter owned by a lady called Carol and her family, who looked after them both really well and helped them immensely in lots of ways, as did the family of a German chap who was in the next hospital bed to Tim.

When Stu and I got back to Germany we tried to keep Tim supplied with English teabags and digestive biscuits, but it was a full-time job because the nurses used to pinch them as fast as we delivered them! Who says the Germans don't like anything English?

Both Keke's and Nigel Mansell's doctors visited Tim, and a number of others did too, so he definitely wasn't short of medical attention. Williams were fantastic: they paid for everything and flew anyone out who Maureen wanted with her. Professor Sid Watkins was constantly checking on Tim's condition with the German specialist and even Mark Thatcher, son of the then prime minister, Margaret Thatcher, who had been a guest of Williams, sent Maureen flowers and offers of help, which was pretty good of him considering that Tim used to take the mickey out of him mercilessly. Tony Jardine, whose cartooning skills will be mentioned later, made a fantastic card and had it signed by loads of well-wishers in the pit lane, including the drivers. There was a 'whip-round' in the paddock which raised enough money to allow Tim to buy a bicycle and some expensive headphones to use as he fought his way back to health. Even the marshals from the Hockenheim circuit sent him a book on Schwetzingen, although after being in the hospital there for three weeks he'd probably seen enough of it.

Tim recovered after the excellent attention he'd received in Germany and eventually returned to work the following season, but he had to take things easier and his duties were restricted to driving the motorhome. It was a very traumatic time for all of us. Motorhomers haven't time to be ill: they are expected to be there and ready for action as soon as the team hits the circuit, irrespective of anything else happening in the world. When an event such as Tim's heart attack happens it bursts the bubble of self-absorption that surrounds motor racing. It was a moving experience to see teams and individuals stepping out of their competitive 'zones', caring, helping and responding to the needs of one of their own. This type of thing happened a lot in the past and I am sure it still goes on now.

Tim and Maureen continued to work at Williams until 1987. Tim sadly died in 1994, but we are still in touch with Maureen.

Many years later, when we were working at Bridgestone, supporting their tyre testing activities, whenever Keke Rosberg was at a test with his son Nico he always asked, 'Hey Di, how's Maureen?'

'Maureen's fine, thanks.'

Stepping forward to the late 1980s and early 1990s, while we were working for Benetton, our Plus 1 business had a contract to provide hospitality to Leyton House in their own motorhome, known unaffectionately as 'the Cucumber' due to its shape and awful colour. We hired Nick Underwood and Sue Goffin after the original people we had contracted left. It was usual to hire couples for the role, and Nick and Sue didn't exactly fit that bill because they only knew each other through a mutual acquaintance, but working and living together in such cramped conditions quickly turned them into very close friends.

Nick, who was a big guy and had the nickname 'Baloo' after the character in *The Jungle Book*, had previously worked at MSL and had driven the early Ford hospitality coach, so on the surface he seemed ideal, but while he was a good chef he was also pretty scatty and regularly left his passport behind in the hotel, or hid his money in a safe place and then forgot where it was. When the Cucumber wasn't broken down it was usually taking a wrong turn with Nick at the wheel, which meant he arrived at the circuit late while we were panicking because we had a contract to fulfil. It was Sue's first time in hospitality; she was the calm if despairing side of the partnership. Her personality always shone through, though, and she was very popular.

We sometimes thought Nick was trying to drive Stu and I prematurely grey. A perfect example of his style was the time in Hungary when he stopped at the local market on the way to the circuit to do some shopping; among his purchases was a tray of peaches that were past their best, as they generally were in Budapest at that time. Being late to the track again, and trying to carry too much at once, he had the peaches clutched to his ample chest. We were waiting impatiently in the paddock and when he came into view I could see he had squashed the peaches into the front of his uniform shirt, which was in a terrible state. I told him to change it before any guests saw him and he calmly replied, 'I haven't got another one. I forgot to pack the clean laundry.' We had to hunt for a similar-sized member of the Leyton House squad and beg a clean shirt from him.

Sue kept smiling through the mayhem, but in 1990, while we were in Japan, I noticed she was looking off colour; she said she was just a bit tired, probably due to the long flight and the late nights at the circuit. The next Grand Prix, the final one of the season, was in Australia, so we told the pair of them that, after Japan, they should go wherever they liked to chill out, so long as they were in Adelaide by the Monday before the race.

They chose to go to Townsville near the Whitsunday Islands at the heart of the Great Barrier Reef, while we were meeting up with a friend in Sydney; we'd told them where we would be and asked them to check in with us occasionally. After a day or so we received a frantic call from Nick saying Sue had been taken ill and admitted to the women's hospital in Townsville with what was thought to be an ovarian cyst; she was due to be operated on the next day. The day of the operation was our wedding anniversary and we had booked a meal at a lovely restaurant called 'On the Rocks' in Sydney. We cancelled the booking and waited in the hotel room for news. About six in the evening a distraught Nick rang us and through his tears told us that the surgery had revealed that Sue had advanced ovarian cancer.

Devastated, we rang Sue's sister in the UK to give her the news. Nick had phoned her the day before to tell her that Sue was unwell, but nothing more, so it was left to us to give her the details. We badly wanted to get to Townsville, but there was an airline strike on at the time and for a few days no one was travelling anywhere. Despite the best efforts of our friend Annie, who worked for Qantas in Adelaide, we were grounded. Sue was in hospital, Nick was in pieces, and we were in Sydney.

A few anxious days passed until Annie finally found us tickets to Adelaide, where at least we could communicate more easily through friends and the circuit office. We had notified Leyton House, who were naturally shocked, but they rallied round and phoned that stalwart, Professor Sid Watkins, who spoke to the medical team in Townsville to get an up to date medical report so that we knew the extent of the problem. Once again motor racing faded into insignificance and the Formula 1 paddock showed its human side. Sue received many messages of love and support; Leyton House were brilliant, particularly managing director Ian Phillips and drivers Ivan Capelli, who had really taken a shine to Sue, and Mauricio Gugelmin. We struggled through the Grand Prix and, with the help of friends and wives who had flown out for the last race, we managed to help at Leyton House and operate at Benetton as usual.

After the Grand Prix, and with the airline strike over, we changed our plans and flew to Townsville where we had a tearful reunion with Nick and Sue, who had been discharged from hospital and instructed to rest. We had booked them into a resort we knew in Mission Beach where the doctor who had performed her operation and his family joined them for a day or so to keep an eye on her. Ten days had passed since the operation but Sue was not passed fit to fly; she had to wait another week for test results to see if the cancer had spread. We all stayed at the resort until it was time to go back to the clinic to see the doctor.

The wait was agonising; Sue was only 25 and had a lot of living still to do. Eventually the results came through and she was allowed to fly on condition she reported immediately to Professor Hudson at St Bartholomew's hospital in London when she arrived back in England. 'Qantas Annie' arranged the flights home. We broke the journey in Singapore for a couple of nights and Sue was able to do some gentle sightseeing, but by that point the ordeal had caught up with Nick and he had a panic attack on a boat trip. Sue, Stuart and I had to look after him, which was a bit of a turnaround. Sue had remained amazingly positive throughout although, as she said at the time, 'What other choice is there?'

Back in the UK we visited Sue in Homerton University

hospital, London, where she endured a gruelling session of chemotherapy, sometimes feeling so ill she wanted to give up. Lots of us in the Formula 1 community tried to help her through it and Sid Watkins, who knew Professor Hudson, kept an eye on her progress. She eventually came through it all and is a perfect example of the power of positive thinking. We've maintained contact with Sue and we always will, as we experienced so much together. She married and had a lovely child called Jessica, now aged 12, by IVF; she didn't marry Nick but they are still in contact. At the time of writing it's 21 years since she was taken ill and on the 20th anniversary we got together to celebrate her good health.

We always think of Sue on our wedding anniversary, and the kindness of all the people in Formula 1 who rallied around her when she needed them most.

Chapter 10

AYRTON'S FIRST WIN, CHIPS AND CHARMS

In 1984 we were effectively looking after motorhomes for two teams, as we were working at Lotus and popping along to make sure that everything was OK at Toleman. That's when we got to know Ayrton Senna.

Our first impression of Ayrton was that he was very polite and quite shy. He had obviously been in England for some time, doing Formula 3, but I think he was a bit in awe of what was going on around him when he first made the step up to Formula 1. He was a really nice boy; neither Stuart nor I could get over how young he looked. Ayrton was never surrounded by PR types and minders – he just turned up, sometimes with his younger brother in tow, and got on with the job in hand. He used to call by and chat about stuff in general and we became quite friendly.

We first met him in the Toleman motorhome and he was obviously a bit confused: he knew we had some involvement there, but he didn't quite understand why we were always turning up in our Lotus uniforms to check on what was going on at Toleman. We had to explain to him that we were subcontracting our motorhome to his team, but we were running the Lotus unit. Thinking about it, I can understand his confusion.

Ayrton was a phenomenon. Despite being in the underperforming Toleman car, I am sure he would have won his first Monaco Grand Prix had the race not been stopped because it was too wet to continue. He was catching Alain Prost lap by lap, Alain was signalling that he wanted the race to stop and eventually, after 31 laps, it was brought to a halt and only half points were awarded. Well, we were in France and Alain was French.

We were retained by Lotus for the 1985 season and we were delighted that Ayrton had signed for the team as we got on so well together. He was paired with Elio de Angelis and it would be hard to imagine two more gentlemanly drivers.

Despite our love/hate relationship with the 'Black Pig', Ayrton really enjoyed being in the motorhome; he didn't like all the stuff that goes on around the race meetings like PR events, dinners and that kind of stuff. He was there for one thing and one thing only and that was to race. His dream had always been to race in Formula 1 and then to become Formula 1 World Champion. He was delighted to be in a team with such a rich history, although he had misgivings as to whether it was the right team for him because of the demands placed on him to attend formal dinners and sponsors' functions. He was happy to hang around with us and sit in the motorhome reading a book; sometimes he went to his hotel after leaving the track and then came all the way back just to relax, he felt so comfortable in those surroundings. However, Peter Warr was quite demanding of the drivers; of course he had to be, because of the JPS sponsorship. The team had made a big thing about the potential of this new driver they had signed. Equally, JPS had made a major commitment to the team and the sport, with Peter Dyke and Geoffrey Kent still attending every race. They were very proud to have Ayrton as it was plain that he was special, but the demands of all this extraneous activity were very stressful to a young driver who just wanted to get on with the business of winning.

Eventually Ayrton realised he had to follow team instructions, but he was never comfortable in those forced and semi-formal circumstances. He was much more comfortable sitting down to what we all laughingly called the 'Senna sandwich', which was his particular and peculiar breakfast. The Senna sandwich was actually a baguette with cheese and ham on it which was then liberally spread with jam. He had that every morning when he came for breakfast, with a glass of sparkling water. He knew we used to think this a bit odd, even by racing driver standards, but he took it in good part and every day, without fail, he would arrive and ask for a Senna sandwich. Sometimes he didn't have his sandwich until after first qualifying, as things were not quite as controlled on the dietary front as they are today (except, of course, for Ken Tyrrell telling Jean-Pierre Jarier that he couldn't eat anything). God knows what the nutritionists in the race teams of today would have made of it!

Our time with Ayrton was memorable in every way. By 1985 his parents had started to come to the races and we all got on very well. We were with him when he won his first race in the rain in Estoril, at the Portuguese Grand Prix. The track at Estoril had a downhill stretch and part way down it there was a gate that allowed access to the track. As the race came to a close, in pouring rain, Stuart jumped down from the pit wall, where he was in charge of the pit board, and ran all the way to the gate. He went straight through the opening and stood by the side of the track to clap as Ayrton went past on his slowing-down lap. I was watching through the motorhome window as Ayrton drove across to Stuart's side of the track, unclipped his seat belts (which wouldn't be allowed now) and hugged Stu, who had leant into the cockpit to congratulate him. One of the Formula 1 journalists wrote the following week that he had never seen a driver stop and embrace someone like that on a slowing-down lap before. It was a first and probably it will be the last time that anyone will do that. Ever since that day I have tried to find a copy of a photograph of that fantastic moment. Ayrton continued with his slowing-down lap and arrived back in the pits where everyone was waiting for him. We were all crying in the motorhome and his mum and dad were just beside themselves.

We have since been asked what kind of relationship we had developed with Ayrton that made him do something so uncharacteristic, and I can only think that he felt we had become part of his extended family, his race weekend family. He seemed so vulnerable when he came over to the UK, with most of his family all those miles away in Brazil. I just think that he felt comfortable and relaxed with us in the security of the motorhome.

Unfortunately, while Ayrton was attracting the attention of the world of motor racing he also attracted the attentions of a stalker! Many men would have been quite pleased to have a female stalker but it made Ayrton very uncomfortable and often he would hide away in the motorhome until she gave up for the day. She looked Portuguese with long auburn hair, wore white high-heeled shoes and a skirt that swirled as she walked, and was about twice Ayrton's age. No one knew her name or how she managed to get into the paddock but she was always around either sitting watching the motorhome or continually walking past trying to get a glimpse of him. We used to spot her coming and Peter Dyke, the JPS marketing director, used to say, 'Here she is! Better warn Ayrton.' Often we managed to get her thrown out but she would turn up again the next day as if nothing had happened.

Sometimes Ayrton was a bit too relaxed, however, as I recall from one particular night in Spa, at the Belgian Grand Prix. A group of we motorhomers had decided we would walk up the hill from the circuit to one of the many 'friteries' that featured the best of Belgian cuisine, namely chips and mayonnaise, when who should come walking up to us but Ayrton.

'What are you doing here?' we asked. 'Shouldn't you be at some PR event?'

He said, 'I didn't want to go so I told them I wasn't up to it – too tired.' Then he asked us, 'What are you two doing tonight?'

We looked a bit shamefaced and said, 'Well, we're just walking up the road, actually, to get some chips at the "friterie".'

'When are you going?' he asked.

'In about 10 minutes, as soon as I have finished washing up.'

'Can I come with you?' was his somewhat surprising response, to which we said, 'Of course you can if you want to – but look, there are crowds of people out there and they are bound to recognise you.'

'I don't care; I would like to come with you.' He was adamant.

We shuffled our feet a bit and said in a rather embarrassed manner, 'Well, there's one more thing; we don't go all the way around past the garages and out of the main gate. We roll under that little locked gate at the top of the paddock near the hairpin. If you don't mind rolling under the gate it's fine.'

So the three of us rolled under the gate, quickly followed by the Williams motorhomers, and we could hardly get through as we were in hysterics at the lunacy of it all. We walked up to the 'friterie' and it was packed with people. There were no chairs to sit on or anything like that, and Ayrton had one of Stuart's caps pulled down round his ears and his collar up because it wasn't all that warm.

When he asked what we were going to have to eat we said, 'Well, we don't know whether you should have this or not as it's a bit fatty, but we are having chips and mayonnaise.'

'I know I shouldn't have this,' he said, 'but I love chips.' So he had fricadelles, which are long sausages, and chips sitting on the kerb by the side of the road in between Stuart and me. The public were going past and none of them looked at us twice because we were not wearing our uniforms. Then Jean Sage, the Renault team director, walked past. Noticing Stuart he shouted, 'Hello Stu, enjoying your chips?' – and then he looked at the rest of us. He did the perfect double take and actually walked backwards to make sure he had seen what he thought he had seen. Then he just said 'Good' and walked off. He was the only person who had recognised Ayrton.

When we'd finished our gourmet meal and were walking back to the track we asked Ayrton how he was going to get back to his hotel. He was staying at the Dorint, some way away. We were all a bit perplexed for a moment or two until we came across Bob McMurray from McLaren, who kindly volunteered to take him back. Ayrton won the race the next day from Nigel Mansell, so plainly fricadelles and chips are fine racing fuel.

At Imola, which was the race after his first win, Ayrton's mum wanted to give us something to commemorate the event and to thank us for being there for him. She sent Stuart an expensive pen in a fine case and me a beautiful silver chain with a blue stone on it, in a gorgeous presentation box. The stone is a traditional Brazilian charm to ward off the evil eye or 'olho gordo'. She attached a little note that said: 'I want you to wear this, Diana, for as long as Ayrton is racing, even if you are not in the same team as him.'

When Ayrton gave it to me he said, 'Mum wants you to wear this,' and I wore it every weekend that he raced. After a while it got quite worn and so I used to carry it around in a box and just wear it on race day. I am not really religious or particularly superstitious, but something compelled me to do it.

Chapter 11

ANTICS, TRAGEDY AND CLOSE ENCOUNTERS OF THE SPOOKY KIND

While we were building the relationship with Ayrton, the usual mayhem was going on all around us. There were so many happy times with the lads at Lotus, and I particularly remember one incident in 1985, when we were in Austria. It was my birthday and Austria being Austria there were masses of logs hollowed out and filled with geraniums all around the paddock; they looked really pretty. As usual, we were sleeping in the motorhome and we woke up one morning to find all the chairs and tables had been moved from under the canopy and dumped outside. The space had been filled with all the flower-filled logs from around the paddock to wish me a happy birthday! Nigel Stepney and Bob Dance were the instigators and they, with four of their colleagues, had come back after their night out and quietly done the deed. The downside for them, of course, was that when they arrived for breakfast we were still trying to move the flowers and find the furniture, so there was a bit of a delay.

Tony Jardine was the Lotus press officer in those days; now he is a well-known pundit, commentator and after-dinner speaker. It's a little known fact that he is a brilliant cartoonist. He used to be at Brabham, driving the truck, and enjoyed the nickname of 'Teach' there as he had previously been a teacher in many parts of the world. He had done a brilliant cartoon on a scroll for my birthday present, which had been signed by the team, the drivers and the sponsors from JPS. The lads also arranged for a cake to be made. I had my photograph taken with Ayrton and Elio de Angelis presenting it to me. That is my all-time favourite photograph, and I will always treasure it.

Some of the antics the lads got up to were really funny, but one or two were very dangerous. On one occasion I was in a car with Nigel Stepney and he got bored with driving the car around the perimeter of the circuit and drove straight through the fence, during a 'race' with Bob Dance. It was all good fun, but pretty hazardous in retrospect.

In those days McLaren had the same sense of fun – although it is difficult to imagine that now – and there was terrific rivalry as to who could get up to the most mischief. I remember Bob Dance blowing up at least six portaloos in Watkins Glen in America with acetylene bombs, after taping the cubicle doors shut. The bombs were put together by shoving a plastic bin liner into the cesspit area of the cubicle, filling it with acetylene gas and taping it shut with a fuse leading outside. All that was required then was a lighter and a pretty good turn of speed. It was discovered just in time that one of the toilets had been taped closed while it was occupied, but fortunately the occupant was released before the bomb was armed. The loos just shot up into the night air. Watkins Glen toilets weren't all that salubrious to start with (as mentioned earlier). We still see lots of signs at the tracks saying 'Motorsport is Dangerous'. It certainly was when Bob was around.

All the mechanics used to get up to stupid tricks, and never more so than when hire cars were involved. I am amazed that the hire companies don't close down when the Grands Prix come to town.

In Monaco in 1984 the paddock was not under the same level of control as it is now, and the rich and famous seemed to be able to get everywhere, even the pit lane. Practice sessions at Monaco are always on Thursday and there is no running on Friday, when the roads are open to the public. Nigel Mansell was driving for Lotus at the time and was particularly concerned about the number of people in the pit lane. He had to weave through them on his way back to his pit after every couple of laps while he was trying to finalise his car set-up during the Thursday morning practice session.

Lotus was using turbocharged Renault V6 engines at the time and they were impressive on track but not particularly suited to slow manoeuvring. Nigel was getting more and more upset and expressed this in no uncertain terms to his pit crew, particularly his chief mechanic Tony Fletcher (Fletch) and John Woodward (Woody). During the lunchtime break Fletch and Woody decided to solve the problem. The team had a small utility van for bringing bodywork and parts from the spares truck, which was parked outside the circuit, into the pit lane. The van had a Klaxon horn installed. Fletch and Woody spent lunchtime whipping the horn off the van and installing it in Nigel's car. They made a pretty professional job of the whole thing and wired it into one of the spare buttons on Nigel's steering wheel. (Normally steering wheels had spare buttons for pumps for drinking water and the like.)

Lotus was also experimenting with carbon brakes and a set was installed during lunch. When the afternoon session started Nigel was told about the new brakes and that he had to come in every couple of laps to have them measured for wear. 'Don't forget they only work when they're hot,' he was told. 'Oh! By the way, push that button on the left-hand side of the steering wheel.' Nigel looked surprised but gave it a try and the Klaxon made everybody jump. His eyes lit up and off he went on two 'installation' laps to make sure the brakes were up to temperature, and then he went on a 'flying lap' to really test them out.

Shortly afterwards there was this huge horn noise from up the pit lane and all the hangers-on parted like the Red Sea, much to the amusement of Nigel and the Lotus lads. What was not amusing him, however, was the new carbon braking system.

'How are they?' asked Fletch.

'Awful. Every time I press the pedal I nearly shit myself,' Nigel responded, giving his usual level of technical feedback. He was told to give them a couple more laps and then come in. Two laps later, while the Lotus lads were trying to catch up on a biscuit for lunch, as they had worked through the official period on Klaxon and brake duty, the horn was approaching again.

'How are they now?' Fletch asked.

'Just as bad; I was shitting myself on that last corner.'

'Grab a drink for a few minutes, we have a different set to try,' Fletch told Nigel, who went off into the garage mumbling and grumbling.

When the brake change was finished Nigel was called to get back in the car and give it another go. As Fletch was helping him back into position Woody dropped two unfinished Jaffa Cakes on to the seat under him. Nigel was wearing particularly thick fireproof overalls and never noticed the uninvited visitors.

While Nigel was on track Peter Warr came into the Lotus garage and asked what had been going on with Nigel's car and why it was making that God-awful noise coming down the pit lane. The lads had to own up, but Peter just laughed and walked off. He had a pretty good sense of humour, which was fortunate.

After a few more laps Nigel came back into the pits, Klaxon blaring, and when he got to his own pit box he decided he would get out of the car while something was done about his brakes. As he emerged, the seat of his fireproofs was an atrocious brown mess. The Lotus lads just said to him, 'Brakes no better then, Nigel?' He looked at them, a bit puzzled, and asked how they knew. 'You must have had quite a scare out there this time,' they added.

'What the hell are you talking about?' he asked, turning towards the garage. Fletch walked up to him and, taking a clean rag, wiped the seat of his suit and showed him the evidence. For confirmation, Nigel looked down on to the seat of his race car, back up to the grinning mechanics, and through gritted teeth muttered 'You bastards!' Then, looking about him, he sidled slowly towards the garage, trying not to turn his back on anyone.

The Lotus lads always seemed to be in trouble in Monaco. On one occasion most of the team managed to get arrested. The Grand Prix is raced around Monaco's streets, so it's fairly important that the principality's rather ornate cast iron lampposts are removed for the weekend. They are taken up and stored, ready to be reinstated when the Formula 1 circus moves on. Just why Bob Dance decided that the Lotus team should take one of the lampposts for a walk is not recorded, but I suspect that drink was involved. Bob lined up about ten of the mechanics and they lifted the lamppost from where it was kept and, one in front of the other, marched it half a mile into Casino Square. Bob had obviously heard what Peter Warr had said about him leaving the scene of the crime because he left the others to it while he went off to his hotel.

As soon as the lamppost and its transport crew arrived in Casino Square all the lads were arrested (no charges were brought against the lamppost) and taken to the police station. After a few hours Bob Dance received a phone call at the hotel and the situation was explained. Bob was, after all, team manager and therefore supposed to be a responsible individual. After handing over a suitable number of French francs, Bob and the guys were put in the back of a police van and taken back to the square to be reunited with the lamppost. By this time most of the other teams had become aware that the Lotus lads were in jail and had come along to watch the fun.

The police insisted that the lamppost be returned to its storage spot and the lads were ordered to lift it up and carry it back from whence it had come. The ensuing spectacle included ten drunks with a police escort carrying a lamppost along a route lined with equally inebriated, cheering and clapping Formula 1 personnel. You couldn't make it up.

I have mentioned that Peter Warr had a pretty good sense of humour, but on one occasion in Rio it was stretched to breaking point. Peter had a hire car while the rest of the guys had a minibus to take them about. One evening, when they had finished work, the guys went off to a square close to Copacabana beach. As they were debating which bar would be graced with their presence that night, they spotted Peter's hire car outside a restaurant. Peter had made an unfortunate miscalculation, as there was a fountain about ten feet away from where he had parked. The Lotus mechanics gathered around the car, a small Fiat, and lifted it bodily into the fountain. They then sat outside a bar to watch the fun.

Shortly afterwards Peter came out of the restaurant and went to get into his car, did a double take and realised it had gone. He looked around and saw it sitting there, in all its glory, right in the middle of the fountain. He knew the guys would be somewhere close to watch what happened and, sure enough, he spotted them across the road. The lads all left their drinks, retrieved the car, and got Peter on his way before the police took an interest. In fairness, he took it well.

One thing that I was proud about was the way that the guys used to look after me at the fly-away races, which was a nice change from the other way around. When we first went to Detroit with Lotus we arrived at the motel that had been booked for us and it looked pretty dire. There was a huge guy on reception who didn't seem to be too interested in checking in this mass of people who had suddenly descended on him, as race teams tend to do. I waited outside and eventually he sorted everyone out and all the guys went off to their various rooms while I waited with the luggage. It was like a comedy sketch, because everyone went in and then everybody came straight back out again.

I overheard Bob Dance and Nigel Stepney saying to Stuart, 'We can't let Mum stay here!' so we all trooped out of the place – but that meant we had to find somewhere else to stay, not such a good idea on a race weekend. It was down to Bob Dance to find another hotel, and it proved really difficult, but eventually after an awful lot of phone calls he found a place across the Detroit River in Windsor, which is actually in Canada. The hotel was marvellous compared with the one we had narrowly avoided, but we did have to get special dispensation to keep crossing backwards and forwards across the border between Canada and the USA every day. Some of the lads from the team eventually told me that the hotel we'd originally been booked into was a 'pay by the hour' motel; others told me it was a brothel! I am not sure of the distinction but I didn't really want to find out.

When we were travelling in our convoy with Williams or McLaren, and maybe one or two others, we had to find a pretty big lay-by to accommodate us all. The Lotus motorhome had a strange configuration, very different from the others. The conventional truck layout was to have a door at the front and maybe one at the back, but the Lotus version had two doors side by side in the middle of the vehicle that both entered on the same landing, which made it even stranger.

One night in France we had all stopped in a lay-by and were fast asleep when we suddenly heard a 'bang, bang, bang' on the door. Stuart got out of bed and leaned over the top step, opened the door and was confronted by a gendarme standing outside. The gendarme stuck his head into the motorhome and looked around while I stayed in bed, trying to preserve my modesty. He seemed to be satisfied, grunted in the expressive way that only French officials can, and then left. Stuart got back into bed but within a minute there was another banging on the other door, just as though Monsieur Gendarme was visiting two semi-detached houses. Stuart opened the door again, said a few things that were definitely not French but needed little translation, and our caller went away looking confused. We then heard further banging and expletives as the hapless gendarme moved down the line of motorhomes. We had no idea what he was looking for, but he obviously never found it.

Working with Lotus gave us the opportunity to meet some really interesting people, including the Harrier display team pilots who performed at lots of Grands Prix. Peter and Bob Dance were very interested in their planes so they made sure that the pilots always came around to our motorhome for meals when they had finished their display. These were British airmen, and not a bit like the scary American airman from Ketteringham Hall who we were destined to meet later... At the 1984 Austrian Grand Prix we became very friendly with the lead pilot and instructor, Bruce Cogram, who was in charge of the Harrier team. Bruce was a gentleman; all eight of them were, and he arranged for us to have a tour of their fantastic aircraft. At the end of the season we were privileged to receive a signed photograph and a note from Bruce, thanking us for our hospitality.

Then, in February 1985, we heard a newsflash about a Harrier accident over Germany. For whatever reason, I had the feeling it was Bruce. The next day there was a small snippet in the newspaper naming him. We rang Bob Dance and he provided the details: two aircraft had collided in mid-air, Bruce's and a German fighter plane; Bruce had been killed instantly, the pilot he was training had ejected. I cut the small article out of the newspaper and mounted it with the photograph. It was strange that I was convinced it was Bruce when it could have been any one of the many instructors in Germany at that time.

At the end of each season we took the motorhome back to Lotus headquarters at Ketteringham Hall. To be fair, we were glad to see the back of it because it had become pretty long in the tooth by our second year, and it kept breaking down to the point that we wouldn't travel on our own and always made sure we were with at least one of the other motorhome couples. On one of our trips we were sitting in a traffic jam at the Portuguese border and the engine, which was always overheating, was boiling over – and so was Stuart. He became so frustrated he took all the air conditioning drive equipment from under the bonnet and threw it over a hedge. Strangely, the engine stopped overheating after that. It was a pretty unpleasant experience to be in one of those great big things when it was broken down as there was nowhere to hide. The traffic would be held up, with everybody blowing their horns and telling us to get out of the way – frankly, we would have liked nothing better. We often felt like just leaving it and thumbing a lift home.

The other reason we were glad the season was over was that one of Peter Warr's friends, Karl-Heinz Zimmerman, who had a hotel in Lech in Austria, had started to turn up and get in the way. Karl-Heinz used to bring along a fresh trout or salmon and want us to turn over the kitchen to him so that he could cook it for Peter and the sponsors. He would always approach us at the same time, just as I was trying to feed the team personnel who had to eat around on-track events. It was impossible to cook both meals at the same time on our tiny cooker, which meant either Peter or the boys had to wait. No prizes for guessing who won.

Some years later Karl-Heinz moved on to run a number of Formula 1 contracts, the most significant of which was Bernie's Bus, where a select band of important people who have no particular team affiliations hang out at races. Karl-Heinz still has the bus at the circuit, and his hotel, where movers and shakers from the Formula 1 industry are regularly invited to stay.

Given the circumstances, then, we were pleased to arrive back at Ketteringham Hall at the end of the 1985 season. We were, of course, late, following our traditional mechanical breakdown. The team knew we were coming and had arranged things so that we only had to press a button on the electric gate to let ourselves in. We drove through and parked just inside the perimeter fence. By that time it was around two in the morning and pitch black, except for a light from one of a couple of cottages in the grounds of the Hall, where team members lived. We were staying in one of them with some friends, Ian ('Duck the Truck') Martin, who used to drive one of the trucks, and Jude, his wife. They were waiting up for us and had no idea where we were, as this was long before the era of mobile phones.

From where we had parked we could see Ketteringham Hall and it seemed to be lit by a bit of a glow. We had left our car in the grounds on a previous visit, when we had gone to pick up the motorhome after another repair, and we went to get it so that we could transfer our personal belongings from the truck. Unfortunately the car had a flat tyre, but we decided to load it up anyway and sort it out the next day. Stuart was filling the car as fast as he could, with his back to the Hall, but I was looking towards it. From the direction I was standing, Ketteringham Hall had three rows of windows on three floors. I suddenly felt very cold and I told Stuart, 'There's someone watching us from one of the middle row of windows and there is a bluish glow coming from behind him.' It was quite eerie; the wind was blowing and we only had a torch and the lights in the motorhome, which were getting dimmer by the minute. We decided it must be a security guard watching us and got on with the unloading. Then I looked again and said, 'Stuart, that person has moved to the top floor and the glow has moved with him. I really don't like this.'

There had been rumours about Ketteringham Hall, which had been used as an air base by the American Bomber Command during the Second World War. Stuart finally took his head out of the boot of the car and he saw it too. Before either of us could speak the person had moved back down to the second floor – and so had the glow. To this day I can still remember the figure looking out at us. We did our best to ignore it, finished loading the car and then had to contemplate the walk through the woods to the cottage with nothing but a dim torch to help us find the path. It was very scary.

We got to the cottage and banged on the door. Jude opened it, took one look at our faces, and said: 'God, are you two all right?'

I said, 'Yes, but tell me, is there any security in the Hall?'

'Well, there used to be, but why do you ask?' Jude replied.

'Someone was watching us, but they kept moving from one floor to another in a split second.'

Jude and Ian looked at each other and Ian said, 'That's OK, we know about that,' and didn't say anything else about it. They gave us a drink and we started to chat and were slowly relaxing when, all of a sudden, the stable-style front door opened, first the bottom and then the top. Then the door between the lounge, where we were sitting, and the kitchen opened as well. It was as though a gust of wind had come right through the cottage.

I couldn't help myself and said, 'Jude, is it a bit ghostly around here?'

Smiling, she said, 'Don't worry, it happens often. Two weeks ago, while Duck was at the race, I was lying in bed and these bright lights were outside. I thought perhaps there was a helicopter landing, but when I looked out of the window there were three American helicopters hovering with their lights full on, and then they just vanished. I asked one of the neighbours if they had seen anything, or was it the police looking for something. They said they saw them too, but then they just disappeared.'

When we finally got to bed we had a bit of an uneasy night, although nothing else untoward happened. The next morning we went to a meeting with Peter who, like us, didn't know at that stage that we wouldn't be going back the following season. We handed him the keys to the motorhome, and our passes, and he thanked us for everything we had done. As the meeting was drawing to a close I said, 'Peter, are there security staff on every floor at night?'

He looked a bit quizzical and then said, 'We haven't got any security. Why do you ask?'

We told him what we had seen the previous night and he just said, 'Oh, don't worry, that was just the airman.'

'What airman?'

Peter smiled. 'The American airman. That's the reason we don't have any security. They won't stay here any more.'

'Was he a ghost, then?' we said, incredulously.

'I suppose he must be; he's been seen around a lot. He was probably only protecting you and checking who you were!'

It started with Colin's room looking like he had just stepped out of it and ended with an elusive American airman. I decided I was never going to Ketteringham Hall again although, as it happened, I did go there just once more – during the day!

Chapter 12

ENGLISH OR ITALIAN, MR BENETTON?

By the end of 1985 Ted Toleman couldn't continue racing, so he sold the team to Luciano Benetton, who owned the clothing empire and had been a team sponsor. During that winter we were told that Peter Collins was leaving Williams to join Benetton. Peter, an Australian, had left a promising career in business and moved to England to join Lotus some years earlier, then subsequently fallen out with Colin Chapman and gone off to join Williams as team manager. We had met him many times in the paddock and we'd become friends.

Peter confirmed that the newly established Benetton team had hired him and he, in turn, asked us if we would like to work for Benetton. The same people whom we had worked with at Toleman had stayed through the name change, and it was still like a family; we felt we really wanted to go back. We knew Mr Benetton as well, and liked him a lot, so we agreed.

We also had a contract to supply hospitality facilities to Ken Tyrrell under our 'Plus 1' banner. The Tyrrell team had secured sponsorship from a company called Data General and, as part of the financial package, the company funded the motorhome. It was reassuring to know that Ken had been happy enough with our previous efforts to offer us the contract; however, as we'd accepted the role with Benetton we had to find some other couple to run the Tyrrell operation from our motorhome. We advertised in the local paper under the heading 'A Unique Opportunity' and had some interesting responses. The people who secured the position, Julian and Jo Peyser, really thought the job lived up to the 'unique opportunity' billing and enjoyed themselves immensely over the life of the contract, but other applicants took some extreme measures to try to secure the position. We had asked for photographs of the applicants, to make sure they looked the part, and one over-enthusiastic lady sent in a picture of herself topless. I never knew whether she thought that would clinch the deal.

The downside of our decision to join Benetton was that we had to tell Peter Warr and Ayrton that we were leaving. It also meant missing the opportunity of working closer with Johnny Dumfries, or John Colum Crichton-Stuart, the 7th Marquis of Bute, as he is now referred to. We had met Johnny when he did some testing for Lotus; he joined the team full-time for the 1986 season, just as we left.

We wrote to tell Peter that we wouldn't be going back to Lotus, and he asked us to go to a meeting to discuss our decision. We went along to explain how we felt and he was OK on the surface, but it was plain that he wasn't happy. It was a difficult meeting and a difficult decision because we liked the boys in the Lotus team and we'd got on quite well with Peter, despite him being a bit overwhelming. Well, that's what we thought at the time, but by today's standards he was probably not frightening after all. After the meeting Peter wrote to say he couldn't understand why we were leaving after all he had done for us, which made us feel terrible, but we also thought we had done rather a lot for the team as well. He also asked if we could find someone to replace us and help the team through the first few races, so we did.

Clive Hicks, the Lotus tyre man, had told us about this chap called Peter Gurr and his wife, Jane. Peter, or Pete as we came to know him, was a chef at the hotel that Lotus stayed in on the A2 when they were at Brands Hatch. Apparently Pete was a fanatical Lotus fan and had asked if he could be considered if a position with the team ever came up. When this opportunity arose we thought we would have a chat with him and fixed to give him an interview. Our hearts sank when he and Jane arrived as they turned up in a black Morris Marina with gold stripes and a liberal sprinkling of Lotus stickers. We instantly thought, 'He's too much of an anorak and he will be too awestruck to do the job properly.'

We went ahead with the interview, though, and he was so keen it almost hurt. Unfortunately he didn't have a Heavy Goods Vehicle licence, as they were called in those days, but the regulations were a bit grey and it was possible to drive on a normal licence if the vehicle was privately registered. Pete had driven vans and assured us he would be fine, and remembering how desperate we'd been to get a chance just a few years earlier, we arranged for them to meet Peter Warr. They were given the job on the understanding we kept an eye on them. Pete was 'over the moon', and he and Jane became firm friends of ours, despite being much younger than us.

We helped Pete and Jane to settle in, as we'd promised, so to a degree we had reversed the procedure. Previously we had worked for Lotus and kept an eye on Toleman, and now we were doing exactly the opposite for the first few races, although Toleman was now Benetton Formula.

Our time with Lotus had been very special for the friendships we'd developed, and it was a wrench to leave, but telling Ayrton was the saddest moment. We had kept in touch with him during the winter, and when we told him we were leaving he asked if it was a monetary problem with Peter Warr and Lotus; he said that if it was he would be happy to top up our salary with £5,000 a year out of his own pocket if we would stay. We told him it wasn't a money issue, that it just felt right to go back to the Toleman environment. He said he understood, and that he hoped we would always stay friends, and asked us if we could find out from Benetton if it would be OK for him to come to see us for a chat when he had time. The old Toleman team members had been upset when he had announced he would be joining Lotus in 1985 and he was unsure of his welcome.

All motorhomers have their own approach to their drivers, which creates a different driver atmosphere from team to team. Our approach was to let the drivers find their own level: if they wanted to chat, we would be happy to chat with them, and if they wanted to be quiet and reflective we left them to it. Ayrton liked our company and chatted about all manner of things. He was very comfortable in the Lotus motorhome, which helped him to relax. I hope he managed to build the same relationship in his other teams after we moved on.

Being back with Toleman, even with a new name, was like going back home. It didn't change when Benetton came in, they kept it like a family and it stayed resolutely different from every other team, although the family grew a little. For the first year it was the same boys in place and it was pretty much like being at Toleman, but with more money. We were still using our little motorhome that first year and were down at the less successful end of the pit lane, but there was a superb atmosphere. Things changed gradually over the initial period, but as the team started to improve more money was made available and the rate of change speeded up.

Peter Collins might have left Williams, but he hadn't cut his ties entirely and he still used to invite Patrick Head around to the Benetton motorhome for dinner fairly regularly. The lads would all be working and the two of them had little to do at that stage except wait around to make sure everything had been finished properly. Naturally there was a fair drop of wine about, and Peter used to make sure that Patrick got the lion's share of it in the hope that he would be a bit indiscreet with a few technical details. Peter used to whisper to me, 'Get another bottle of red wine out,' and I knew what he was up to. After a couple of bottles of wine Patrick would be quite vocal and Peter would be winking at me. I am not sure if anything useful came out of it all, or whether Patrick knew exactly what was going on, but it was quite amusing to watch.

The Benetton family owned the team but they didn't interfere with the day-to-day running of it because, at that stage, they didn't really know much about the way it all worked. Mr Benetton was a most delightful man, who always pretended that he couldn't speak English, but one of Stuart's jobs was to pick him up from the airstrip when he arrived at a race and from the moment he got in the car he always spoke English to Stu. In meetings he always used his 'lack of English' to his advantage. Mr Benetton may have been very quiet but he never missed a trick; he could see what was going on. It slowly became a proper business and it was plain that some things needed to be changed.

One thing that hadn't changed, though, was the character of the team. We had some very interesting people who had started at Toleman and went on to make big reputations for themselves in Formula 1. Rory Byrne, who was chief designer, Gordon Message, the team manager, and Pat Symonds were all with Toleman in Formula 2 originally, and they had stayed with the team throughout its trials and tribulations.

The title of 'Mum and Dad' had followed us from Lotus to Benetton and it spread like wildfire. Gerhard Berger and Teo Fabi were driving for the team in our first year and they had very different temperaments. Gerhard thought my name was 'Pam' for a long time, because he reckoned he had heard a lot of people calling me by that name. In the end I had to say to him, 'Gerhard, it's not Pam.'

'But everyone calls you that,' he said, looking extremely confused.

Then it suddenly clicked and I said, 'No, you've misheard, they are saying Mum.' Gerhard went on to become a friend and got us into a few scrapes with his practical jokes.

Some of the drivers never spoke much and Teo was one of them because he was quite shy, but despite his shyness he was very quick when he got in the car, and he scored Benetton's first ever pole position, in Austria in 1986. Throughout our career we were lucky because, although they were all very different, we never worked with a driver we didn't really like.

Motorhomers were a family too, as I've said, and if one had a problem we all shared it. In March 1986 we were at the Paul Ricard circuit; we had just finished a test and were packing up the motorhome. There was only Stuart and me, along with Tim and Maureen, left in the paddock when the police came to speak to Tim to explain there had been an accident and ask for team management contact details. Frank Williams and Peter Windsor had rushed off to try to catch a plane at Nice airport and their car had left the road. Peter wasn't seriously injured, but Frank's neck was broken just above the spinal column, causing him to be confined to a wheelchair for the rest of his life. We were allowed to stay in the paddock that night in order to be near a telephone, in case Tim had to go to the hospital. It was all very difficult because, of course, neither of us had a car, just the motorhomes. We supported them in the best way we could.

There seemed to be a never-ending stream of talent joining the team in the late 1980s and into the '90s; in addition to Pat Symonds and Rory Byrne, Pat Fry turned up too. Pat Fry was a particularly pale-looking chap and I remember distinctly, when he moved from the research and development department in the company and joined the test team, thinking that it might put some colour in his cheeks – and I wasn't wrong. I was usually drafted in to help out with the team uniforms, assisting with the original measuring and then sorting the mountains of stuff out when it arrived, trying to match it to the person who had been measured for it. I had been sorting Pat out because, at the following week's test, he was due to make his pit-lane debut and needed some kit. Stu and I then went off to Jerez to make sure everything was in place when the guys arrived some time later.

We were all set up, waiting for the test to start, but we weren't expecting the test team to arrive until the next day. As it was going to be Pat Fry's first experience of the pit lane he and 'Symmo' came to the circuit a day early so he could become familiarised beforehand. We hadn't realised they were coming, however, and Maureen from Williams and I were sunbathing topless on the viewing area on the roof of our motorhome. It was a perfect day, and we were quite relaxed and admiring the scenery when we suddenly heard some footsteps on the stairs leading up to the roof.

'Someone's coming,' Maureen said, but I just replied, 'It will only be Stuart, don't worry about it.'

No sooner were the words out of my mouth than Pat Symonds's head popped up, closely followed by Pat Fry's. Symmo didn't turn a hair as he had seen us around the swimming pool topless before, as that was the fashion at the time; we were a slightly different shape then, too! But Pat Fry didn't know where to look (although Stu says he probably had a pretty good idea) – I had been hoping Pat would get some colour into his cheeks on the test team but there he was, scarlet with embarrassment, and he'd only been there two minutes. It had just been a week since I was making sure he had all his race kit and there I was without mine. Stuart said that this encounter had given a whole new meaning to the 'viewing deck' and that Pat had become much more familiarised than he had bargained for.

Pat Fry was certainly an interesting guy. He used to get terrible headaches, and he said to me more than once: 'Do you think I have got a brain tumour?' I said I doubted it and I was probably right as the last time I saw him, over 20 years later, he was standing on the Ferrari pit wall as the head of racetrack engineering.

However, some things don't change, and in keeping with

the Toleman tradition most Benetton dinners ended up with a bread-roll fight and red wine poured everywhere. We really appreciated that, when the team had gone off to their hotels leaving us to clean up all the mess before we went to bed. Rory was usually in the middle of the shenanigans but never in the middle of the clearing up – unless he was asleep, of course, and then we had to clean around him.

There was always a lot of banter between the Benetton boys and the guys from Williams. Nigel Mansell was driving for Williams then and, as I've mentioned, he has always had a tendency to appear injured, with one bit or another bandaged up. All the guys really admired Nigel's driving but were less impressed by this other aspect of his character. I think, at that point in the season, the two teams were about equal on points when Nigel appeared in the pits with his elbow bandaged, so to wind Williams up, all the Benetton mechanics went on to the grid before the race with their elbows bandaged too. It was obviously a mark of respect.

Every time I think about Rory Byrne I have to laugh because he could fall asleep anywhere. He was even worse than Stuart, because he could fall asleep in the middle of a conversation. Sometimes he would 'drop off' during a meal and his chin would fall into his soup. This often happened when the team all went to a restaurant together; the other guys would get up from the table on the count of three and leave him, so when he woke up he would be stuck with the bill. When he came for breakfast the next morning he would just say 'I had to pay again, 14 of us this time.'

Rory went down in paddock folklore for actually falling asleep on the pit wall in the rain, standing up, and had someone not caught him he would really have dropped off. He was always considered to be 'on the edge' of everything, including the Formula 1 regulations! Rory always pushed the boundaries of the rules to bending if not breaking point, and he always seemed to have a different interpretation of the rulebook from everyone else. He usually proved his point, but occasionally, during the Benetton period, his understanding of the rules was deemed to be wrong. He used to sit and think about things, in silence, while all the lads would be hanging around waiting to set the car up for the next day and we would be waiting to go to bed. We often waited hours for his instructions.

From my point of view I could never understand why the team, which had qualified well on Saturday afternoon, used to pull the car apart on Saturday night, then sit about waiting while Rory was in one of his trances, thinking everything through. I used to look at the engineers and it was plain to see that they were sitting there thinking 'Come on, what are we doing?' and drumming their fingers while Rory, who was chief designer, scribbled away and didn't speak for half an hour as he was deep in thought. No one dared to interrupt him. It might be midnight before the lads were given their list of jobs and could start rebuilding the car and incorporating whatever Rory had dreamed up.

I remember when we were at the Phoenix Grand Prix it was really hot, which as Phoenix is in the desert didn't come as a huge surprise to anyone. However, Rory had a brainwave and decided the lads should start cutting holes in the bodywork to allow more air into the car – at two o'clock in the morning! Apart from him I was the only one in the motorhome at that unearthly hour and I had to say: 'Rory, do you mind if I ask you something?'

He looked enquiringly at me, cocked his head to one side and said, 'Yes, Mum?'

'Did we know it was going to be hot here?'

'Yes.'

'Then why didn't we bring bodywork with some holes already cut into it? Don't we do that sort of thing?' I asked, to which he replied, 'That would have been a good idea,' and wandered off to get another coffee and watch the lads cutting his holes until 4am.

Incidentally, one of the local traders was much more on the ball than Rory. He used his local knowledge to manufacture a truckload of straw hats with solar-powered fans in the middle of them. Everybody in the pit lane was given one and they were all wearing them in an effort to keep cool; unfortunately they were all wearing them when Bernie Ecclestone walked down the pit lane and made everyone take them off. His instructions became law – and lore – in the paddock. 'No silly hats in the pit lane, no silly hats in the pit lane' was a Bernie-ism that lasted for some time.

Perhaps I went off at a tangent there, but Rory was off at a tangent a lot of the time. He had a wart on his nose and when he was deep in thought he would twizzle it, and the more agitated or excited he got the more he would twizzle. The lads would say 'Oh, no! He's in top twizzle mode now; he's tuning in his radio to tell us something.'

Rory announced his retirement from motorsport twice, and we had two collections for him. He did actually leave for a short period to go diving in the Philippines, but not long afterwards he turned up at Ferrari. Rory had his own unique interpretation of the rules, including the rules about retirement collections but, as Stuart always says, 'Well, that's what he's paid for.'

Gerhard Berger scored his and Benetton's first Formula 1 win in Mexico in the penultimate race of 1986. The race was coming to a close and we were leading. I was standing at the back of the garage and could barely watch; I had to keep going off to do something. I could never stand the tension when we looked like winning. Someone from the FIA came up to me and said, 'When you win, what national anthem do you want playing?'

'I've no idea,' I replied. 'I'll go and ask.' Fortunately Luciano Benetton was in the garage, not on the pit wall like he often was, so I walked over and asked him the question.

Mr Benetton thought about it for a second, then looked straight at me, smiled and said: 'British, of course.'

'Not Italian?'

'No, British.'

I will always remember that. When the race was over we stood at the back of the garage and he put his arm around my shoulder; it was very emotional. 'I haven't won a Grand Prix before,' he managed to say. We had, of course, but not with Benetton.

I always think about that conversation when I hear that interminable Austrian national anthem played after Milton Keynes-based Red Bull win a race. It's just a different approach, I guess.

Chapter 13

ELIO DE ANGELIS

Elio de Angelis was a strange combination of concert pianist, perfect gentleman and hugely competitive racing driver. He drove for Lotus between 1980 and 1985 and then left to join Brabham for the 1986 season. Elio had many claims to fame, but one of the oddest was that he kept all the other drivers amused during a stand-off with the FIA which caused a drivers' strike at Kyalami in South Africa before the first race of the 1982 season. The drivers were angry about a change to their terms and conditions they had to sign up to in order to qualify for the super-licence they needed to race in Formula 1. On the Friday morning of the race weekend they disappeared off to the banqueting suite of the Sunnyside Park Hotel in Kyalami so they could maintain some solidarity and show they were serious about their objection to the changed terms. While they were holed up in the hotel Elio kept them all entertained with his piano playing.

Elio was a Roman and he was accompanied at the races by his father, who had a large building company in the city, and his delightful girlfriend Ute, an ex-model. Elio, Ute, Stuart and I became firm friends while we were together at Lotus, and even after we had all left the team Elio always came back to chat with us at races and tests. At one test at Paul Ricard in France in 1986 Benetton happened to have one of the only motorhomes there, despite the fact there were a number of teams testing. Elio and Ute came by to say 'hello' and we made them some pasta for lunch. We sat around chatting and then John Gentry, who was Elio's race engineer at Brabham, came along and said: 'Right Elio, your turn!'

Elio gave Ute a peck on the cheek, saying 'bye' to me and that he would see us both later. I told him to come back and have a drink after the session and off he went.

Shortly after he had gone out on track we were aware of that eerie silence that comes over a race circuit when everything has stopped for an accident. We could see black smoke in the distance and knew something serious had happened. I was in the kitchen of the motorhome and could see drivers starting to walk back into the paddock with their crash helmets off. I was counting them back and mentally ticking off who I had seen. I went outside and Ute was obviously doing the same. I looked at her and thought, 'God, don't let it be Elio.' I didn't want it to be anyone, but I knew it had to be someone.

I saw Nigel Mansell coming towards me and I mouthed to him 'Who is it?' He whispered back 'Elio' and then Keke Rosberg came by and looked from Ute to me and whispered the same. By now it had dawned on Ute that it was him and she set off to run towards the track before Stuart grabbed her and said 'Ute, stay here, stay here.' Then Gordon Murray, the Brabham designer, and John Gentry came to her with tears in their eyes. John's hands were terribly burnt from trying to pull Elio out of the car. It was obvious that the situation was very serious and Ute was distraught. We had to keep hold of her as she was desperate to go to him. Eventually, after what seemed a lifetime, a helicopter arrived and he was taken to hospital.

The wing had come off his car at 180mph and it somersaulted, coming to rest upside down on a run-off close to a tree. Elio was hanging there from his seat belts with the car on fire; John and Gordon tried desperately to get him out but couldn't get near. The circuit medical and transportation facilities have improved beyond measure over the years, but at that time there were no helicopters standing by, or any of the current safety measures. When the helicopter did arrive it was half an hour after the accident.

The test was called off at that stage and we packed up as quickly as we could and set off, in silence, along the winding Cote d'Azur coast road. We knew there wasn't going to be any good news. We later heard on the radio that Elio had been taken to hospital in Marseilles and that he was in a critical condition. He died the following evening. Incredibly, he had only suffered relatively minor injuries from the crash, but he succumbed to smoke inhalation.

We never saw Ute again. She couldn't bear to go anywhere near a racetrack. We received a message from her by way of one of the German journalists to say she was OK, and we exchanged a Christmas card or two. I hope she's happy; she deserves it.

There is a small plaque at the circuit, close to a tree at the point where he was killed. The track layout has changed now and it's no longer close to the action. The last time we went to Paul Ricard I asked someone to take me down there so I could leave some flowers, and a few tears.

Elio's music lives on and he can be seen and heard on various YouTube sites.

Chapter 14

TRUCKED!

After using our original motorhome in the first season with Benetton we found that the company had commissioned a new one 'more in keeping with their image'. Benetton wanted to raise standards in every area and, as one of the changes, had designed and built a new motorhome. This was going to be the first hospitality truck in the Formula 1 paddock with pop-out sides, although they were regularly used in American motorhomes. Peter Collins took us with him to Treviso in Italy, where it was being built, to give it a quick 'once over'. When we arrived at the factory we were confronted with the ugliest thing I had ever seen. The truck was purpose built on a normal articulated 14-metre trailer. It didn't appear to have any windows in it, although it had two side doors, and it was painted matt green, matt pearl grey and dark grey. It was a hideous forerunner of some of the huge motorhome assemblies we see in the paddock today. The side pods popped out on RSJs to increase the motorhome's interior space; then, as hydraulic feet came down, the sides opened out to finally reveal the windows. We named the truck 'The Transformer'.

We looked at it and had to say, 'Look Peter, it's a fantastic piece of Italian design but unfortunately it's totally unsuited for the job in hand. We will need ten people to build the thing.' Obviously Peter wasn't about to tell his bosses that they had made a big mistake, so we were stuck with it. We tried to help with the overall design of the motorhome, to make it more user friendly, but we were ignored and some fairly fundamental flaws made it through to the finished product. One of the more obvious problems was that it wasn't possible to move from the office at the front of the motorhome to the area at the back of the same structure without coming outside, walking along a balcony and then going back in.

A major inconvenience from our perspective was that, although it had quite a large kitchen, we needed to hoist a heavy three-phase cable up through a flap in the roof to power it up. Nine times out of ten Stuart forgot all about it when we were packing up and, as the pods were retracting, they would rip the cable out of the roof, which was not the perfect getaway. The whole thing was a nightmare to set up, and during the period we were working with it Stuart had four hernias, mainly due to the solid wooden internal walls which were really difficult to erect. To compound the difficulties, when it came to dismantling we needed at least six hours after everyone had vacated the unit to be able to clean it sufficiently to allow the side pods to be concertinaed back into their original position, as it would not be opened again until it was delivered to the next Grand Prix, and there was never that amount of time available. A combination of the nominated Italian driver wanting to leave virtually as soon as the race had finished and the team wanting to have their race debrief in it (until they had to rush off to the airport) meant we often didn't get the chance to clean as thoroughly as we would have liked. There was no way we should have been allowed to leave the kitchen like that until the next race, but there was no option.

The final problem was actually the *coup de grâce*: Stuart wasn't allowed to drive it. We first collected it on the motorway close to Circuit Paul Ricard, where it had been delivered, and then had to drive it to Silverstone. We stopped just south of Paris for the night; it was Stuart's first time driving an articulated lorry since passing his test. I was in the cab with him and he said to me, 'Look, we are going to have to get up really early because there is no way I am driving around the *périphérique* in Paris when everyone else is on the road.' So we left the hotel at 4am. It was pleasant driving, as there was nothing about at all – until we got to the *périphérique*. I think every truck in France was on that bit of road at the same time. It was horrendous and very scary, but we got it to Silverstone with no damage.

We finally got it set up and everything was fine, but then it was discovered that Stuart, despite having driven the unit from France to the UK, was apparently not licensed to drive it. Under prevailing Italian licensing laws his UK Heavy Goods Vehicle licence was not valid to drive an Italian-registered truck, so an Italian contractor named Gaetano was hired to drive it instead. When we first met Gaetano we noticed his glasses were like bottle bottoms and thought, 'Get on with it, then.' We gave him the keys and decided he could find his own way back to Dover. Hockenheim was the next race and Gaetano turned up there without mishap, but after the race he said, 'How do I get back to the motorway?'

Stuart told him, 'Look, you follow me, and when I flash my hazard lights you turn on to the motorway because we will be carrying straight on,' so that was agreed upon in a mixture of sign language and grunts. We set off and came out of the housing estate surrounding Hockenheim, past the railway, on to the main road and then we got to the motorway. Stuart flashed his hazard lights, as agreed, and we carried straight on. A few seconds later Stu looked in his rear-view mirror and turned to me, saying, 'That bastard's still behind me.' Not really having any alternative, we turned off into an industrial estate that I had spotted just ahead. There was a huge Ford dealership on the corner so we pulled up just past it and Gaetano pulled up behind us. Stuart told the hapless driver, 'You'll have to turn it round and go back down the road, then turn off where I flashed my hazards.'

Gaetano started to turn the truck around in the big wide entrance to the Ford dealers. He was doing all right, with Stuart watching his manoeuvres, although he was getting a bit off line; Stu came round from the back of the truck to the front to tell him it was going wrong. Unfortunately Gaetano carried on going backwards until he reversed into an aluminium flagpole. The flagpole proceeded to break off, close to its base, and slowly but surely it fell right across a Ford Taurus. By this time Stuart was yelling all kinds of abuse at him; he couldn't understand but I think he was getting the drift. Eventually Stu made him get out of the truck and he completed the manoeuvre. Then he tried to appease the people in the Ford dealership who, incidentally, had been Ford's guests in our motorhome over the weekend. They seemed to have enjoyed themselves but that didn't stop them charging us the equivalent of £400 for the repairs.

Gaetano disappeared over the horizon in search of the motorway and we never saw him again because Gastone replaced him. Gastone was quite a character and we will hear more about him later. The truck was withdrawn from Formula 1 at the end of 1988 and we were delighted to see the back of it.

Fortunately there were some real positives in 1988 and, as usual, they revolved around the drivers we were working with. Our drivers were Thierry Boutsen and Sandro Nannini. Sandro was a real character and I'll write in detail about him later. Thierry was probably the best Formula 1 driver Belgium has ever produced, despite being very quietly spoken. We became close to Thierry and his wife Patricia, who was a great source of paddock gossip. Patricia's nickname was 'Speedy' because she always seemed to be in a hurry, and as a result of her rushing about she was quite accident-prone so her antics gave us lots of laughs. Patricia and Thierry had been together since early in his career and she travelled everywhere with him; they were a great couple – Thierry the quiet one and Speedy the crazy one. When Thierry announced that he was leaving Benetton for Ligier Patricia supported his decision, but privately she and I sobbed together in the kitchen of that awful truck. It was a sad day for us all. We didn't lose touch, though. As their son Kevin grew a little older Patricia always brought him round to see us, irrespective of which team Thierry was driving for. Kevin never quite sorted out our two names and to him we were known as 'StuandDi', and it stuck. We often visited them in their apartment in Monaco, but sadly they eventually split up, which was a great shock to Stu and me. They are now both remarried and happy, and we are still in contact with them both.

Chapter 15

'DI, WHAT'S THAT NOISE?' – ENTER FLAVIO

We first came across Flavio Briatore at the Detroit Grand Prix in 1988. Steve Madincea introduced us to him. Steve was working for Rod Campbell at Campbell and Company, which was looking after all the Ford Motor Company PR at the time, and Ford was supplying Benetton with engines through its Cosworth association. Flavio was introduced to us as 'Mr Benetton USA' because he was responsible for all US-based Benetton stores then. At the time we assumed that Flavio was just another of the Benetton guests, but we soon came to realise there was more to his presence than met the eye.

The team attended a test in Brazil at the start of the following season. Stuart and I were surprised to see that Flavio had turned up again and went to say hello to him.

Flavio said, in his inimitable style, 'I see you in Detroit. How are you doing?'

We said, 'It's good to see you again, Mr err...' because we couldn't remember his name for the life of us.

'You just call me Flavio,' he said helpfully.

There were minimal facilities in Rio, just some old huts that served as the debrief room, the kitchen and everything else combined, and it seemed a really strange place for a guest to show up. After a while he settled down and started to read the newspaper. The cars were all droning round and I was trying to cook lunch for the team on two gas rings. Eventually Flav looked up from his paper and said to me: 'Di, what's that noise?'

'What noise?'

'That noise that give me headache.'

I realised then that he meant the cars out on the track, so I told him: 'It's the cars. The teams are testing.'

Flavio floored me by asking, 'What are they testing?'

I thought, 'Well, this chap knows nothing,' and so I told him, as politely as I could, 'Well, they are testing drivers and technical changes for the new season.'

He just looked at me and said, 'All they do is go round and round, seems stupid,' and went back to his newspaper.

Slightly put out I said, somewhat unsubtly, 'You haven't been involved in motorsport before, have you?' to which he responded, 'I only know about clothes.'

Actually, all these years later, his point has been proved because there is now a ban on 'in season' testing to reduce the massive budgets required to run a modern Formula 1 team. Perhaps he did know something, then, after all. There was an awful lot of time and money wasted in those days at the track, and it seemed to be a badge of honour to be the last team to leave the garage on the Saturday night before the race on Sunday. Even the team that had qualified in pole position couldn't help pulling the car completely apart and rebuilding it before they left the track at three or four in the morning. Nowadays the cars are in *parc fermé* following qualifying, which means the teams are not allowed to touch them. Maybe it's no coincidence that all the cars are much more reliable and a considerably higher number finish each race. I used to take the lads' supper to the garage and find the cars in bits all over the floor. 'For goodness sake,' I would say, 'we need more women in motorsport. They wouldn't operate like this.' With the influence of Flav and Eddie Jordan there were soon more women in motorsport, but they were mainly sprawled over the cars having their photos taken without much on.

Flavio came to the circuit once or twice more, after which Stuart took Peter Collins aside and said, 'I think you should look out for that Italian chap because I can see he has his eye on you.' We were a bit wary of Flavio at first, because we all got on well with Peter. Obviously Flavio had been tasked by Mr Benetton with finding out exactly how the team was being run, and that is what we'd suggested to Peter. We were quite close to him, because in our kind of job we are in the middle of what is going on but certainly not in a position to take sides. It is amazing what people talked to us about when they started to relax and, as I've mentioned before, sometimes it was information we'd have preferred not to know. But we would never betray confidences and we knew where to draw the line.

The Benetton family had become involved with Formula 1 by initially sponsoring the Alfa Romeo team, but they had been determined to own their own team and use it as a marketing tool for their business. Initially the owners had left the management of the team in the hands of the existing staff, but as their business plan developed they started the gradual move away from having pure racers running the team to businessmen running the overall operation, with someone lower down the pecking order in charge of the motorsport activity. Over the years this has become the norm rather than the exception. Flavio was appointed the team's commercial director and he was looking at how the money Benetton provided the team with was being spent; that new business approach was at odds with the views of Peter Collins, who was trying to run a race team along traditional lines. Peter's ideas were being superseded. Benetton wanted to up the image and by then global TV coverage had created the opportunity to bring their products to the attention of a world market. As Flavio slowly wrested control of the team from Peter Collins, there was almost as much activity in the motorhome as there was on the track.

That test in Rio, where Flavio had started his slow insinuation into the team, had been significant for other reasons because it was the test that would make or break Johnny Herbert's Formula 1 career.

Our first real meeting with Johnny had been at the previous British Grand Prix when he signed a contract to drive for Benetton in 1989. This little crazy kid came up the steps of the motorhome and stuck his head around the door. We knew Johnny was going to be trouble straight away because, as the Grand Prix came to a close, he turned up back at the motorhome to ask if we had seen his car keys. We hadn't, so we then had to scrape through the mud outside the motorhome looking for them. We had known Johnny vaguely because he was racing for the Jordan F3000 team, which Benetton sponsored.

Not long after he had signed the deal with Peter Collins, Johnny had had an awful accident at Brands Hatch and almost lost both his feet. It looked like being the end of the dream for him, but Peter still had faith in him. 'Look, if you can prove you can drive a race distance then you are in,' he told him. Over the next few months we got to know Johnny well – he was still laughing and joking on the surface, but physically he was in a mess. Peter sent him to a clinic in Austria to get his feet sorted, but when his test opportunity came up it looked like being a little too early; the medical team that had been looking after him doubted whether he would ever be able to walk properly again, let alone drive a Formula 1 car. Maybe, in retrospect, testing then wasn't such a big mistake because if Johnny had continued to rest he might never have got back into a racing car again.

He had had the accident in September and there he was in February, being given the opportunity to prove he was ready to drive for Benetton at a test in Brazil. Interestingly, Peter Collins didn't attend the test but Flavio did. Was it a sign of things to come? Peter asked us to watch Johnny and we all knew what was at stake. Driving a race distance was what stood between him and the fulfilment of his Formula 1 ambitions: a seat with the team. When we went to the airport at the start of the trip it didn't look promising; he couldn't even walk to the plane, which prompted us to call him 'jelly legs' – not perhaps the kindest nickname in the circumstances. When we got to the circuit he had a little bike and managed to cycle around the paddock, as he couldn't walk to the garage. Stuart actually had to lift him into the car at the start of his sessions.

The first obligatory check was to test his ability to get out of the car in a given number of seconds in case of an accident. By some act of will Johnny actually passed it: he just hauled himself up and somehow made it out, although he would never have been able to run away if the car had been on fire. When it was time to start his race-distance test Stuart lifted him into the car and, again, I have no idea how he actually managed to complete it. Stu then had to lift him out at the end of his stint; he couldn't even get back on his bike so Stu ended up carrying him back to the office. We rang Peter and told him that Johnny had done it and he was delighted. Flavio was an interested observer.

The full team then came out for the Rio race, which was the first event of the season. Johnny amazed everyone by coming fourth and I cried again. I have done quite a lot of crying, for one reason and another, at racetracks. Johnny's wife Becky was there and she was shaking; completely beside herself. Unfortunately the dream couldn't last as Johnny's feet were taking a terrible hammering, and once the season had started he couldn't take time out for treatment. Stu and I did everything we could to help. I had to take his socks off at the circuit because his legs and ankles were locking up, and it used to make my stomach turn over because there was still grass coming out of the cuts. His feet were a mess; in fact they still are. Johnny was taking huge numbers of painkillers, which concerned Stuart and me, but he was just so determined to keep going he wouldn't listen to our concerns.

Johnny was extremely single-minded, and when we went to race in Mexico he somehow walked all the way up the Aztec steps, just to prove he could do it. We had gone out for the day with Johnny and Peter Collins to see the steps, but when he started to climb them I had to say to him, 'Johnny, you just can't do this. I'll stay down here with you while the others go up.' But he wouldn't listen and he walked to the top. I will never know how he did it. He must have taken so many painkillers he didn't know what he was doing, but it showed the grit of the guy. What a hero.

Mexico was followed by the US Grand Prix in Phoenix and then by the Canadian Grand Prix, where Johnny failed to qualify for the race. That was when the whole problem came to a head. Johnny just couldn't do it any more without some time to recuperate; he couldn't even press the brake pedal down. The result was that Johnny was 'rested', and although he was devastated at the time Flavio probably did him a favour. It was the right decision because he would either have had a big accident or been unable to walk for the rest of his life. Physically he was just going downhill; and if a driver can't put any pressure on the brake or accelerator he is a danger to himself and everyone around him. Emanuele Pirro was his replacement for the rest of the season, but Johnny wasn't finished in Formula 1, or in the lives of Stu and me for that matter.

Flavio blamed Peter Collins for sending Johnny to the clinic in Austria, suggesting that he was doing things he should never have been doing with the injuries he had. He hadn't just suffered broken bones; his feet, as has been well documented, had been hanging off after the accident. This disagreement over Johnny was Peter Collins's swansong at Benetton and he left shortly afterwards, with Flavio formally taking control of the team.

Chapter 16

THE DREAM TEAM

When we heard that Nelson Piquet was joining the Benetton team in 1990 we just thought, 'Benetton are signing another "has been" but this time he's a rude one, so that's great!' Nelson wasn't Mr Popular in the paddock because he was so outspoken. We didn't really know him at that point, but he had driven for Williams and our friends Tim and Maureen knew him well. They told us he was great and that we would be pleasantly surprised. The rest of us used to say, 'You are joking! He's so offensive, and he can't be a very nice person,' but they insisted.

We decided to reserve judgement, but the pairing of Nelson and Sandro Nannini actually became our 'dream team'.

Nelson had done a deal with Flavio whereby Flav wouldn't pay him much of a basic salary but would put him on a points-related contract. In the event Nelson did well and earned a considerable amount of money. Each time he had a good result he would come in the motorhome, rubbing his hands, and say, 'That's a bit more off Flav,' with a huge grin on his face. He was a fantastic guy to be around, although he often came out with things that made me cringe. A good example was when he said that Nigel Mansell's wife Roseanne shouldn't be allowed in the paddock because she was too ugly. I didn't think Roseanne was ugly at all; she was a friendly, homely English wife.

I told him, 'Nelson, you just can't say things like that.'

'Why not?'

I would be stuck for words on occasions like this and say something like 'Because it's not nice.'

'But it's the truth! Di, you cannot deny that I never tell a lie,' he would say, though I sometimes wished he had.

I don't know how our relationship got started, really – he was just the next driver to join the team – but we must have something that encourages drivers to feel comfortable with us. We're not management and we're not mechanics; we're just someone they can talk to. It's as though they need people around them who understand enough about what they are doing but are on the fringe of it all; the drivers can unwind and chat knowing we don't want anything from them. The motorhome is their area for relaxation and when people are relaxed they chat. It's been the same throughout our career.

One morning Stu and I were at our hotel in Estoril, in Portugal, at a test and we were down for breakfast early, as was Nelson. For some reason we didn't have a hire car on that trip and we were using taxis back and forth to the track. We all had breakfast together and then we told Nelson we were off to get our cab; he asked us what time we were leaving.

'Now.'

'I'll take you,' he said. It was rush hour and we were staying on the coast, a long way from the track. We got in the car and we were terrified for the whole journey. Nelson went on the path, on the inside of the traffic and in between the trees almost all the way to the circuit. He never worried if there was a line of traffic waiting; he just drove on whatever was available, even if it was a footpath. I don't know who was more afraid – us or the pedestrians.

On another occasion we were at a test in Monza and he hadn't turned up; he had missed the whole morning's session. Nobody knew where he was until we suddenly heard a helicopter coming and, on looking up, saw Nelson with his arm out of the window, waving. We eventually realised that he wanted us to clear a space in the paddock so he could land the thing. He had got lost coming to the circuit because he had forgotten to put his map in the front seat with him – it was in the back of the helicopter in his bag.

He said later, 'I was trying to decide how I was going to fly it and get my map out, so in the end I followed a road and it took me all the way to Switzerland.' We'd been quite worried but everyone else had already decided that he was probably with one of his many lady friends (which of course he was). He had gone off for the night, got up in a hurry the next morning and not quite got himself organised. He was not allowed to land in the paddock for safety reasons and had to use a field next to the track where all the teams' cars were parked. Nelson was angry – angry with everyone, including himself, for getting lost. When he came into the motorhome he was throwing things everywhere, so we found chores to do elsewhere around the paddock and kept our distance.

Later, after racing at Paul Ricard, there was a test scheduled in a week's time at the same circuit. Nelson asked us when we would be arriving for the test and we said it wasn't worth us going anywhere – we would be staying over after the race and sleeping in the motorhome.

Nelson had his boat moored in the harbour at Bandol and he said to us, 'Well, come to Bandol and spend an evening on the boat.' Initially we said we couldn't because we had our neighbour's 16-year-old son Mark with us, helping out on that trip, and we couldn't leave him.

'Don't worry,' he said, 'I will send Geraldo down to collect you.'

Geraldo, Nelson's brother, duly arrived on the appointed evening, but we had been forced to work late and by the time we got to Bandol, where we were to meet Nelson, we couldn't see his boat anywhere. Geraldo had only just arrived in the area before he'd picked us up and hadn't been to the boat, so he didn't know where it was either. He was embarrassed and said, 'I can't see the boat.'

We replied, 'Don't worry, we'll just go back to the motorhome.'

While Geraldo walked off to see if he could locate the vessel we stood looking out to sea, listening to the 'put put' sound of a small outboard motor. Suddenly, out of the darkness, a face and two hands appeared below us on the harbour wall. It was Nelson, saying, 'My boat's out there. Can you get there?'

I was terrified. Three of us had to find a ladder to climb down into this 'craft' and when we finally wobbled our way aboard there were Stuart, Mark, Nelson and I in a two-man rubber dinghy. We had lost Geraldo. I thought I was going to die and, with the water up to the top of the dinghy sides and the sea getting really rough, we slowly made our way in the pitch black to Nelson's yacht. I swear it was at least a mile away, although it was probably only a few hundred yards. Eventually we pulled up alongside his massive boat called *Pilar Rossi* or *Red Pillar*; it was over 33 metres long and we were faced with the problem of getting on board as the dinghy and the boat were both going up and down in the swell. Stuart managed it, and I was trying to clamber up the best way I could. In the end Stu was trying to pull me aboard while Nelson was standing in the dinghy with both hands on my bum trying to shove me up over the rail in the dark. Eventually we all made it. Mark couldn't believe his luck; he had eyes like saucers. Since then Nelson has upgraded his boat a couple of times and now has a 64-metre monster with outriggers. I am really glad we didn't have to climb on to that.

The arrangement was that we would have dinner on board and Nelson's girlfriend Katharina was there cooking, quite unconcerned, when we all struggled into the cabin. We had an enjoyable meal, but the sea was getting choppier and choppier. Suddenly Nelson pushed his chair back and said, 'Right, Stuart, Mark, I need you.' We looked at him in confusion and asked what was going on, to which he replied, 'I've had a call. We have a mooring, but I can't park it on my own.' So Mark and Stuart, neither of whom had any idea what they were doing, had to guide Nelson into his mooring.

Unfortunately it was right next to where Gerhard Berger was already safely anchored, and he was standing there watching the pantomime. Despite Stuart telling Nelson he was too close there was a loud scraping noise as we ran all down the side of Gerhard's boat. Nelson just said, 'Ah, he won't mind,' and carried on. Gerhard, in the meantime, ran through his full vocabulary of English swear words which, incidentally, is pretty impressive.

When the test was finished Nelson asked what we were doing next.

'Nothing much,' we said. 'Mark is going back in the Benetton truck and then we are taking a break.'

'Come on the boat for a while,' he suggested, so we did. The weather was beautiful and we cruised the south of France's coastline. We'd come back and moor at Juan les Pins each evening and Nelson used to say, 'Come on, I have to go training.' Well, Nelson never trained much, so we went along with it. We were fitter in those days so we readily agreed when he suggested a run/walk. He was always at the front with Geraldo and we would be bringing up the rear. Unfortunately the two of them had a ritual farting competition while they were running, with the number of farts deciding the winner. Following those two was no place for sensitive people or sensitive nostrils, and the whole thing was made worse by the fact that they would wait until they were passing someone in the street before letting off the most enormous eruptions. We would all stop for a coffee along the route and then set off back again.

Nelson claimed that his record was 168, or something similar, and he boasted that he always beat Geraldo. I hoped it was nothing to do with our food. We stayed three nights and four days on the boat and we just couldn't understand why he was bothering with us; he could have spent his time with anybody, but he chose to spend it with us. It made us very proud because, after all, we only made the tea.

Nelson had a habit of scaring us all and one of his more frightening escapades came at an event in Brazil. The motorhome accommodation was still pretty spartan and we all had to share the same room at the circuit. The engineers' and drivers' debrief was taking place after the day's running. I had put a plank on top of the fuel barrels to form a worktable to put my gas rings on and was trying to concentrate on cooking the evening meal. Nelson's engineer was a guy straight out of university called Christian Silk, and Nelson used to give him hell; at the time Christian sported a ponytail, which Nelson found hilarious, and he often threatened to cut it off. Nelson was always telling Christian he didn't know what he was talking about and that he shouldn't be doing the job. I used to turn round and look at Nelson in an effort to tell him to leave the poor lad alone, but he would just wink at me. I expected Christian to burst into tears at any moment.

On the occasion in question Christian was in full flow. Nelson unexpectedly said to me, 'Could you pass me my bag, Di?' I passed him his bag and he rummaged around. Suddenly he pulled out a gun and put it to Christian's head. Christian's face went white and everyone stopped talking. Nelson wriggled the gun around, still holding it to the hapless lad's temple, and said, 'You are not a bloody engineer, and you should never be allowed near a racetrack.' To Nelson that was a huge joke – guns were nothing to him, and he was used to carrying one – but Christian didn't see the funny side and we were all a bit shocked. Incidentally, despite his early trauma at Nelson's hands, Christian stayed in Formula 1 and he was working with Renault when Nelson Junior was with the team. I hope it didn't bring back too many unpleasant memories.

Some time later that day when Nelson had terrified Christian, Nelson sent a message to me that he wanted something out of his bag – racing gloves or tear-off strips for his visor or something like that – and would I take them to the garage. When I opened the bag there was another gun in there. I carried on looking for what he wanted, hoping against hope that I didn't shoot my hand off. Nelson had received a number of kidnap threats over the years and his guns were licensed, but I wish he had warned me.

We had to do a bit of covering up for Nelson over the years, and keeping his women apart was almost a full-time job. Sylvie, who claims to be his first wife, although Nelson maintains they never married, was usually around. Then there was the attractive lady Katharina, his partner at the time, who used to sit inside the motorhome with Nelson while Sylvie sat outside on the motorhome steps. Nelson and Katharina had a son called Laszlo whom Nelson adored. He was a good kid and used to call Stuart 'Stu Stu'; I think he just liked saying the name. If this set of relationships wasn't enough for us to cope with, someone else would come along whom we knew he was seeing and I used to think, 'How are we going to handle this?' I still don't know why I spent so much time covering up for him; perhaps I should have let him drop himself in it. But you don't, do you?

One day Sylvie, who was Nelson Jnr's mother, turned up at the motorhome with a chubby child sporting blonde curly hair. Right in front of her Nelson turned to me and said, 'Do you think this is my baby?'

I had no idea what to say, but I think I muttered, 'Well, she is blonde,' which Nelson definitely wasn't.

He considered this for a minute and then said, 'It's not mine! But she says it is and I have got to support her,' which in fairness he did. Sylvie was OK with us but Nelson had to fund her Monaco lifestyle. He had led her a bit of a dance, though, and I guess she deserved to be looked after.

I remember one night we were sitting with Nelson and we tried to count up the ladies he was 'seeing' at the time. After a while we came up with the number seven, and then he looked at us in a very serious fashion and said 'No, there are 11!' We stared back at him in amazement and then he said, 'Do you want to count the children?'

Stu and I just said, 'No thanks, Nelson, we don't want to count them or we'll be here all night!'

'You're probably right, because I am sure there are a lot that I don't know about,' he admitted.

His pranks, particularly when there was a female around, were legendary. We had a female photographer called Pam Roe with us for a few days at a test in Kyalami and, true to form, Nelson always chatted her up. She had taken lots of photographs for *Autosport* and she was due to fly home overnight and go straight to the magazine office with the films. (This was in the pre-digital era and the photographs had to be developed in-house.) Before she left for the airport she made the mistake of leaving her camera in the garage while she went off to the ladies' room. Nelson, who was in the garage at the time, spotted the photo opportunity. Unzipping his overalls, he pulled out his proudest possession and recorded the sight for posterity on the luckless Pam's camera, swearing all around him to secrecy. I didn't actually see her leave but I know the photos were delivered as planned and then developed. Pam was mortified when she was presented with the results of her weekend's work, but unfortunately for Nelson he didn't manage to keep the identity of the 'model' secret. He had forgotten that race overalls have the driver's name embroidered on the belt; his was, like everything else, revealed in glorious Technicolor. The photo didn't make that week's publication...

If a pretty girl wanted his autograph he would write 'Nelson' in his normal way, then emphasise the 'P' of 'Piquet' in such a way as to make it look like a large penis. Most of the ladies didn't realise what he had done until they studied it (the autograph!) later. And ladies weren't the only target for the famous Piquet humour; the whole team got caught out sometimes. At another Kyalami test Nelson had been pounding around incessantly and then, on one particular lap, it seemed to take him forever to get back to the pits. We had heard nothing from him on the radio and were all really concerned. Then the car came very slowly back down the pit lane and parked. The driver got out, took his helmet off – and it wasn't Nelson. He thought he would play a trick on the lads and swapped his place with 'a learner driver' who was marshalling on the other side of the track, and the rookie had driven the car back. Can you imagine that happening now?

Stuart was often one of Nelson's figures of fun. On one particular occasion we went to Kyalami for a test paid for by Pirelli. Only a couple of weeks earlier Stuart had been operated on for a hernia and he shouldn't really have travelled because the doctor had said he should rest for a minimum of six weeks; to Stuart that meant a maximum of 10 days. (The hernia had been brought on by the Benetton motorhome we have already referred to.) Nelson was doing the driving at the test and, knowing he was always 'friendly fighting' with Stuart, I had to warn Nelson while Stuart was out shopping that Stu was 'sore in parts', and that his lower anatomy was an eye-catching black colour. When Stuart got back Nelson rushed over to him and I thought he was going to be really sympathetic but, true to form, he demanded to see Stu's 'black banana' on the grounds that he had never seen a black penis on a white man. Stuart declined to show him, but for the entire test he ended up being called 'black banana man'.

Nelson was a very genuine mate but he definitely had his peculiarities.

I didn't know Sandro Nannini until he turned up at Benetton, all twinkly-eyed. His first two requests were 'Where's the espresso machine?' and 'Can you hide my cigarettes?' Sandro's family own the Nannini coffee and bakery shop chain so I suppose it was a bit of an occupational hazard. He could never understand my name. Everybody called me 'Mum' or 'Di', but in Italian 'Di' means 'of', so he got very confused. He ended up joining the others in calling me 'Mum' because he couldn't get his head around 'Di' or his tongue around 'Diana'. Sandro was the craziest of the dream team; he just didn't care. He was fast as a driver but a little bit slow in other matters.

Quite often we got to know the drivers at tests rather than race weekends because testing is all short bursts of activity surrounded by long periods of boredom. At one test, in Jerez, Sandro had a massive accident at the bend coming into the straight. Wheels were bouncing everywhere and the car was a wreck. Sandro was taken to the medical centre and then he was brought back to the motorhome; he had no serious injuries but he was told to sit, relax and keep calm. The doctor gave me a package and said, 'This is his medicine but he also has something else he has to take.'

I left Sandro sitting quietly in the motorhome and got on with my work; eventually he called to me and asked for a glass of water. I was pleased he was being sensible and taking his medication so I poured him a glass and took it into the drivers' area. As I walked in I caught him just about to put a large pill in his mouth, which I thought I recognised. I said to him, 'I don't think that's supposed to go in your mouth. Have you still got the packet?' He fished the packet out of the bin and, sure enough, his pill was a suppository. I had to explain: 'You don't put that in your mouth.'

He looked puzzled and said, 'Well, where do I put it?'

I had to tell him as politely as I could. 'It's got to go in your bottom.'

He looked puzzled and then said, 'Will you do it?' He was extremely bruised after his accident and had trouble moving, let alone reaching around to insert the 'pill', but I still declined. I will do most things for my boys but I had to draw the line at that. He said in his Italian way, 'Well, why they have given me this?'

'It's probably to relax your muscles and get the medicine into the bloodstream quicker,' I offered.

A look of understanding crossed his face and he said, 'Ah, I understand, to shit out the shock!'

Sandro was one on his own. He developed a taste for what he called 'English toast', which was actually cold fried bread left over from the mechanics' breakfast; he had stolen a piece one day and thought it was wonderful. Sandro drank 12 espressos a day and he would even be on the grid, waiting to start a race, then run back for another espresso and a cigarette. I used to say to him, 'You can't have it, you'll be hyper.'

Smiling, he just looked at me, shrugged and said, 'Hyper? I need it!' before swigging down his espresso, taking one massive final drag of his cigarette and rushing back to the grid before Flavio saw him.

Sandro was quiet, in his own way. He didn't speak English as well as his team-mate but he learned the appropriate swear words, mainly from Nelson. When Sandro and Nelson were together there were one or two fall guys and chief among these was Flavio. Nelson always said he had something on Flavio and Sandro, being Italian, had done a bit of local research; they used to have long discussions on the subject. When the problem blew up many years later about Nelson Jnr deliberately crashing his Renault into the wall during the 2008 Singapore Grand Prix, I knew Jnr would be telling the truth. Nelson would never have allowed his son to lie; he would have had him by the throat until he was sure he was getting the truth. As I have already said, 'Like it or not, he will tell the truth.'

When Sandro had his helicopter accident we were just about to leave Paul Ricard, following a test prior to the Japanese Grand Prix. Sandro and Nelson were due to visit the factory in England before the race, but they were both going home first – Sandro to Sienna and Nelson to Monaco. Nelson made it home but Sandro's helicopter crashed as he was landing in Sienna, and as he pushed up his arms to try to shield himself, his right forearm was cut off by a helicopter rotor.

We had only just left the two of them and we were still on the road home when we received the call. Nelson had dropped everything and rushed to Sandro's bedside. Unless you knew them well you wouldn't believe Nelson would have given a toss, because the two of them bantered all day long, which was fantastic fun. Now he just wanted to be by his team-mate's side. Sandro required microsurgery to have his arm put back on and Nelson actually told him not to have it done. He had a friend who had lost a leg in an accident and had his leg reattached, but he'd regretted it afterwards. Sandro ignored his advice, but I think that if he had the decision to make again he wouldn't have had it done. His arm gets in his way and he can't do anything with it; perhaps he would have been much better with a prosthetic arm. Sandro proudly showed us his arm next time we met, but it was like a wrung-out towel, thin in some areas and thicker in others. The tendons never worked after the operation and the hand is like a claw.

Nelson used to take the mickey out of Sandro, but he had a really soft spot for him. He wasn't as hard as his reputation suggested. Unsurprisingly, Nelson was a better driver than Sandro, as you would expect from a three-times World Champion, but it didn't matter to Nelson; he would never have wanted to get one over on Sandro. They were mates, which was fantastic to see, and that's why it was the best partnership, the 'dream team', for us. We have worked with equally nice drivers, but with those two it was just fun.

Chapter 17

CIRCUIT SHORTS

In our early years a number of the circuits were quite unlike they are today and, to be absolutely honest, a lot of them were downright dangerous places. Facilities in the late 1970s and early 1980s were very limited and the electricity supply was often inadequate for the number of teams in the paddock. Understandably, the garages and pit area took priority, which resulted in the hospitality area, which was generally at the rear of the pits, perhaps having one 'electricity box' for every four teams. Unfortunately all the hospitality units wanted their electricity at the same time – mealtimes – which in turn created a problem because the whole system became overloaded and 'blew'. For the first couple of years I had to boil kettles continually for cooking and washing up, a very long job. Consequently, the drone of generators firing up almost outdid the cars on track for noise.

Some circuits are particularly memorable, and usually for very different reasons.

Japan

The first time we went to Suzuka in Japan we had Tetsu Tsugawa to help us rent hire cars, book hotels and sort out everything we needed. There's a lot more about Tetsu in a subsequent chapter, but suffice it to say here that he is a brilliant character, well known in the world of Formula 1 and very famous as a journalist in Japan. In Suzuka in the 1980s there were no English street signs – no reason why there should be, really – so if we got lost going to the circuit it was like being on another planet. We couldn't stop and ask anyone for directions and we couldn't even write down the name of where we were going. When we went out in the evening we used to have to carry our room key with its tag showing the hotel's name and address in Japanese, in case we got lost; we had no way of communicating otherwise. I remember Bernard Ferguson telling me that he had some business cards translated and printed in Japanese at his hotel. Unfortunately, every time he handed one to a normally polite Japanese person they would burst out laughing, so he wondered if he had upset the translator in some way. It's a lot easier for us all now as the whole place is much more cosmopolitan.

The circuit provided no space for us at all in our early days. We had two tiny Portakabins; one was full of the drivers' kit and we shared our cooking area with a couple of desks full of engineers. For cooking purposes we had two sets of two gas rings and no running water. We used to cook in the same room where the team held debriefs. The lads ate their meals in the garage on whatever they could perch. It was difficult enough with very few facilities, no separate room and no space but the big issue there was 'What on earth are we going to cook?' We sent out lots of tinned food from England, but because of the freight weight restrictions we never had nearly enough to last a weekend. Tetsu helped a lot and luckily there was a theme park adjoining the circuit where, walking around taking the air on our first night, we walked past a stall selling baguettes. We had stumbled across a French baker, of all things, in a Japanese theme park. At first we thought we were dreaming, but it was real enough so we ordered our daily bread from there. We told one or two close friends in the business about our find but not everyone, as we wanted to make sure we got what we needed. The only trouble was that we ended up with a bread bill for the equivalent of about £500 each race just for baguettes. The next problem was finding something to put in them. The tins we had sent out from England were fine, but we couldn't find anything fresh and local that the lads would eat in a sandwich. We bought what we thought was ham and started to fill the sandwiches with that until we realised it was *carpaccio* of some fish or other, which was definitely not a big hit with the team.

Sharing the debrief room as we did we couldn't help hearing the team talking about all the intimate details of strategy and set-up while we were chopping the vegetables and washing the pans. I can't imagine that happens any longer, somehow, although at a more recent event I remember overhearing Martin Brundle, who was partnering Michael Schumacher at the time, saying things like, 'The car feels like a speedboat with a caravan on the back.' Even now we hear him come out with similar classics on his TV commentary which is, incidentally, excellent. There we were back then, though, trying to make a hundred or so sandwiches while there were about eight engineers around the debrief desks. It was a relief when the cars went out on track and the engineers got out of the way, but by the time I had claimed the desk/worktop space everything would go quiet and they would all trail back in and I'd have to find somewhere else to put the sandwiches.

We had some odd culinary experiences in Japan. We had some big flasks with taps on the side and we used to fill them with cold drinks to go into the garage, usually orange juice or something similar. We'd sent quite a lot of sachets of juice out from the UK to mix at the track but, again, because of weight restrictions, we hadn't enough and had to buy some locally. We went out and looked in the shops for something we recognised and found some large jars of orange powder that looked very much like the stuff in our orange juice sachets. Unfortunately it didn't taste too much like orange juice. I mixed up the first batch and luckily I asked Stuart to test the strength of it before I took it to the garage, because the lads didn't like it too weak. Stu gagged, but said fairly politely, 'It tastes a bit soapy.' It was only after checking with Tetsu that we realised we had bought bath salts!

Several of us motorhomers fell foul of the next problem, which was the milk. We bought what we thought was milk and filled the milk flasks for the hot drinks, only to find we had filled them with very runny yogurt. There was no actual sliced bread but we could buy four very thick slices in a pack that were capable of making some pretty big 'doorstep' sandwiches. Unfortunately, to make around a hundred sandwiches we needed quite a lot of packs, so it sold out quickly.

Tetsu introduced us to the manager of a little supermarket locally and we used to order some items similar to those being served in the theme park. The Japanese are a wonderfully polite race of people and when we spent a lot of money in the supermarket all the checkout staff and the shelf stackers used to line the exit and bow us out. There we were, with our four trolleys of assorted runny yogurt, fat bread and bath salts, being given a hero's farewell. We felt very embarrassed and I suspect the supermarket staff had a pretty dim view of the English diet.

I shouldn't admit it, really, but we used to take a holdall full of bacon and sausages with us when we went to Japan, risking customs. It was totally illegal but the odd thing is that, once we arrived, no one ever once asked us where we had got the stuff from. Like many places when visitors go through the customs area there is a red and green traffic-light system and I used to say, 'What on earth are we going to say if it's red?' But it never was. So, like the pony express, the bacon and sausages always got through. At least the lads got their traditional breakfast, even if it was washed down with some pretty odd drinks. It was just a good job there were no sniffer-dogs at the airport or we would have had to hope they were vegetarian.

We have had to do similar things since then, particularly when we were rallying during the foot and mouth restrictions and weren't allowed to take meat out of the country. To some extent it was a bit disappointing that no one ever congratulated us, or said, 'How on earth did you do that?' Some of the other teams asked where we'd got it from and I had to decline to answer, which of course told them everything.

Despite all the problems, I enjoyed the Japanese experience. When we did go shopping and had our uniforms on we were asked to sign autographs, as if we were famous. The drivers all stayed inside the hotel in Suzuka, so I guess we were a pretty poor substitute, but the Japanese crowds were so enthusiastic that it was a pleasure to be able to help. The other amazing thing I found in Japan was that when the crowd cleared after the race and we looked across to the stands there wasn't one speck of rubbish; everyone took it home with them.

I loved the Japanese people and that feeling was to be reinforced in the future when we spent several years with the Bridgestone tyre test team.

Hungary

The first time we went to Budapest, in 1986, the Russians were still there following their invasion many years earlier. The Formula 1 motorhome personnel had a meeting in Hockenheim in preparation for the trip and we were told that we needn't make any special food arrangements as anything we needed would be available in the city. We were also told that, as the motorhomes would be the first Formula 1 vehicles to arrive at the border, we had to arrive in Vienna en masse and cross together. Of course, as Hungary wasn't part of the EC we had to have all kinds of paperwork listing what we were carrying into the country. I defy anyone to be able to list the contents of a motorhome but we did our best and eventually, by fair means or foul, we got through customs to be met by a police car and a van. The van had obviously come from the airport because it had a big illuminated sign on top saying 'Follow me' – in English, fortunately.

We followed the van from the border all the way to Budapest and we just stayed on the main road except for this one town, which, for some reason or another, we had to bypass. We were taken to the circuit and once we were there the police washed their hands of us. We were each given an interpreter and Stuart asked where the biggest supermarket was. He followed the directions he was given and found that the 'Supermarket' was a disused railway station with the tracks filled in; the platforms were filled with local produce. We would have described the scene as an open market and to confirm this there were long queues of locals. Stu made straight for the meat counter and the first thing he saw were bags of chickens' feet; apart from these, and some bags full of fat, there was nothing – or certainly nothing much that he was prepared to buy. The vegetables were all misshapen and unpleasant-looking and nothing looked attractive. Stuart was standing there with enough money in his hand to buy the entire stock, but the shopkeepers preferred to serve the locals with two potatoes and a carrot rather than take his money, which was fair enough, really. Bananas couldn't be found anywhere, despite the fact they were available in abundance in Austria, just over the border, but there were masses of watermelons for sale at the side of the road and mangy apples available on every street corner.

The shopping was so bad that we agonised, 'What on earth are we going to feed our people on? There is absolutely nothing!' We ended up phoning Benetton to tell the lads to bring food with them. Unfortunately the first ten to arrive all brought an iceberg lettuce, so we then had to get a bit better organised, making a list and sending it back to Gordon Message, the team manager. Everyone had to bring a pack of bacon and various other bits and pieces. Manfred Oettinger from Arrows had relatives living in Vienna, which was a few hours' drive away, and he got one of his relations to bring a van full of food across the border, which was a pretty hazardous exercise.

The second year we went we were a bit better prepared and, before we set off for Hungary, we went to the big shopping centre in Vienna, bought a fridge freezer and stood it in the motorhome kitchen. Then we kept the generator running until it was down to temperature and went back to the shopping centre to buy enough food to fill it up. Unfortunately we had to drive all the way to Budapest with the generator on. The border was a very nasty place at that time and we could have been arrested for bringing in all that food. There were a number of truckies who were beaten up there.

Vanessa from Zakspeed had someone driving over the border with a consignment of long-life milk because the local milk was in clear polythene cartons, full of lumps and looking very yellow. The only shops that remotely looked like a small version of a supermarket were called ABC and all we could get from there was bread; large, unpleasant loaves of bread. There was a freezer in one little shop that Stuart said smelled of urine, but I tried not to breathe in while I was there, so I'll take his word for it. I did, however, move one of the unidentifiable meat packages in there and uncovered masses of maggots. There was nothing we could have fed our chaps on. There were no flowers available either; the only ones for sale were gladioli and the only place to buy them was outside the cemetery. The second year I bought some flowers in Vienna and also put some artificial ones in the awning.

One of our fridges broke down and our interpreter, Jacob, found the only fridge for sale in the whole of the Budapest area. It was all such a shame, because Budapest is a beautiful city and has wonderful architecture, but the suffering of the people and the conditions they had to tolerate at that time ruin my memories of the place. The racing did contribute to the wealth of the area, but it had some adverse effects, too, as the Marlboro flags hanging from every bridge didn't exactly add to the natural beauty of the area. Things gradually improved, but it took at least three years. Appearances were kept up as well as they could be, however. If we went in a restaurant there was always a big menu but the waiter would point at a couple of things and say, 'You can have that or that.' Prostitutes and Russian tanks were everywhere and we felt that we shouldn't be there because the people had so little. There was nothing in the shops, but there were sentry boxes with armed soldiers all the way down the motorway. The red star was still on all the buildings.

When we left after that first race we were directed out of the country via a different route from the one we went in on. We hadn't been driving long when we were stopped by a police road block; they didn't want any money or anything, but they took a tray of Coca-Cola from us. I don't know if they had radios, but not much further down the road we were stopped again and it was the same situation. At one point we passed a convoy of Russian tanks stopped by the side of the road, and the soldiers manning them were just kids, wearing what looked like one-size-fits-all uniforms; they really did look a rag-tag bunch. I was afraid all the time I was there that first year and my enduring memory is of broken-down tanks, abandoned and left to rust away.

Hungary is completely different now. The people are very smart, the restaurants are well stocked and the food is wholesome. Budapest is a very cultured city – and it now has a Tesco, which doesn't add to its charm but certainly helps out the motorhomers.

Canada

Montréal was another circuit where there was no space to work, but it's a truly wonderful place. Stu and I used to go over to the island to the supermarket and I will always remember the lads used to go to the same area because there was a particular hairdresser's that they liked to frequent. Over the years it became a bit of a regular jaunt for them all. It was our fault, really; we had spotted the establishment on our way to the supermarket and Stuart had told them about it. The main cause of their interest was that the hairdresser was topless. While she was cutting their hair her boobs would rest on their cheeks or round their ears, depending on which way they were leaning. We had the best-turned-out mechanics in the pit lane.

Brazil

There are a number of stories about Brazil that crop up in other chapters, but the country has always been one of *the* classic problem locations for us, whether we were in Rio or Sao Paulo. In those early years all we had to cook on was a shelf at the back of the garage. There was a drain underneath where the rats used to run from garage to garage; we also had the gas rings perched on top of the fuel barrels, which used to drive the fire marshals crazy.

Of all the interesting times we have had in Brazil the worst trip was when the local currency, the Real, was devalued. When we arrived the cash was so worthless that it was lying in the gutter, literally and metaphorically. Stuart was meeting a doctor close to the airport to buy US dollars from him at a pretty miserly rate because the cash we had was of no value. The race was almost cancelled at one point because no one could buy anything. The race organisers started sending people to the circuit who would let us have a small amount of money in dollars every day, but it was nowhere near enough to allow us to get the job done. From memory it was about 40 dollars for each team.

We had no personal money and, to add to the problem, Nelson Piquet asked me if I would buy him some soap and toothpaste because, as is usual with drivers, he had forgotten his. I also needed some 'feminine hygiene' products and I had to decide 'him or me'. Needless to say, he got his toiletries and I had to scrounge around the other motorhomers. To add one final problem to the trip the hotel bill had to be settled somehow. Flavio managed to organise the head of Benetton Brazil to collect some cash from somewhere on the Monday morning and the long-suffering team manager, Gordon Message, had to cross Rio in a taxi to collect the money. He was presented with a carrier bag full of it to pay the bill, which was, of course, very, very risky!

We have seen much worse things than money lying around,

though. Driving to the circuit one morning we saw a dead body in the road, with everyone just driving around it as though it was a new mini-roundabout. Life always seemed to be very cheap in Brazil. On another occasion we were eating dinner in a Chinese restaurant near the Copacabana beach in Rio. The restaurant was a little unusual, in so far as it had those ranch-style doors that burst open in all the best Western movies, although they rarely seem to feature in China. At one point in the evening the doors suddenly burst inwards quite violently and a man fell through with a knife sticking out of his shoulder. We were quite close to the door, on the end of a table, and he fell at our feet. The waiters just dragged him outside, got the mop and bucket out, cleaned the floor and carried on serving. I decided I didn't like it there and went without pudding that night.

In the years we were travelling to Rio with Benetton we rather took to one of the street boys, and we found out that his name was Maximilian. I can still picture him: he was about nine or ten when we first met him, and one of a group of kids who used to swarm around us when we sat outside, some trying to sell bits of tat and some just begging. We knew someone around the corner was operating them all, but this one young lad stood out from all the others; he had no parents or any relations and he just lived on the beach. The team took to him and adopted him as the Benetton boy; when we left at the end of the race all the lads gave him a gift, like their trainers or something similar, which I suppose in retrospect was a bit silly because they would have been taken off him as soon as our backs were turned. Stu and I just fed him. We bought him food and told him we wouldn't give him anything because he had nowhere to put it, as he lived under a palm tree on the beach. If we gave him money he had to take it round the corner to his handler.

The years passed and he grew up; he was still living on the beach but he developed into a nice kid – still being operated, but a nice kid. One night, one of the truckies, Del Boy, suddenly noticed his favourite watch had gone, so when Maximilian turned up, as he always did, the guys told him what had happened. Max disappeared and a short time later he came back with the watch, still in perfect condition; he knew exactly where it had gone. Over time we realised that when the little chaps came to try to sit on our laps at night they were actually taking note of who had what. They certainly caught me out, because I had a gold chain round my neck one evening and one of the little urchins must have noticed it. When we came down the steps of the hotel the next morning he was there with his friend and they snatched it from my neck, even though it was tucked inside my shirt, and ran off down the road. Stuart went to run after them but I held him back, saying, 'For goodness' sake, they will stab you as soon as you get round the corner. Let it go.' It made a bit of a mess of my neck, though. The poor souls were stealing to live, but the police still cleared them out over the years.

One year we went to the race expecting to see Max, as usual, but he wasn't there. We recognised one of his friends and asked where he was and we were told he had been murdered: shot. We were very sad. We had grown up with him for six years and then he was gone and no one seemed to care. He didn't have anyone to look after him, and he lived and died on the beach.

Barry Griffin from Goodyear went out jogging on Ipanema beach one morning, which was not too smart, because someone grabbed him and stuck a broken bottle to his throat. As Barry was wearing shorts, a T-shirt and trainers it was plain that he didn't have any money on him, so he was marched back to the hotel. The night porter was made to hand over the key to his safety deposit box and empty it. Barry lost his passport, money, watch – the lot. We decided it was always better to be carrying a little bit of money in the long run (!).

On a trip to Sao Paulo we were staying at the Novotel at Marumbi, which was a bit unusual. On one side of the hotel was an asylum with no glass in the windows, so all night long we could hear the inmates screaming. On the other side of the Novotel there was a 'Love Hotel', with cars coming and going all night, and there was almost as much noise coming from there as there was from the asylum. Even shopping was hazardous. There were security towers in the car park with armed 'spotters', and inside the supermarket each till had an armed guard. It wasn't the place for a leisurely and comfortable shopping expedition, particularly when you are carrying enough money to buy provisions for a race team.

Every night seemed to bring a new incident. On one occasion we were walking towards our car, to drive to a restaurant, when two men on opposite sides of the street started shooting at each other. We all had to dive behind parked cars.

It says a lot about the nature of the lads that, even there, they managed to have some fun. The minibuses ran on alcohol (so did the lads quite often). The group figured out that if they revved the minibus up as far as they could, then switched off the ignition and promptly switched it back on again, they could drive down the street with the exhaust backfiring like a gunshot and the pedestrians ducking for cover. On one occasion we were unwilling passengers during one of these episodes and we saw a man walking back to one of the shanty towns, or *favelas* as they are called, that surrounded the circuit, carrying a dead cat. I hope he was taking it to give it a decent burial because I don't like to think of the alternative.

The circuit facilities in Brazil were abysmal. Whenever I went to the toilet there were always frogs or newts on the floor and the flushing system either never worked or never stopped. On one occasion when I flushed the toilet it wouldn't stop flushing and the lid was flapping up and down like something from the set of *Jaws*. I just slammed the door and ran because the contents of the sewage system were slowly starting to come back over the pan in true horror film fashion.

Some of the local residents, who lived in the *favelas*, were employed as cleaners and sweepers at the circuit for the race weekend and their poverty was all too obvious. They looked longingly at the food that we had bought to feed the team.

At one particular race we noticed a young girl cleaning and sweeping around our motorhome area and we managed to communicate with her, to some extent. When we asked her where she lived she waved her hand towards the *favela* nearest the circuit, indicating she lived 'over there'. On the Sunday of the race I managed to let her know that she could have any food that was left after the race had finished; she rushed over and told her father, who was also working at the circuit as a cleaner. I spread the word among the other motorhomers and they all said that they would donate their leftovers to the locals. The food was all gathered together and when the girl's dad saw what had been left he promptly disappeared and arrived again shortly afterwards with a beaten-up old pick-up truck which he filled with a mountain of leftovers. The two of them were so grateful that they thanked us with tears in their eyes.

The whole episode made me realise that there was so much waste in Formula 1, and it set a plan in my mind to try to organise for this kind of activity to be formalised at every circuit, with refrigerated trucks supplied by the Red Cross or a similar organisation collecting all the unused food and distributing it to the needy. It would both have helped the local poor and also Formula 1's image for conspicuous consumption. Bernie had no objections to the plan, but unfortunately we moved away from Formula 1 before it came to fruition; however, I suppose someone would have scuppered the idea sooner or later by declaring that it contravened health and safety regulations!

Brazil is now one of the new world powerhouse economies. I hope they spend some of it on their race circuits.

Mexico

We were in Mexico City in October 1986, just a year after the massive earthquake that had hit the country. All the buildings were in a terrible state, with collapsed structures everywhere, and our hotel had cracks that in some places went right through the walls. It was difficult to maintain any level of sanitation.

When we first arrived at the circuit we were confronted by ramshackle offices damaged by the earthquake – some buildings had fallen down and were left where they had dropped; others were teetering, just like the whole of the city seemed to be. There was no usable water; it was only suitable for washing tyres, which was useful in the garage but not much help to the locals. The authorities had opened a shop of sorts in the paddock area so we could buy bottles of water, but we still had to buy purification tablets to dissolve in this bottled stuff to be doubly sure it was safe. When we held a glass of untreated water to the light we could see all sorts of unidentified floating objects. The whole situation was pretty unnerving; after all, we were feeding drivers and team alike. Everyone was in the same situation, but we certainly didn't want to be responsible for the team or its drivers being unable to compete because of food poisoning.

The organisers had told everyone not to buy food from roadside stalls for fear of poisoning, as there had been a large number of deaths due to food being boiled or washed in contaminated water. We followed the advice to the letter, but were amazed to see the crews of Air Mexicana tucking into whatever was on offer. Perhaps they knew something we didn't.

The electricity supply was very hit and miss, and large numbers of power lines had been destroyed. It seemed a bit inappropriate to complain, though, when there were families whose homes had been destroyed living by the roadside and under bridges. Basically, we should never have been there. To make the trip even more memorable Stuart, like lots of other people, suffered food poisoning; I have no idea how he managed to fulfil his pit-wall duties for Gerhard Berger, but he kept going as we were due to take a couple of days' break in Hawaii after the race. However, Stu ended up in a clinic on a drip for a week; at least he got a rest.

On our other trips to Mexico Stuart used to go to the shops on his own, as I refused to go because it was so dangerous at the time and the police were very corrupt. To minimise the number of trips Stu always stocked up with a car full of provisions. On one trip he came out of the supermarket car park, went around the corner and a hundred yards further on he was stopped by the police.

'There is a problem at the bridge,' the policeman said.

'What bridge? I haven't seen a bridge. I have only driven a hundred yards.'

'Follow me,' the policeman instructed, and Stuart had to follow the police car around the corner until they stopped. Straight away another police car pulled up behind him. 'Money. Dollar,' the policeman demanded.

Stuart's polite 'Can I have a receipt?' wasn't well received by the uniformed officer, who was starting to get a bit grumpy. It was plain the answer was 'No!'

The following year Stuart prepared in advance and bought a couple of those old-fashioned international driving licences with his photo inside. They used to cost about £1 and were not really valid for anything at all. When, inevitably, he was stopped at the side of the main road into the circuit and asked for his driving licence, he pulled out one of these worthless documents. He was asked for dollars again, but he always replied, 'You will have to come to the circuit, because my money is there.'

The policeman would say, 'If you don't pay you don't get your driving licence back,' so Stu just started the car and drove off, and through his rear-view mirror he would see the policeman looking at the document in dismay.

We didn't have all the fun. For some reason nobody really understood, the police stopped the Williams minibus as it came out of the circuit. One of the lads in the back of the bus started to write down the policeman's number, when suddenly the officer's pistol came through the open window and pointed at his head. The offending paper had to be handed over, together with a 'thank you' of about $400 before the gun went back into the holster.

Estoril

At some circuits security was terrible. Estoril in Portugal was a prime example. After a spate of thefts of big items like televisions, fridges, chairs and tables it was finally discovered that they had been 'confiscated' by the security staff.

Zeltweg

Not every circuit was bad news and one that all the motorhomers loved was Zeltweg in Austria. This paddock actually had a 'Gosser' bar (Gosser being local Austrian beer), so it meant that the people who were sleeping in the motorhomes had somewhere to go after they finished work. There were some really good times in a very congenial atmosphere, with beautiful mountain views over the top of the stands and stronger-than-it-looked beer. One downside of this was that the teams often stayed for a 'quick one' and left in the early hours. We have particularly vivid memories of the father and uncle of one of our drivers making it their base for the weekend, to the point they were found sleeping nearby one morning, having failed to make it back to the hotel. Another downside to the circuit was that the paddock security woke us all up every morning shouting *Achtung Fahrenlager* which didn't mean 'have another beer'. It meant 'Attention paddock!' This early morning call happened every day at 6am, even on days when there were no cars due to run; it was very unpopular.

Zandvoort

Zandvoort in the Netherlands was another charming circuit, mainly due to its position near the beach and the town centre. The downside was that the sand blew everywhere, on to the circuit, into the garages and in the food. Spectator facilities were quite dangerous, particularly when a walkway collapsed on the Saturday of a race, injuring people hoping to get a close-up view of the action from above the pits. Luckily no one was badly hurt. Access to the paddock for the support trucks and motorhomes was via the circuit, so the drivers had to align themselves to get under the bridges and walkways; that was fine until the Renault truck was heading off in a hurry after the GP and took a bridge with it. Needless to say, photos were taken and distributed around the paddock for the next race. Ironically Michel, the driver at the time, now works for the sport's governing body, the Fédération Internationale de l'Automobile (FIA).

Barcelona

On one trip we left Estoril in Portugal and the next stop was the new circuit at Barcelona. We were all given directions and told a specific motorway exit to take. One of the McLaren truckies, Steve Cook, or Tatts as we all referred to him, got completely lost. He did what we all usually did when we were desperate and stopped a taxi driver, asking him to drive to the circuit while he followed. The taxi driver duly obliged, but unfortunately he took him to the old track in the middle of the city, Montjuic Park. We were all wondering where he was and couldn't understand what had happened to him. He was very late.

When we arrived the circuit wasn't really finished and we noticed that all the banks around the track had been painted green; we had no idea why. Eventually we realised that the grass hadn't grown and Bernie had insisted on a certain standard of presentation, so the local builders had sprayed all the soil and mud that had been excavated green. Needless to say it rained, and green sludge came down into the paddock like something from a horror film. There were no drains so it just settled, making life impossible.

Overall, at the older circuits, when the paddocks had originally been laid out, no one had anticipated the future needs of the teams from the hospitality point of view. Water, electricity and drainage are the lifeblood of the hospitality business. On arrival at any circuit we sought out the nearest drain to our parking spot and then hopefully ran a hose into the drain from our waste outlet. At that point, as long as there was water coming in, electricity to keep the show on the road and a drain going somewhere hygienic, we were in business. The British contingent became quite adept at doing this job, but other nationalities sometimes had a bit of a relaxed view on it all and just let their waste run anywhere in the paddock. The Italians and French were the worst, and it was not unusual for team members and guests to have to pick their way through dirty waste water containing rice, pasta and anything else that had been cooked.

It is amazing that teams and visitors alike have always turned up at a track with no idea that such basic problems exist – but then, why should they? Sorting them out was our job. However, even in those early days, some circuits stood out above all the others and our favourite was Adelaide.

Adelaide

Everyone in the pit lane was really excited when it was announced that there was to be a race in Victoria Park, Adelaide, starting from 1985. A new venue always gives everyone a lift, but the possibility of finishing the season in the November sun on the other side of the world was something to really look forward to. Unfortunately we couldn't look forward to it with much anticipation that first season because the Australian organisers were offering free hospitality at the venue and, understandably, Team Lotus decided to take advantage of the opportunity and left us behind.

Fortunately things changed for 1986. We had moved to Benetton by then and our new deal required us to attend every Grand Prix. The hospitality provided by the circuit in 1985 had created some problems, so quite a number of teams decided to take their own personnel. The food and all the other arrangements had been fine, except for the fact that there were set eating times for the teams, with no flexibility, which is virtually impossible to impose as the guys just have to eat when they can because all kinds of technical situations can arise right through the day and night.

So we attended the 1986 Grand Prix and the city of Adelaide did an amazing job of welcoming everyone. There was a band to greet us all on the tarmac at the airport, and the whole city turned itself over for 'Grand Prix party time'. Banners were everywhere; the bars and restaurants loved anyone who was involved in Formula 1. Victoria Park was no longer a park but a full-blown racetrack and, in the sunshine, everyone in the Formula 1 community had an 'end of term' feel about them. Even the garages were good for that era, especially considering everything was constructed just for the occasion.

Initially the actual hospitality facilities were quite basic caravans, but later we were provided with Portakabins as offices and a seating area in the garage. Needless to say the traditional Aussie barbecue, which we hired locally, came into its own. At that time the Australian barbecues were considerably more advanced than our half-an-oil-drum contraption, so a lot were bought outright by the teams and sent back to Europe with their freight.

To underline the 'end of term' atmosphere a lot of Formula 1 personnel flew their families out for holidays after the event. Often the spending money was generated by selling their race uniforms at the end of the race. The Anglo-Australian détente was pretty strong and a lot of new relationships were forged, some ending in long-term ones while others, sadly, caused the odd divorce. There were quite a few instances over the years when a band wasn't the only thing at the airport: when the lads arrived there was more than one lady waiting with a bundle in her arms. Enough said on that subject.

Another 'relationship story', albeit brief, occurred when we were sharing our hotel with a group of Cosworth lads. On the night in question Stu and I had gone to bed early when we were woken around one in the morning by two Cosworth mechanics accompanied by two local ladies tiptoeing very noisily along the corridor past our room. One of the Cosworth lads, in a stage whisper, told the girls to be quiet because Mum and Dad were in bed. The girls burst out laughing saying, 'You brought your Mum and Dad all the way to Australia?' The girls must have thought they had made a very bad choice but all must have turned out pretty well because we were woken again at about six in the morning by the girls being escorted back out of the hotel.

The people of Adelaide could not have been more accommodating and anything we needed was made available, however obscure our requests may have seemed. I think I can speak for everyone who went to that delightful city in the ten years of the event that it was always our favourite spot on the race calendar. We forged many friendships with both local people and companies that continue to this day. It was a sad day for everyone when the Australian politicians got involved and the race was moved to Melbourne.

Spa

Naturally we have visited many other circuits, but sometimes we used to forget where we were because we had the same neighbours, doing the same thing and generally holding similar conversations each weekend irrespective of where we were in the world. It was just like living in a bubble. The drivers definitely all have their own preferences among the circuits, but if you ask their opinion on which is best, Spa features heavily, with its sweeping *Eau Rouge* corner and beautiful scenery – when it can be seen for the rain, that is. We particularly remember one year in Spa when the track had been resurfaced and hadn't settled before the race weekend. It was uncharacteristically hot and the track surface started to melt but racing carried on through Saturday when, unfortunately, the track broke up during one of the support races. A decision was taken to postpone the Formula 1 race until October, a time of year when there was often snow falling in the area. Unfortunately news of the cancellation had failed to reach many of the fans and they were still streaming into the circuit as we were all streaming out.

Monza

Monza was probably the second most atmospheric and memorable circuit we ever visited in our long Formula 1 career, although it also provided us with some interesting and unique challenges.

The circuit was, and still is, situated in Parco di Monza, a park open to the public and usually crowded with both locals and the many people who descend on it from nearby Milan in the hope of a breath of fresh air. The Grand Prix was traditionally held in September, when the weather was stiflingly hot and the humidity high; it was the signal for thousands of fanatical Ferrari fans, known as Tifosi, to flow in a sea of red through the park gates and into the circuit. It's impossible to get out of the circuit against the tide so we never tried; we knew we would never get back in time to cook lunch.

All the teams and team members had to be extra vigilant during the Monza weekend because it was so easy to 'lose' anything remotely connected with the Grand Prix. Fans did their utmost to climb into the paddock to claim anything that they fancied and, on occasions, we lost cutlery, Parma hams and even chairs during the night; plainly someone was short of dinner at the campsite. Drivers lost helmets and overalls while the mechanics had to keep their hands on their tools. When a car broke down on the track guards were positioned to protect it from being stripped where it stood.

The Tifosi sit in the grandstands opposite the pits for hours, just to catch a glimpse of a car or driver, and at the first sight of the Ferrari team opening their garage door a huge roar will reverberate around those stands. The most unusual characteristic of Monza is the fact that the Tifosi are allowed on to the track immediately the race finishes: they rush down to the podium to gather in their thousands at the foot of one of the best rostrums in Formula 1. If a Ferrari driver makes it on to the podium the atmosphere is electric, but even if there isn't one in the top three it's still impossible to see an inch of the track surface beneath the red and yellow Ferrari flags. Monza is home to the Tifosi, the Ferrari team are their heroes, and nothing will ever change that.

Monaco

If Monza is the second most atmospheric circuit in the world then there is only one choice for first. It wouldn't be possible to talk about Formula 1 circuits without mentioning Monaco because there just isn't anything to compare it with, anywhere in the world.

The place doesn't make any sense, which is what makes it so wonderful. If it were anywhere else all the drivers would refuse to race there because it is too dangerous. There are no 'run-off areas' to slow the cars down, just concrete walls, or on the odd occasion an excursion into the sea in the harbour, but despite this the race has been run around the principality since 1929. Much of the justification for continuing to race there is that the cars are travelling far more slowly, but the glamour of the setting plus the fact that all the drivers seem to live in the area for tax purposes will keep it on the Formula 1 calendar for the foreseeable future.

The teams are often indifferent to the glamour, as working conditions are unbelievably poor in comparison to the newer, permanent circuits. Things have improved over the years, but chronic lack of space has always been a problem. Everyone in the pits knows how difficult the weekend is going to be when they set off for the race, but the 'buzz' has always overridden the downsides and they travel prepared for anything the place can throw at them.

In the 1970s, and indeed right through to quite recently, there were no pits as such, just a row of temporary structures and storage areas for the teams. Things have moved on a little now; rudimentary pits have been constructed, although the facilities are far from ideal. The top teams are allowed to park on the harbour wall and work under awnings that come out once a year. However, the other teams have to work in the underground car park below the palace, which is situated virtually on the opposite side of the harbour; the cars have to be pushed and manhandled to the team's allocated pit by the overworked crew.

The pit lane is incredibly narrow and very dangerous. Stuart was designated pit-board man for many years, and he and his counterparts in the other teams added to the hazards of driving in Monaco by waving a heavy board over a low wall above a narrow track.

At Monaco the race is run on the streets, and even the days the cars practise and qualify are different from everywhere else in the world. The roads are closed to the public for Formula 1 practice on Thursday and reopened on Friday so that everyone can go about their business. They are then closed again on Saturday for qualifying and Sunday for the race, so in theory we all get the day off on Friday – in theory. The atmosphere is amazing, as the principality just embraces the Grand Prix for a period in May each year, and the residents put up with all the disruption.

On race day the track is full of folk who don't need to be there – they are there to be seen rather than to see. The annual Cannes Film Festival takes place around the same time as the Grand Prix and lots of the stars come along the coast to add even more glamour to one of the most glamorous spots in the world. There is always a clamour among the rich, famous and infamous to grab an invitation from a team or from Bernie to be seen at the event. Sometimes it's difficult to see the cars for the stars.

Sponsors pay a fortune to have a yacht berth in the harbour for the race weekend, from where they can throw parties, walk in to the circuit and sit around being seen. We motorhomers who were sleeping in our vehicles often thought these yachts spoiled our view, but I guess our vehicle didn't improve the view from the yacht much either. Sometimes we were lucky enough to be invited on to a yacht by one of the team's sponsors, which was always a bit special. Not as special as Shaune's 40th birthday, though.

Ron Dennis hatched a plot with Bob McMurray, Shaune's husband, and invited Bob and Shaune with some of their friends on to the *Sea Goddess* to celebrate her birthday. The *Sea*

Goddess was the yacht on which several of McLaren's guests were staying. Bob was sworn to secrecy, so on the night Shaune thought we were all just going into Monaco for a meal to celebrate her big day. As we passed by the *Sea Goddess* we suddenly found ourselves taking a sharp right and being ushered up the gangway by Bob. Shaune started screaming, 'We can't go up there, it's a private function.' Ron was really welcoming, which was a terrific touch, and Shaune certainly had a birthday to remember.

Some people had an even better time on the yachts in the harbour. We were often parked opposite craft where some of the goings-on were well worth staying up late to watch. Once we were facing a boat with James Hunt on board, and what we didn't see, hear or smell on that occasion isn't worth recording; let's just say he and his friends were having a very lively time, as only James could. We did lots of people-watching from our awnings as evening turned into night. One year, when we were working for Benetton, Flavio came walking by. He was staying on a boat with his girlfriend of the time and was out walking her dog; he stopped for coffee with us and it was quite nice to see him in a different role. I have also seen the sun rise over the harbour sitting with John Barnard and Tom Walkinshaw, enjoying the odd gin and tonic and gazing at the view, putting the world to rights while the lads worked into the early hours.

A number of we motorhomers calculated we had actually been Monaco residents for at least six months of our lives over a 20-year period but, unfortunately, without the tax perks.

Behind the scenes, Monaco in the early days was incredibly difficult and it hasn't improved much. Just driving into the principality is a nightmare for the truckies and motorhomers; they have to be exceptional drivers to negotiate the narrow, busy roads. All the trucks supporting the race have to congregate in a holding area, which is often as far away as Nice, to await permission from Monaco Automobile Club, the race organising body, to start the drive into the circuit one by one; this was to avoid all the trucks arriving at the same time and the whole place becoming gridlocked. A whole day of our lives could pass by in frustration while we waited for our turn, a complete contrast to every other track where all the trucks just pulled off the nearest motorway junction and drove sedately, or not so sedately, into the circuit.

Anyone who has been to Monaco and actually thought about how it all came together would probably marvel at the skills of these drivers. All eyes are naturally on the racers, but it's not only their daring which makes the circuit what it is. It would actually be interesting to see some of them have a go at parking a motorhome on the harbour wall, shunting back and forth with the only driver aids being other drivers shouting, 'About three more inches.'

'Stop!'

'Forward!'

'Back!'

Shopping was incredibly difficult as there wasn't even a large supermarket in the area. We had to trudge to the open market, which was an experience in itself; we weren't able to use a car as the streets were closed and it was a long, steep walk, culminating in a trip through a warehouse, to get to the motorhome. The market was so attractive and the goods so enticing that, despite arriving armed with shopping bags, we always bought more than we could carry.

Over the years we got to know some of the stallholders and, as we had specified our order the previous day, one of them used to bring his van down to the harbour wall before the streets closed at 6am to deliver our produce into the awning. Monaco was probably the only track where we could walk out to the shops (even if we couldn't carry the shopping back), which in its own way was quite a change from being trapped in the circuit. Fontvieille, which is known as 'Monaco new town' and is where a lot of the drivers live, or at least have addresses, has a Carrefour hypermarket now, so the experience has changed a little.

The Monaco atmosphere can't be compared with anywhere else, but by the time race day comes everyone in the team is totally shattered, which is just down to the logistics of working there. At the end of our career in motorsport it will probably be the one Grand Prix we will visit just to watch from a terrace, or wherever we can find a decent vantage point. When we worked at the Grand Prix and everyone left the motorhome to go to the pits we were on our own, without a clue about what was happening out on track. One day we will watch it in comfort.

Chapter 18

FLAVIO TAKES THE HELM

When Flavio Briatore took formal control of the Benetton team he quickly worked out what needed to be done. He'd been studying the team's activities for some time and had developed a unique perception of the strategic direction that Benetton, in particular, and Formula 1, in general, should be taking. Flavio had the charisma to be able to come into the business and run a team when he knew absolutely nothing about racing. He learnt it all pretty quickly, though, and soon became one of the major movers and shakers in the industry. Flav turned Benetton from a team into a business, which was astute, because things needed to change; he set about bringing his commercial know-how and contacts to the sport. He wasn't the first to introduce personalities to the track but he certainly developed it into an art form with the approval of Bernie Ecclestone, who became his close friend.

As Flavio's influence grew the rate of change speeded up. I didn't see the value of bringing scantily-clad models to the track and draping them all over the cars to make them go quicker, although I guess I was in the minority because most of the lads approved wholeheartedly. I suppose I was a bit 'old school' and thought that we were there to try to win races; I felt it was a distraction. However, it was all part of the Benetton plan and one of the reasons they joined the Formula 1 circus; it wasn't just to sell sweaters. Under Flavio's direction and promotion Benetton became one of those brands that everyone knew, even if they weren't sure what the company did. All of this was supported by the fairly shocking posters that Benetton put out at the time. The chap who produced them used to come to the races and we saw some of the proofs in the motorhome before they hit the press, like the black and white horses copulating and the nun in white kissing the priest dressed in black. The posters were great, but the guy who designed them was completely off the wall, as you would imagine.

Another obvious visual change from the outside was the approach the team management took to team uniforms – they came up with some fantastic designs, even though they didn't suit all the lads who had to wear them. Somehow Italians seem to look great in anything, whereas some of the other nationalities suffered a bit by comparison as they had been hired for their mechanical and electronic skills rather than their shape. No one could deny that the uniforms were colourful, though, and very much in line with the Benetton retail image.

The first season each member of the team was given coloured shirts to wear, but they had to wear a different colour each day. There was even a uniform colour chart to study, so no two mechanics working together were wearing the same colour on the same day. As an example, I had to wear pink one day and Stuart blue, and the next day the colours were reversed. It's not too difficult to imagine the potential for confusion that this caused, particularly if the lads had been out late the night before. The company also designed red T-shirts with silver fluorescent arrows on the back, so that if the TV camera showed a pit stop from above the arrows would flow around the car as the lads changed wheels; the red shirts were teamed with bright green Benetton trousers. The next innovation was red and white striped overalls and bib and brace dungarees, which predictably weren't too popular. Benetton's ideas were wonderful and certainly brightened up the paddock, but the company was smart enough to appreciate that the team was on show when they were travelling to and from the races and they became the front runners in supplying more casual 'fly-away' uniforms in the form of quilted jackets and cargo pants. Now every team has designer uniforms and they all look a lot smarter.

Through all these changes we got on very well with Flavio and he did confide in us quite a lot; sometimes we had to agree to differ, but it was never a problem for him. I think he respected us for standing up for our point of view. One of our major breakthroughs came when we managed to convince Flav to replace that hernia-inducing truck – what a relief that was. Stuart was the prime mover in getting the Van Hool family involved; we had remained in touch with the company since the early days when they had sponsored Surtees. They had always wanted to get their vehicles into Formula 1 and Stuart introduced them as a supplier by arranging for Benetton to move from the previous monstrosity to a custom-designed coach. Stuart designed it from the chassis up and he always said to me that the Benetton coach was the first hospitality vehicle he had driven in all the years in Formula 1 that he felt confident would always get to its destination. It was brand new, had diesel instead of petrol engines and was designed to last. That first Benetton coach was finally scrapped after 21 years, so it certainly stood up to some punishment.

The vehicle had permanently fitted interior walls and the floor was lowered to get two storeys in. On the top floor there was a press office at the front, lounge and drivers' area in the middle and Flavio's office, which was also our bedroom, in the rear. On the ground floor we had a small kitchen area and, with the extension to the awning around the back of the coach, we had an outside cooker and extra fridges. The layout of the kitchen was smaller than in the previous truck but far more practical. We were self-contained, and we could carry everything inside the coach – the tables, chairs and the canopy, as well as an outside fridge. Today some of the teams have in excess of 45 trucks to carry the hospitality facility around, while the team principals sit around discussing how to make the sport 'greener'.

The coach was a major success and Flav called us into his new office one day saying, 'I make you rich.' We were a bit sceptical and asked him how and why that was going to happen. He replied, 'I want to buy a bus.'

Flav had gone into business with a London lawyer called Jepson and they decided to buy a motor coach which they then leased to Ford and we got a (small) slice of the lease payment in return for making sure it was running smoothly. We had a couple called David (Foggy) and Claire Fogden as front of house for the first three years and then Luigi, who had left Ferrari, pestered Flav until he gave him the job. The Ford and Leyton House coaches were also made by Van Hool and specified by Stuart; with Stu's help, the company produced seven coaches for a variety of teams over the next couple of years, but we never did get rich.

Under Flavio's control, the motorhome was thrown open to the wives and girlfriends of the drivers, or WAGs as they are now known in other sports. We had a different name for them: the 'stitch and bitch club'. They were mainly the Italian wives and girlfriends with the exception of one Belgian, 'Speedy' Boutsen, and Flavio really encouraged this as he loved anything continental; he liked to be surrounded by ladies, so the arrangement suited him just fine. It was terrific to see them all sitting around the awning, probably about eleven of them in total. They would all chat happily together, but when one of them got up to go anywhere you could tell those still around were all bitching about the one who had just left. We would have expected the Ferrari motorhome to be the natural magnet for all these gorgeous ladies, but the team didn't seem to encourage them quite like Flav.

Our new coach was a major step forward in presentation, but however hard Flavio worked on the team's image it still left space for the pranksters in the team to have some fun. I remember one race weekend that one of the team, John Mardle, stole into the motorhome just after it had been set up for the weekend and peeled the one-way paper lining from the toilet window. Traditionally it had been possible to look out of the window without anyone seeing in, but the removal of this lining allowed people in the motorhome opposite to see straight in; the trouble was that no one noticed for a whole race weekend, or if they did they never let on. John must have had a thing about trousers coming off because on another occasion he and some of the other lads wanted to eat in the restaurant at the hotel where they were staying. John, however, was wearing jeans and was politely told he couldn't go in the dining room wearing them. He promptly took them off, stuck them under his arm and walked into the restaurant in his underpants. The staff looked on in amazement, but he got his dinner.

Sometimes the lads got a bit too out of control and it actually worked to the team's disadvantage. Gordon Message, the team manager, had tried for years to book rooms at Hotel Jerez in Jerez as it was on the right side of town for the GP circuit. One year he finally managed to secure the elusive rooms after assuring the management that everyone would be well behaved (the hotel had experienced a lot of problems with teams in the past). It all went wrong on the very first night when 'Dangerous' Dave Butterworth threw his bed out of the window. Apparently he was dissatisfied with the fact the bed was more of a put-you-up than a four-poster, and decided to demonstrate his dissatisfaction. Gordon found it impossible to keep the rooms for the next year and had to work hard to stop the whole team being kicked out there and then. The job of team manager can be very hard in lots of ways.

Benetton were renowned for having music playing all through the race weekend in their garage; Ian Harrison was a Brit working for Zakspeed, a German team, who were always located in the garage next to Benetton. Ian used to nip by on the first evening after the garage had been set up and tap into the Benetton sound system, running a wire next door to get the same music at minimum cost and effort. The Benetton lads were aware of this but didn't let on until the German Grand Prix in Hockenheim, when they changed the sounds on the system to play nothing but stirring war tunes like the 'Dambusters March'. Ian had to race around and disconnect the whole thing pretty smartly before a third world war broke out.

Eventually, whatever the environment, everybody meets their match and our mechanics met theirs on one of our trips to Rio when we encountered a certain Ronnie Biggs, one of the Great Train Robbers. Biggs had fled England after escaping from Wandsworth prison and ended up in Brazil via France and Australia. Brazil didn't have an extradition treaty with England so he was able to wander around freely. Julian Bailey, who had been driving for Tyrrell in Formula 1 but wasn't involved that season, obviously knew Biggs and brought him to the bar where we were one evening. Biggs was trying to sell ten-shilling notes with his signature on. He had a drink with us and, to be honest, none of us liked him very much because he was a bit of a 'Flash Harry', but he started turning up at the bar with his young son every night when we got back from the circuit. He latched on to the Benetton boys and thought they were a bit of fun; then he started saying, 'Look, on the Sunday night after the Grand Prix, I am going to treat all you Benetton boys and girls.'

When the night finally arrived he turned up, and while we sat outside taking the air he kept buying champagne, one bottle after another, until he suddenly said, 'Excuse me, I have just got to go to the toilet.' He took his son with him and was gone quite a while. I started to think, 'He's done a runner, hasn't he? He's bought all this drink and gone.'

Just then his son ran back to us saying, 'My dad's been beaten up in the toilet. Can you help?' Two of the lads went to see what was going on and Biggs had a bandage round himself and 'blood' coming through his shirt. Fake blood is obviously not restricted to Halloween and Harlequins rugby players. His son said, 'We've got to get him to hospital,' but the lads realised it was a scam and got Biggs up against the wall. One of the guys was threatening to throw his son out of the window, but it was pointless because there was no money. He'd also been trying to sell T-shirts with a picture of a train on the front bursting through a £10 note. What a waste of space.

It wasn't only in Brazil that we sometimes felt vulnerable. One night in Phoenix we were walking through a none-too-salubrious suburb to get back to our cheap hotel, feeling a bit exposed as we passed this mission hall with lots of down-and-outs sitting around. Suddenly a pick-up truck drove past, screamed to a halt, turned round in the road and roared back towards us. Pulling up alongside, the driver leapt out of the cab, ran towards us and just as we were about to try to run off he shouted 'Mum and Dad?' We were amazed and cautiously replied 'Maybe.' He then passed us a grubby piece of paper, saying, 'I've just been reading about you in a book. Would you mind signing this?' Apparently he had been reading a book by Gerald Donaldson in which we had received a mention; we thought we were about to be mugged but nothing was further from the truth. Perhaps we shouldn't be fooled by appearances.

Flavio continued to imprint his own charisma on the team and his reputation as a deal-maker was complete when he pulled off a coup by signing Michael Schumacher from under the nose of Eddie Jordan in 1991. Nelson Piquet and Roberto Moreno were driving for the Benetton team from the start of the season but, despite doing reasonably well, we were not really getting the results that Flavio needed to develop the brand. Michael had done a brilliant job in qualifying his Jordan at Spa and suddenly everyone was talking about him, despite his car breaking early in the race. Flavio decided that Michael was the missing ingredient he needed to move the team forward, and while we'll never know how the finances were worked out, nothing was going to stop him getting what he wanted. It helped that Bernie wanted a German driver in a successful team and it didn't seem like Eddie Jordan had Michael's contract watertight, so it all took on an air of inevitability.

As the Spa weekend progressed the whole paddock was talking about the battle for Michael's future. There was a high level of scurrying and intrigue and the journalist pack was camped out watching the comings and goings. Stuart was in overdrive, fetching and carrying messages, and most of the deal was done over that weekend. We stayed up until God knows what time, waiting for some lawyer to come from Italy – not out of interest, but because the meeting was in our bedroom! Flavio also wanted us to stand by in case we were needed to witness any contract documents, but in the end the deal wasn't finalised in Spa and the whole circus carried on until the early part of the Monza weekend.

Roberto Moreno had come into the team when Sandro Nannini had his helicopter crash. He had known Nelson from their early years in karting and they got on really well. Roberto was like a little monkey, but a nice little monkey. I used to call him 'Little Monkey' and of course he called me 'Mum'. He was a real character, always had a grin on his face and forever fooling around, but this situation was no joke; he was just a pawn in the power struggle that was going on. Eventually all the power brokers had finished their meetings, the lawyers had left with their signed documents and the journalists had disappeared to write their versions of events, but I'll always remember Roberto's face as he walked into our little kitchen in the back of the motorhome. He was crying and he just said: 'I have to go.'

I didn't really know what was going on then. We had heard rumours, which are the lifeblood of the paddock, so we tried not to take any notice, but the press were outside and they already knew. I said to Roberto, 'Go where?' to which he just replied, 'I go, Jordan's, Flav, he doesn't want me. I can't finish the season, he doesn't want me.' His little face was a picture of sadness and it was the first time I had ever seen him like that as he was normally grinning. He had been quite successful on the track, but in the end that just wasn't enough.

As they say, 'As one door closes another door opens' and on this occasion it was the door of the Benetton motorhome on Thursday, 5 September 1991, at Italy's Monza race circuit. As I related in the Prologue, I was in the kitchen filling flasks with tea for the mechanics when there was a knock at the door and a chubby-cheeked, curly-haired chap standing there asked, 'Are you Mum?' After a little confusion on my part, he said, 'I'm Michael Schumacher, your new driver,' and with that a whole new chapter of motor racing history and a very special friendship had started.

His new team-mate, however, was less impressed. Nelson and Roberto had been friends for a long time, as I've said, and they were still close despite the traditional team-mate rivalry. Nelson let the team management know exactly what he thought of the decision to 'transfer' his mate: he told Flavio and his right-hand man, Tom Walkinshaw, that he believed Roberto had been 'shafted'. Roberto was very popular, but in sport when someone comes along with something special that will take the team forward, that takes precedence over popularity. Once he had vented his feelings Nelson had to admit that Michael was probably going to be a bit special, particularly after Michael finished ahead of him in his first race for the team.

Michael wasn't the only new blood to join Benetton in 1991. We also saw the arrival of Rory Byrne as chief designer and Ross Brawn as technical director. Ross had previously worked for a number of Formula 1 teams and, most recently, the Jaguar World Sportscar Championship team, while Rory had rejoined after a short sabbatical with the short-lived Reynard Formula 1 operation. The stage was set for a brilliant collaboration, but even this prompted humour from the irrepressible engineering group.

As most people who know anything about Formula 1 realise, Ross Brawn is and always has been a fanatical fisherman. When he arrived at Benetton all the lads renamed him 'the Cod'; what wasn't made clear was that this had nothing to do with his fishing. Ross, like a number of men, became more handsome as he grew older, but in his early years he tended to look a bit, shall we say, 'lippy', and that was the reason for his nickname. Everyone in the team had a nickname; most of them were based on some personal characteristic or foible.

In his early months with the team Ross came up with so many ideas to improve the car's performance that everyone was working flat out, day in and day out, trying to make them work which initially made him pretty unpopular. In exasperation, one of the engineers, who went on to become extremely well known in the pit lane, had some T-shirts made which featured a picture of a cod's head within a red circle with a red diagonal line across it. These were distributed to the whole team – except Ross, of course – and we had a team photo taken early one morning before Ross arrived at the circuit. Michael Schumacher was in the photo and he had no idea what it was supposed to represent, but he wore one too. Michael asked the rest of the lads what it was all about and they told him it was something to do with cod fishing, so he sat there obliviously throughout the photo session. It was another great example of the Benetton sense of humour.

By the end of 1991 Flavio had confirmed himself as one of the leading team principals in Formula 1 and established the foundations of a structure which would develop into a World Championship-winning organisation at Benetton and bring together the group which would eventually transform the fortunes of Ferrari.

In 1992 the Benetton driver line-up was changed again, with Martin Brundle coming in to replace Nelson Piquet as Michael's team-mate and Alex Zanardi arriving as our test driver. Martin had a slow start to the season, with quite a few DNFs, but as the season progressed he notched up some impressive results and put a lot of pressure on Michael, so everyone was more than a little surprised when he was released after only one year and replaced by Riccardo Patrese. Martin was easy to get along with and was very kind to Stuart and me, often inviting us out for dinner if we had a free evening, usually at tests because we were all a bit busy at race weekends. He brought his wife Liz and his brother Robin to most Grands Prix, which made it a real family affair, and we were sorry to see him go. At the time we never envisaged that Martin would make such a fine television commentator, using all the knowledge he had gathered through his career to bring both race commentary and interviews to life for the viewer. His son Alex is now racing.

Riccardo was a perfect gentleman and a pleasure to be around, but we never really became that close to him because he was quite shy. On one occasion, however, Stuart got a bit too close to him when Riccardo drove too near the pit wall and Stuart almost hit him on the head with the pit board. That was one of a number of adventures Stu had during his pit-wall duties. Riccardo had a passion for model trains and he was happy to demonstrate his knowledge on the subject to anyone who would listen. Susie Patrese was a different proposition altogether and very outgoing. She used to keep me up to date with all the paddock gossip; she was scandalous, but very funny.

Alex Zanardi was bored quite a lot of the time and he used to help me make the sandwiches. I had a sandwich-sealing machine and he was so fascinated by it that when he left I had to get him one to take home. I asked him why he wanted something like that and he replied, 'When I go to the testing I take my own sandwiches, although now I know you are here I won't bother, but I would still like one of those machines.'

Every time Alex came to a test he used to sit there making sandwiches, always wearing a new sweater knitted by his mother. I couldn't help taking the mickey and I used to say, 'Oh! It's a green one this week, then' – but he didn't react; his mother must have been as fast with the needles as he was in the car. I can't say that I liked all the sweaters, but he obviously did. Alex's initial period in Formula 1 was promising but it never really took off. Instead, he went to the USA, where he was hugely successful in the Champ Car series, becoming rookie of the year and twice winning the championship before coming back to Formula 1 with Williams. Again, things didn't work out and he was dropped after one season, returning to the States to restart his Champ Car career.

Alex had a massive accident at the Lausitzring (or EuroSpeedway Lausitz) in 2001: he lost both his legs when his car spun, coming out of the pits, and was hit by Alex Tagliani. His life was saved by some brilliant medical work at the trackside. Alex's crash was yet another sadness in a catalogue of similar events, but he seems to be coping. In fact, he is probably coping better than Sandro Nannini with his arm, because Alex was back behind the wheel of a racing car within two years.

There was soon another addition to the team, and although our new boy wasn't as well known as the drivers and designers he certainly left his mark. Ronnie Dean arrived and brought one of his 'inventions' with him. There was no major scandal or massive fines involved in this bit of technology transfer, but it certainly generated a whole lot of black looks because Ronnie brought his 'Lung Tester' with him, which was supposed to be a device for testing people's health. The cover story was that some people would be spot-checked to make sure they could stand up to the rigours of the job. A whole cross-section of people, including drivers, mechanics and unfortunate bystanders, was selected 'at random' to take the test and persuaded that it was both in their interests and a legal requirement.

The 'Lung Tester' was a clever arrangement that looked like a tin can with a windmill on top of it. There was a spout for blowing into and that was linked to a tube which ran through the can and came out of the top to push air on to the windmill-shaped gauge. The gauge was graduated with numbers that purported to measure lung strength. Unfortunately there was a bit of a knack to using this tester because the pipe that one blew into was effectively split into two separate pipes. The upper part blew air on the gauge and the lower part blew air into the can, which had a small split in it and contained black paint powder. Someone would tell the luckless 'testee' to watch and then demonstrate that a quick blow would produce a rotating windmill and a positive reading on the gauge (failing to point out that the demonstrator's tongue had been covering the lower part of the pipe). When asked to reproduce this, the person being tested would blow like crazy while being egged on by a small but interested group of advisors, with a negligible impact on the gauge but a significant impact on their appearance. Unknown to the victims, they always ended up with a black face and white eyes like a panda because the natural reaction when anyone blows hard into something is to close their eyes. In case this all sounds like 'Double Dutch' I've included a sketch that will hopefully help out.

On completing the test the person being tested would be told, 'OK, thanks for that, we'll let you know the results shortly.' An awful lot of people were caught by this piece of tomfoolery, including Michael Schumacher, Martin Brundle, Mark Blundell, Johnny Herbert, Flavio Briatore and Riccardo Patrese as well as a lot of new engineers. I remember catching Martin; I was standing behind him just after he'd joined the team and I asked him if he had had the lung test. He replied that he had passed the FIA medical, but I had to advise him that Benetton had its own test equipment and it was essential to pass that. I told him that the equipment was on the truck and I would get one of the lads to rig it up. Later in the day Martin went off to undergo his 'examination' and Stu and I waited around to see how he fared. He came back absolutely black.

The 'Lung Tester' was probably just another example of 'Motorsport is Dangerous', because I can't imagine it did anyone much good, but we had so much fun with the device – it went on all the fly-aways, with anyone the boys fancied having a go at getting the treatment. Most people took it in good part. We only had one mechanic who failed to see the funny side, although after his test Flav was in a 'black' mood for the rest of the day. We also had one poor chap who was trying to strengthen his lungs all week, because he was a smoker, and he had been running up and down the hills of Monaco in order to get himself in shape to set the performance record. It was the smokers who always tried the hardest to prove they hadn't been affected by their habit.

There were other surprises in store for Flavio and lots of the team members during the year, the most unusual of which was probably their Christmas card from Nelson Piquet. After leaving Benetton Nelson had gone to try his luck at the Indy 500 in 1992 and he'd had a huge accident. His legs were badly smashed, particularly the right one which he nearly lost. He was rushed to the Methodist hospital in Indianapolis and had his legs X-rayed to check the extent of the damage; the right one was also photographed. After he had been in surgery and was recuperating the doctors showed him the photograph, so that he could see what a mess it was, with the objective of dissuading him from trying to get back in action too quickly. Nelson asked for a copy of the photograph and, for whatever reason, the hospital agreed. I'm sure they would have been horrified if they'd known that he had the photo reproduced as Christmas cards and sent them to all his nearest and dearest. It was something only Nelson would do.

That wasn't the only nasty shock Flavio received in those early years. I remember being in Estoril and, as usual, all the high rollers from each team stayed at the Atlantis Hotel, which was situated right in the middle of the circuit. It had become quite run down, or should I say it had a certain faded glory. Flavio came into the motorhome one morning, grimacing and saying, 'Di, last night I had a terrible time.'

Never knowing what Flav was going to say next, I reluctantly asked, 'Why?'

He replied, 'I went to my room, not a very nice room and a little dark, but there was something on the bed. I thought it was my socks, but it was a rat!' Needless to say we had to take him and his bags, presumably with his socks, down to the coast to find another hotel.

It was a pleasure to help Flavio out with his hotel, though, because he had been very good to us the previous season when we took a break after the race in Mexico. We had decided to visit New York and the Rocky Mountains en route to the Montréal Grand Prix. The New York trip was memorable; we were travelling with Nick from Leyton House. We had subcontracted a motorhome to the team and Nick was working for us, looking after it. We had got a really good deal on rooms at Trump Plaza near Central Park and everything seemed to be going to plan. We had checked in at the reception desk and were on our way to drop our luggage in our rooms; however, when we got to the lift, the door opened and who should be coming out but Flavio. We just stood there, amazed, thinking, 'What's all this about?' Naturally we had no idea that he would be there; no one ever knew what he was doing next.

As he stepped out of the lift he said, 'What you do here?'

And I replied, 'We are having a break for a couple of days.'

'You come with me!' he insisted.

I was becoming a little concerned. 'Look, Flavio, we're paying. We're not charging this to Benetton.'

'Come with me!' he said, stalking off to reception with us in tow, protesting all the way. Flav called over the most senior-looking guy behind the counter and said something to him that we didn't catch because we were dragging our luggage back from the lift. The man opened the door into the back office and we were ushered in behind Flav, feeling extremely guilty – even if we didn't know why. Nick opted out and waited outside. Flav looked at the official and then pointed to us. 'What's going to happen now?' we were thinking.

Flavio told the concierge, 'I pay for these people's rooms.'

I stuttered out a 'Pardon?' but Flav just said, 'He wants you to sign to cancel the rooms you have just booked because

I pay for these.' I tried to tell him that he shouldn't and that we always paid for ourselves when we were between races, but when Flavio decided something he didn't change his mind. What we didn't know at the time was that Mr Benetton and Nelson Piquet both owned suites on the top floor of that hotel, and Flavio was staying in Mr Benetton's. We have experienced a massive number of coincidences in our years of travelling, but that was one of the strangest. We had picked the hotel out of the blue because we had read there was a deal available and neither we, nor Flav, had any idea what the other was doing – yet we had turned up at that lift at the same time. Incidentally, we ended up in better rooms than we had booked in the first place! It's an object lesson in always telling the truth.

Travelling with Benetton was sometimes a bit of a trial. We never had a stack of Benetton sweaters to carry around with us (unlike the condoms at Surtees and the cigarettes at Lotus), but the customs police always thought we had some stashed somewhere and would spend an awful lot of time searching while Stuart stood around fuming. I have no idea why we were stopped so often with that particular team, sometimes being pulled over at the side of the autoroute with sniffer dogs bundled on board. We would always ask why we had been stopped and would always get the same reply: 'We have phone call.'

There are so many cupboards and drawers in a motorhome – it's every motorhomer's dread that, one day, someone will put something dodgy in one of them and expect to retrieve it at the next race, and in the meantime we might be stopped and accused of knowing it was there. I always told Flavio that if anyone left anything in the motorhome I would personally open it, and if we felt it was in any way suspicious we would dump it. It wasn't that we didn't trust the team, but all kinds of people were invited into the offices, and if one of them left something illegal in there it would be Stuart and me who would be in trouble. In fairness, none of those roadside checks ever found anything doubtful at all, apart from Flavio's personal drawer full of monogrammed silk underpants. (That wasn't a crime, although perhaps it should have been!)

However, we got a big, big surprise one afternoon when Bernie Ecclestone arrived just before the race was due to start and asked if I could get Flavio for him. This wasn't unusual, as they were friends, but as I headed upstairs to let Flav know that Bernie was waiting for him I noticed a large brown envelope in Bernie's hand. Flav came down the stairs and Bernie handed it over to him, and after a few words he looked at his watch and set off for the grid. Flavio needed to go to the grid as well, so he turned to me, stuffed the envelope in my hand and left, saying, 'Di, you keep, you keep.' We had a little cupboard above the fridge and, thinking nothing more about it, we stuck the envelope inside and got on with looking after the guests.

We didn't have a good race and neither car finished, so Flavio left early for the airport. The next day, as we were packing up the coach, I opened the cupboard above the fridge and immediately saw that Flav's envelope was still there. Bearing in mind what we had said about packages being left behind, I thought I should ring Rosella, Flavio's PA, and get her to tell him his envelope was still in the truck. I told her that I didn't know how important the envelope was, but it was from Bernie. She went off and got Flavio to come to the phone, but he just said, 'It's no problem. Just keep it until the next race.' We explained that we really needed to open it to make sure there was nothing in it that we wouldn't like to find, and his reply was 'That's OK, you can open it.' When we did we couldn't believe our eyes: it was full of dollars, and there must have been $20,000 or $30,000 sitting there. When we'd got over the initial shock we were quite pleased to think that Flavio trusted us with that amount of loose cash, but equally we were a bit concerned that it was sitting around in the motorhome because, as I've said, we were always getting stopped. I don't know what it was all about, but I expect that it was just one of the regular bets the two of them enjoyed winding each other up about.

It wasn't always so fraught when Bernie came to the Benetton motorhome. Usually his car would drop him off outside our awning in the morning and Stuart would always look up over the heads of the regulars who were sitting eating breakfast and raise two fingers to Bernie, followed by just his middle one. This wasn't a way of telling him to leave quickly but a simple question: 'One egg or two?' Some of the things we have heard in the motorhome over the years are frankly unbelievable, but I would never dream of telling anyone about them. The public face of the whole paddock was quite different from the reality, and at any one time the big news story might be that Flavio and Eddie Jordan had fallen out and Bernie wasn't speaking to either of them – when they would actually all be sitting in the upstairs office having a chat. Journalists have a lot of column inches to fill every week so a bit of intrigue was good for business.

Fortunately, the journalists weren't around the Benetton garage at the end of the Friday of the 1993 Canadian Grand Prix in Montréal. Stuart had been told to collect a young lady from the gate and bring her to the garage, which he duly did. What he didn't know at the time was that this was a special present for Pat Symonds: a stripper. I happened to go along to the garage, to take some food for the guys who were working, and unusually they didn't seem too interested in eating because they were all watching 'Symmo' receive his present. When I could finally see through the crowd I was confronted by the sight of Pat sitting on a chair with the stripper standing in front of him doing her stuff. I hoped he wasn't comparing her with what he'd seen on the motorhome roof a few years earlier! It was his 40th birthday and the other lads thought it was their birthday too. It's amazing how many people had jobs to do in our garage that day. I somehow don't think that behaviour would be condoned in the environment of the current Formula 1 paddock.

Strippers weren't the only people who needed to be smuggled into the paddock. When the driver merry-go-round started towards the end of every season, Flavio used to send Stuart on dozens of missions, always to get hold of a driver or his manager or someone whom he didn't want the press or the driver's existing team to know he was meeting.

'I need to see this driver or that driver. Tell them to be here at three o'clock, but make it look like you haven't gone to see him. Pretend you're borrowing some sugar or talking to the man who runs the motorhome.' It meant we were always involved in these interesting and devious plans about how someone could be taken to somewhere his team would prefer he wasn't, to have a chat with someone he shouldn't, without anyone knowing. People were so used to seeing us about that we were, to a degree, invisible. Some weeks we ended up delivering more messages than our postman at home.

It was while we were at Benetton that we instituted the 'benches'. People used to come round to us for breakfast who were not part of the team – they could be from Arrows, McLaren, all over the place; we often prepared pasta for Martin Brundle and Mark Blundell when they were Brabham's driver pairing, because the team didn't have its own motorhome. They showed their gratitude by giving Stuart and me] a Mont Blanc pen each at the end of 1991. Two influential members of the FIA, Charlie Whiting and Herbie Blash, worked for Brabham then too, and they regularly called round for a bacon buttie.

We didn't have room for all these callers under the canopy – and besides, it wouldn't have looked good to have all those other teams under our team's awning – so we started to place a bench around the rear of the cooking area. The lads would queue up behind the motorhome and sit on the bench, waiting for one of our breakfasts, and it just caught on. If we had any guests or celebrities or anyone unusual we would ask them to sit on the bench for a second, have a drink and then sign the bench.

We have got through four of these benches, sporting the signatures of Senna, Prost, Lauda, Herbert, Frentzen, Schumacher, Phil Collins, Adam Faith, Chris Rea and Sid

Watkins, to name just a few. We still have the benches, but some of the signatures have faded over the years. Phil Collins's 'bench' is special because he is an excellent cartoonist and did a cartoon of himself with his drums and then signed it.

The 1992 and 1993 seasons were a development period for Benetton. Michael went from strength to strength, while Martin came and went, as did Riccardo Patrese. The Williams team was unstoppable in both years and the Alain Prost/Ayrton Senna 'war', which is covered in detail in lots of other publications, was at its height. At the end of 1993 a whole catalogue of rule changes would be introduced into the sport, Ayrton finally joined Williams after years of courtship and Alain Prost retired. But no one could anticipate the story that would unfold in the coming season.

Chapter 19

DIVERSIONS AND DEVIATIONS

Long after he retired from racing James Hunt used to make a point of going to the Dutch Grand Prix in Zandvoort because he liked to visit Amsterdam. On one legendary occasion he organised a route for us called the 'James Hunt Naughty Tour'. He had made quite a study of the various 'entertainments' on offer in Amsterdam, and although initially he hadn't planned to come with us on this particular trip, he did leave us the route and a series of instructions.

There were six of us – Bob and Shaune from McLaren, Tim and Maureen from Williams, and Stuart and myself. Stuart and I never had a car when we were travelling, but Bob and Shaune were always good enough to transport us around, otherwise we would have never left the paddock. James still hung around McLaren and had maintained his friendship with Bob and Shaune. We knew him too, which was nice, because we used to be Hesketh fans when he drove for the team all those years earlier. We liked him a lot, but he was certainly crazy. On the evening in question he had arranged this route for our tour and left the list of destinations with Bob. We started in a bar and then did the usual tour of the streets before starting on James's highlighted shows, all of which he considered 'musts'. Our first stop was a live sex show, with only about 12 seats in the room – which made it quite intimate in every sense of the word. On stage a couple were 'performing' right in front of our faces and it put me right off my red wine. I had no idea what I was doing there but, as I always say, 'When you think it can't get any worse, you're deluding yourself.' We eventually got out of there with a new understanding of the word 'stamina' and a growing trepidation as to what was coming next.

Eventually we arrived at this one particular bar where we knocked three times on the door (really!) and a hatch opened. The face through the hatch asked us what we wanted and Bob said, 'We were told to come here by a certain person.'

'Who?'

Bob gave the doorman James's name and we were ushered in. 'This is not a bar, it's a convent,' we were told, and I began to become really concerned, wondering what on earth we had let ourselves in for.

We passed through a room that looked like the vestry of a church into a second room decorated in purple velvet drapes with religious artefacts. When we got to the third room there was a bar and we were told to sit at it. I wasn't completely naïve at that point, but pretty clueless just the same. There were quite a few people sitting around, but as we sat at the bar we realised there was no space behind it for anyone to stand – it just extended backwards like a stage. While I was taking all this in two doors opened, one at each end of the bar, and some ladies came in and started performing on the eye-level 'stage' right in front of us. It was pretty clear that this was an entertainment aimed more at the men than the women, but we were there and we would make the most of it, so I ordered another red wine.

At that point James, who must have had a change of heart, came in. The girls were all over him, as might be expected. The main sport of the evening concerned a bottle on which the punter was encouraged to place a guilder note. The note had to be folded in two, and then folded again to allow it to stand on the neck of a bottle. The idea was that if the lady performing on stage when the bottle was 'loaded' could pick it up, without using her hands, she got to keep it. I will leave you to work out how she managed it. Stuart described the main exponent of this particular skill as being nimble, versatile and Scouse (she was from Liverpool), but I think I'll just gloss over that. Suffice it to say she collected quite a few quid from incredulous customers. As usual, Stu had to embarrass me by asking her, 'Didn't your Mum ever tell you not to mess with money because it's dirty?'

After all this we were expected to say a prayer – I just prayed she would put her money in her handbag in a more conventional fashion and that Stuart would shut up! I expect all these religious overtones were either to make it seem even more risqué or to cover up the fact that they had no liquor licence. We certainly saw life in all its strange forms in those days.

Nudity wasn't restricted to the stage, however. There were lots of occasions when I would be standing in the motorhome and one of the drivers would say, 'Have you got a towel, Di?' and I would turn around to find our star driver starkers. At one time there was nowhere else to change, so they didn't have any option. Well, that's what they told me anyway. I suppose I could have looked away, but when I was standing at the kitchen sink with nowhere else to work it was a bit difficult. That's my excuse...

Michael used to have his massage in the upstairs area of the motorhome, along with whoever else was lined up to be rubbed down. Sometimes I had to go up there at the same time and attend to things – it was all part of the job. People have often asked me which driver looks best with nothing on, but of course I always averted my eyes so I can't answer the question. Although, if pressed, I have to say Michael doesn't look bad.

Another of our driver episodes involved Gerhard Berger, who was driving for McLaren at the time, although we knew him from his Benetton days. Gerhard arranged for us to go white-water rafting in Austria after the Grand Prix. He'd said to Bob and Shaune, 'Bring your friends,' so the usual six suspects went along.

I really didn't want to go, because Gerhard was always doing crazy things. There was one occasion in Monza when he threw Ayrton's carbon-fibre composite briefcase out of their helicopter to find out whether it was as indestructible as Ayrton claimed. Opinions differ as to whether it was ever found, but I know that all Ayrton's stuff was in it and that Bob had to take him to Milan to get a new passport. Gerhard and Ayrton got on really well and had a lot of fun in the earlier days, and they were always playing crazy practical jokes on each other; that was before Ayrton took to religion. Kimi Räikkönen seemed to be the same. He hardly spoke over the race weekend and then, when he'd had a few beers, he became a different guy altogether. I remember him getting thrown out of a nightclub in London for trying to have 'intimate relations' with an inflatable dolphin. A lot of the 'characters' have gone out of Formula 1 since those days. That's why Nelson was such a breath of fresh air; he wasn't quiet and he didn't care what he said.

Anyway, back to the story. We assembled at the white-water rafting centre where we found that Gerhard had arranged everything and paid for everyone. He claimed we would enjoy it, but the day had dawned wet and cold and, looking at the water, I said, 'There is absolutely no way I am going to do this.' In the end, of course, I had no choice; Gerhard forced us to go into the changing rooms to don our wetsuits, lifejackets and other paraphernalia. When we all came out, looking like Jacques Cousteau, he was still in the clothes he had turned up in. I said, 'What about your stuff then?' to which he replied indignantly, 'I'm not coming, it's too rough!'

By this time the six of us plus two staff were in the boat and about to set off. I had never done anything like it in my life before (and only once since). The weather was foul and I was looking at the raging torrent, wondering how to get out, when Gerhard said, 'Look, you have to sit on the side of the boat.' So we did.

The pilot asked, 'Is there anyone who can't swim?'

Stuart and I said with one voice, 'Well, we can't swim in

this.' The others felt the same, but they didn't own up. As we were looking at each other, the second in command pushed us all into the water in turn, so that we could 'experience what it was like to go in, just in case we fell in!' Apparently, the theory was that if the body was already cold and you suddenly fell into the water your heart wouldn't stop. Mine already had.

I couldn't get back into the boat so they all dragged me over the side in a fairly unladylike heap, and then we were off. I felt sure I was going to die, but what really wound us up was that halfway down the route we passed under a bridge and there was Gerhard standing on top of it, waving. In fairness, he met us at the end and when we were dry he took us all off for a meal. I remember him asking if I had enjoyed it and I was impolite enough to say, 'No, not at all,' or words to that effect, which only made him laugh more. Looking back on it now it was really kind of him. I think.

I have been known to enjoy the odd diversion without the rest of the group. I remember one day in Monaco when Thierry Boutsen was driving for Benetton. I was talking to his wife Patricia and he was just about to take out his new Riva boat. It was a Friday, when there are no cars on the track, and he turned to us, saying, 'Come on board and we'll have a little spin. We won't be long. We'll just go out there' – pointing in a general offshore direction. Paola Nannini and Susie Patrese were on board, looking slim and attractive in their bikinis, and there was me, twice their size, in my team uniform. I have no idea why he asked me to go on board, but it was really nice of him – and he never asked me to make the tea! We were gone for two-and-a-half hours and went all the way down the coast to St Tropez; I was supposed to be getting lunch for the guys at the track so poor old Stuart had to do all the sandwiches and everything on his own. When I got back and told him I had been to St Tropez he had a bit of a sense of humour failure.

Stuart was highly thought of in the Formula 1 paddock and, at one time, he was the man people went to when they wanted to get a motorhome sorted for the coming season. It was a bit of a distraction, but we managed to fit it in reasonably well. As I have already explained, we hired coaches from Van Hool on behalf of Sauber, Williams and Simtek, but Stuart also had a hand in producing Prost's coach after Alain decided he wanted one; in fact, he wanted two. It was just before Spa and Stuart took Alain to meet the Van Hool people, explaining to him that their coaches were a little more expensive but, in the end, you got what you paid for and theirs would be the best in the long term. The two of them went to the factory, got the full tour and talked in detail about the proposal, after which Stuart said to the Van Hool people that from now they should deal directly with the Prost team as he didn't really have anything to do with it.

After some discussion that deal fell apart because Alain thought Van Hool should provide one coach free if he paid for one – a view not shared by the factory. Alain found someone else in Spain who could provide coaches and were in a position to start working on them straight away, which Stuart felt was probably indicative of something a bit negative. Undeterred, Prost carried on and again asked Stu to help him out, so Stuart visited the Spanish factory a number of times. It was something of a culture shock. When one visited Van Hool it was like a town: there were coaches everywhere, some partly completed and some awaiting delivery. When he arrived at the Spanish company there was one bus outside, not many people about and hardly any cars in the car park. Inside, the factory was almost empty; there was no machinery and hardly any equipment. None the less, they made a start on the coaches for Prost, but Stu was very concerned. He had a number of meetings with the Prost management and kept saying: 'I hate to keep saying it, but this is how it was done at Van Hool when I had all the others built. They won't start until everything that you are supplying to go in it has arrived, because there are no circumstances where they're going to stop production to wait for you to deliver something.' The Prost guys nodded, smiled and basically ignored him.

On one of his trips to the factory Stu found that the toilets were incorrect and, without going into too many gory details, when the lid was lifted we could look right down into the sump. Ordinary household toilets had been fitted which were definitely not suitable for a motor coach. Stu explained to the girl who was in charge of fitting out the unit that there would be some significant problems with all of this, particularly for those with a sensitive nose, and she just burst into tears. It might have demonstrated her commitment but it wasn't particularly helpful.

Stu kept banging on, saying, 'You need to get all your TVs, telephone equipment and everything over to Spain otherwise there will be problems.'

'It's no problem,' the Prost team responded, 'our sponsor Alcatel will provide everything.' Needless to say, nothing ever appeared and the coach makers just carried on building the coach.

Stuart would ask, 'Where are you going to fit in all the electrical and telecommunications equipment?' and the Spanish would wave vaguely at a mass of wires hanging out of the walls and say, 'Televisions can go there and phones there.'

Eventually, when we turned up at the first pre-season test, Doug Denhart from AVS had to come out with another guy and completely rewire the whole coach for the TVs and videos otherwise they would never have worked. One of the selling points of the coach was explained to Stuart as 'The Spanish coaches are much more stylish than anything Van Hool could produce, because the Van Hool coaches are very flat at the front but the Spanish coaches are much more sculpted.' The reason the Van Hool coaches were flat at the front was to give much more space between the front window and the back wall. The downside of the raked design was that it reduced the available internal space in the coach and the front window was exposed when the canopy was being fitted, which Prost found to their cost when they had to keep replacing it. At the end of the season Alain came and apologised for the way his people had behaved and for all the advice that had been ignored and, most importantly, he paid Stuart.

Sometimes our deviations and diversions were just plain misunderstandings. During one particular test session in Kyalami quite a few dignitaries had been invited, one of whom was Cyril Ramaphosa, Nelson Mandela's Secretary General of the African National Congress at the time. He arrived with his wife for lunch one day and, as Nelson Mandela is a man that I, along with half the world, admire, I asked Mr Ramaphosa, 'Is Nelson coming, by any chance, because I should love to meet him?'

Mr Ramaphosa said, 'Yes, he is wonderful. I also admire him greatly,' and he then went on to say that he had been with Nelson the evening before at dinner and although it was not planned for him to be at the track he thought he would probably come.

I was thrilled and, barely able to contain myself, I carried on preparing lunch. About an hour later Mr Ramaphosa said, 'Nelson has arrived for lunch as well.' At that moment the garage door opened and there was Nelson – but Nelson Piquet, not Nelson Mandela! It suddenly dawned on me that we had been talking about the two different Nelsons that we admired so much. It was always good to see Nelson Piquet, but on that occasion I felt just a bit disappointed.

The track is the ideal place for diversions and distractions, and I wasn't the only one to get my wires crossed. When our friends Tim and Maureen finally left Williams in 1987 their places were taken by Pete and Jane, who had replaced us at Lotus – although thankfully they no longer had the black and gold Morris Marina. It was after Frank Williams had had his accident and we were in Hungary, where the track was below the level of the motorhomes. Frank wanted to watch the race, and by then he had had a device similar to a tyre trolley adapted to hold him secure so that he could stand up. The trolley also had a drinks container attached so that he could have a drink when he needed one.

Frank's nurse had found a decent vantage point and wheeled his trolley behind the motorhome so that he could watch the action. The nurse made sure he was comfortable and then Pete brought out Frank's drink and a bendy straw so he could reach it. Just as he was positioning the straw the phone rang in the motorhome, so Pete ran in to answer it and never came back out. I kept looking out of my motorhome kitchen window and I could see Frank was getting hotter and hotter and redder and redder and I realised that, in his haste, Pete hadn't managed to put the straw close enough so, try as he might, Frank couldn't reach it. I turned to Stuart and said, 'I am going to have to go out there and do something.' In the end I went out and moved his drink into place and he said, 'Thanks, Di, thanks ever so much.' I then went into the Williams motorhome, found Pete and said: 'You've forgotten Frank!'

'Oh, bloody hell,' he said.

'Have you got a cap for him, because he is burning up out there?' I continued. Disaster was avoided, but only just. I don't think Frank was very impressed, though.

In earlier years, when Tim had been required to take Frank to the pits, he sometimes left Frank for too long in his wheelchair at the bottom of steps while he went off to seek out Bob or Stuart to 'help provide a lift up'. But Frank took the temporary abandonment in good part and would laugh about it.

Frank was a bit of a lad, though, and he could get diverted. I remember that he used to have a bit of a twinkle in his eye when Jane was around, and he usually practised his arm exercises just when she was passing by. He used to have to flap his arms to keep the circulation going and he often practised this when she was bending over, giving him his dinner or something similar. His timing, and the flapping motion, all combined with the fact that Jane was pretty well endowed on the bosom front, used to result in quite a lot of hand/bosom interface situations. She used to come round to see me and she would be a bit annoyed.

'He's done it again,' she would say – but what can you do!

Chapter 20

IMOLA 1994

Over the years the chain that Ayrton's mum had given me after his first race win was wearing thin; in fact it had become quite fragile. I had stopped wearing it for the full race weekend but I still carried it in a box and put it on as part of my pre-race ritual at every event. When Ayrton called to see us at the Brazilian Grand Prix in 1994, as he usually did, I had to say to him: 'I still wear the chain your mum gave me all those years ago. It's getting really worn and I am afraid it may break. I would love another just the same if you could ever get one.' He said he would make sure that he did.

At the next race in Japan I started to put my chain on, exactly as I had done every race day for the past nine years, and the charm shattered, completely and inexplicably. It just turned to dust. I had never seen or heard anything like it before. When I saw Ayrton later I told him I really needed to replace the chain and the eye. I couldn't tell him it had broken. By that stage in his career Ayrton had become very religious and quite superstitious; I really didn't know how he would react. I was nervous right through the race and, in the event, he crashed out after being hit by Mika Häkkinen and then by Nicola Larini. Afterwards Ayrton was disappointed but he told me he would definitely bring me a replacement chain and charm to Imola; he said he had already got it but had forgotten to bring it.

I never got the replacement chain. The world knows what happened at Imola in 1994. It was the worst weekend of our lives and I'll never forget our horror as the events unfolded.

The weekend got off to a dreadful start when Rubens Barrichello crashed heavily on the Friday afternoon after sliding over the sloped kerbing and being launched sideways across the grass run-off area and high into the tyre wall. The car dropped on to its side and the accident looked very serious; we feared the worst as Rubens was quickly transferred to the circuit medical facility. Although he was quite young at the time, Rubens was very close to his countryman, Ayrton. The session was stopped and Ayrton drove back to the pits, got out of his car and walked off to the medical centre to check on his friend's condition. He seemed to have some difficulty getting in, but eventually he was allowed to see Rubens who was mercifully conscious and able to confirm that he was well. Ayrton returned to his pit and drove the rest of the session, but he was a troubled man.

That season, in addition to our Benetton role, we also had the contract to provide hospitality to the new Simtek team. We had employed Pete and Jane (who had replaced us at Lotus) to look after the team on a day-to-day basis but, as usual, we kept an eye on what was going on. I had just been to the Simtek motorhome on the Saturday morning to check that all was well and had spoken to Roland Ratzenberger. We all knew Roland as a really nice chap with a great sense of humour. I wished him good luck for qualifying. It's difficult to believe that an hour or so later Roland would be dead.

As I left the motorhome to go back to the Benetton hospitality area I noticed Nick Wirth, the Simtek team principal, Bernard Ferguson, the Cosworth commercial director, and Roland sitting down to chat with a couple of the team members. Bernard later told me that the discussion had bounced around from topic to topic before settling on the sort of 'wind up' that usually occurs when five or six blokes get together. There was a bit of banter about Roland's sponsorship by the Monaco-based 'Barbara' sports management operation. The group was relaxed and laughing as they got ready for qualifying.

Everyone from the Simtek camp who was not actually

involved in running the car gathered in the garage to watch events unfold on the television monitors. There were monitors everywhere around the paddock, in all the garages and motorhomes, and there were also big screens placed at various points around the circuit. In those days the television pictures were provided by the host country's national television operator, which in Italy was RAI.

As qualifying progressed Roland was well down the timesheets. He was struggling, but he was really pulling out the stops to try to make the race. The group in the garage held their breath as they watched the TV coverage switch from car to car as lap times came down. Nick Wirth's wife was at the back of the garage watching as intently as everyone else and willing Roland on. Suddenly the television screen flashed to images of Roland's car careering off the track at the Villeneuve corner, sliding across the grass run-off area without slowing down and smashing into the trackside wall. The picture was replayed over and over, at full speed and in slow motion, while everyone in the garage watched in horror. Roland's head seemed to have struck the wall as his car impacted at almost 200mph.

The circuit became silent except for the noise of a helicopter, stationary above the crash site, beaming live pictures of the efforts to release Roland from his wrecked car. In the garage no one moved. They could hear the helicopter outside and see the extremely graphic pictures on television, but they were completely unable to take it in. The coverage continued as Roland was lifted clear of his car and laid on the grass alongside the broken chassis. Someone started to pump Roland's chest as he lay on the floor. The spell was broken. Nick's wife buried her head in her hands; a Simtek mechanic was the first to react and leapt to turn off the TV monitor. Outside, the helicopter blades continued to turn noisily above the silent circuit. Simtek team members were in tears and all around the racetrack team personnel, drivers, sponsors and spectators were numbed by what they had witnessed.

Roland was the first driver to die during a Formula 1 weekend

The small family car.

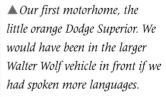

▲ *Our first motorhome, the little orange Dodge Superior. We would have been in the larger Walter Wolf vehicle in front if we had spoken more languages.*

◄ *A sought-after sticker from Team Surtees days: it was often issued with the sponsor's products.*

Previous page: With Stuart in the Ford motorhome, finding time to relax for a change. Not a cup of tea in sight. (Photo courtesy Steven Tee, LAT)

◄ *The full complement of Team Surtees personnel at Niagara en route from Montréal to Watkins Glen in 1978 – no travel uniform in those days.*

▲ *Meeting my favourite Dallas character, Ray Krebbs (played by Steve Kanaly), in 1984, with Nigel Mansell looking on.*

▼ *All good parties end up in the jacuzzi. At the time I told Nigel this photo would end up in print one day. His wife Roseanne was close by.*

▲ *Team Lotus in 1985.*
Elio is in the car with
Ayrton and Hazel
Chapman to his right.

◄ *Elio and Ayrton*
presenting me with a
birthday cake in the pits
in Austria.

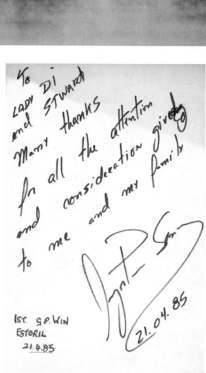

▲ *Ayrton's first win, in the rain at Estoril, Portugal, in 1985. The faded message from Ayrton reads, 'To Stewart and Dianna. Many thanks and love from a good friend'.*

▶ *Ayrton wrote this card after the Estoril win when we were relaxing with his mum and dad. The stain is where he leaned on it in his wet race suit.*

◀ *The 'United Colors of Benetton' in Monaco.*

▼ *Follow the arrows: fine dining for the Benetton lads.*

▲ Luciano Benetton changed the face of the paddock with his colourful uniforms.

▲ Follow my leader in 1986 on our first trip to the Hungarian Grand Prix.

▼ Possibly the last photo of Elio and his girlfriend Ute on that fateful day at Paul Ricard in 1986, at our Benetton motorhome, with a fan. An hour later the accident occurred.

▲ One of Stuart's other duties: telling Sandro Nannini he was in front of Ayrton in the Japanese Grand Prix of 1989.

▲ One of those precious F1 passes – Stuart was around everyone's neck all season.

▼ The way we were. Thierry Boutsen queues for his 'Full English'.

▲ *Nelson – one half of the Dream Team!*

▼ *Nelson laughing at Sandro's lap times.*

▲ *Up close and personal: Stu and I with Nelson and Katharina.*

▼ *Not only tea cups made it to the motorhome; these are the trophies for first and second in Japan 1990.*

▲ *Celebrating with Micky Cowlishaw and Flavio Briatore after Nelson's win in Montréal in 1991.*

▼ *Stuart gives Nelson a helping hand in Hungary.*

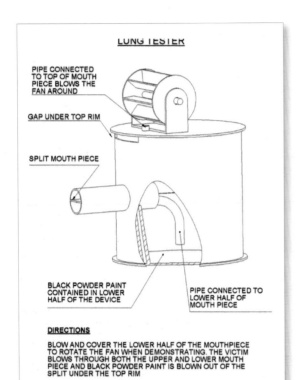

LUNG TESTER

PIPE CONNECTED TO TOP OF MOUTH PIECE BLOWS THE FAN AROUND

GAP UNDER TOP RIM

SPLIT MOUTH PIECE

BLACK POWDER PAINT CONTAINED IN LOWER HALF OF THE DEVICE

PIPE CONNECTED TO LOWER HALF OF MOUTH PIECE

DIRECTIONS

BLOW AND COVER THE LOWER HALF OF THE MOUTHPIECE TO ROTATE THE FAN WHEN DEMONSTRATING. THE VICTIM BLOWS THROUGH BOTH THE UPPER AND LOWER MOUTH PIECE AND BLACK POWDER PAINT IS BLOWN OUT OF THE SPLIT UNDER THE TOP RIM

◀ *The lung tester unveiled.*

▼ *Caught out… Why the black look, Flavio?*

▲ *Adam Faith admires his handiwork on one of our famous benches.*

▶ *Chris Rea is not to be outdone…*

▲ *Michael Schumacher and I wearing our 'Cod' T-shirts – see pages 169-170.*

▼ *Michael borrowed our Honda Prelude at Silverstone and gave it a serious track test.*

▶ *Michael soaked in champagne after sealing the World Championship in Adelaide.*

▼ *Michael, Corinna and Jenny the dog with Stuart's mum and her friend Meg.*

▲ *Near tragedy in the Benetton pit at Hockenheim in 1994 as Paul Seaby is engulfed in flames.* (Photo courtesy Steven Tee, LAT)

▼ *Michael presented a pair of his gloves to me after securing his first World Championship title.*

▲ *George Harrison explains the finer points of strategy to Stuart and me – or maybe he is asking for a cup of tea and a Mr Kipling Country Slice.*

▶ *George standing on a chair in the Benetton garage in Adelaide to get a snap of Michael: everyone has their heroes.*

▲ *Mr E asking Stuart's advice? Imola 2000.*

▼ *Celebrating Johnny Herbert's win at Silverstone 1995.*

A precarious trip from Italy to Argentina for Ford's rally cars – a definite list to starboard.

Refuelling Ford's hospitality coach and kitchen in Sweden: it's minus 25 degrees C.

Graham, Tracey, Stuart and me 'Dancing with Wolves' at the Swedish Rally. At least these fans were a bit warmer than us.

▲ The road-blocking Toleman motorhome.

◀ The Lotus 'Black Pig' alongside the TAG and Williams vehicles, parked up en route to Portugal; it was safer to travel with company rather than alone.

◀ The harbour wall at Monaco – more relaxed times in the mid-1980s.

▲ *An early Benetton motorhome.*

▶ *The hernia-inducing Benetton vehicle with pop-out sides, know as the transformer – it certainly transformed Stuart.*

▶ *The interior of the same vehicle with its heavy-duty walls in place.*

◀Michael Schumacher arrived at a Paul Ricard test in style; we came by bus.

◀Ford's last bus in F1 before transferring it to World Rally.

▼ Big is beautiful? The Red Bull Energy Station in 2011… motorhomes and coaches have long gone.

▶ *One of Tetsu Tsugawa's cartoons in the book he had published in Japan.*

They have no children
But, Mam & Dad of GP.

▼ *Spot the personality. Tetsu's work again.*

To Stu & Di,
Many Thanks for all
the help & Support
Plus the "Best Food"
in F1
Lots of Love

▲ *Johnny Herbert in relaxed mode.*

◄ *Bernard Ferguson, co-author of this book, with Johnny at the Goodwood Revival.*

for 12 years, since Riccardo Paletti's fatal accident in Canada in 1982. The manner in which Roland's final moments had been broadcast live and in such detail had a significant effect on many of the drivers who were competing that weekend and led to many TV corporations reviewing their procedures. Nick Wirth was rushed out of Italy, as is usual under the circumstances. Remarkably, the team opted to race the following day and Roland's team-mate David Brabham showed incredible courage by racing flat out until his car's suspension failed after 27 laps.

Ayrton was particularly distressed by Roland's death, especially as it had followed so quickly after Rubens's accident. Ayrton had often appeared troubled in recent times, even before the accidents, and he had become quite religious, as I mentioned earlier. He was often seen with a Bible.

Ayrton and Thierry Boutsen were very good friends and we were still close to both Thierry and his wife Patricia from the days when he drove for Benetton. Thierry was racing in Germany that weekend, but Patricia was pregnant with their second son Cedric so hadn't gone with him. Thierry and Patricia had already asked Ayrton to be Cedric's godfather and Ayrton had spoken to Patricia just before the weekend of the race.

The race started well for Ayrton, despite his concerns, but another of our 'boys', JJ Lehto, stalled his car on the grid and an unsighted Pedro Lamy smashed into the back of his Benetton. Once again we were concerned, as JJ had only just made a comeback following an accident causing cracked vertebrae in his neck during a test at Silverstone. Fortunately he was uninjured, but the safety car came out for three laps while the debris was cleared.

It was around 2.12pm on 1 May 1994 when Ayrton died. For the second time that weekend the eerie silence, that only those who have been there can recognise, descended over the track, broken only by the sound of a helicopter. Flavio Briatore had come back to the motorhome to tell us what we already suspected, but it had not been officially announced. As we have previously said, no one ever dies at a sporting event in Italy. Michael Schumacher won the race and after a minimal podium ceremony he came back to our small kitchenette. He was very upset; we all were. He had been following Ayrton and had seen him go off the circuit and hit the wall.

Michael said, 'I am just not going to do this any more. This is it. It's all over.' His manager Willy Weber persuaded him to carry on, but his initial reaction was that he would never be seen at a race circuit again.

The world of racing was truly shocked. There had been so many years without a fatal accident and now there'd been two in the same weekend. Probably the only driver on the track that day who had been involved in a race where a death had occurred was Gerhard Berger. The drivers had been brought up to believe it could never happen again. When it happened to, arguably, the greatest driver of his generation, it shook them all. Michael was particularly disturbed by it. He felt that, if such a thing could happen to Ayrton, it could happen to anyone.

The Williams team packed up and left as quickly as possible. We were staying at the same hotel, the Donatella, and went to meet the incoming Benetton test team. The boys were arriving at the hotel to support a test planned to start the following day. We told them there would be no test and why. Most of the lads were unaware of what had happened as they had been flying into Bologna while the race was taking place.

Betise Assumpção, or 'B' as we called her, was in the hotel reception area. B was Ayrton's PA and she was there with his brother Leonardo and two Brazilian journalists; they were all beside themselves. I whispered to Stuart, 'We have to do something, we can't just leave her. She's distraught.' I went over to her and asked, 'Can I do anything?'

In response she just looked at me and said, 'Would you come to my room with me and help me sort his things?' Ayrton had been staying elsewhere, but he kept lots of his equipment with B so that she could ensure it was all transported around.

I wasn't sure about that at all and I didn't think I could face it, but I knew she needed support. 'Do you really want me to do that?' I asked, and she nodded dumbly. So I went with her to her room and Ayrton's stuff was all around, just as it had been left. It was the most difficult thing I have ever done in my life. We put his things together and gave them to his brother to take home.

As I've mentioned, Thierry Boutsen and Patricia were not together that fateful weekend and so were unable to console each other. And of course Ayrton was never able to become Cedric's godfather.

I don't believe that any other incident has had more impact on motorsport than Ayrton dying. I'm not saying that just because there were a whole series of technical changes to the engines and cars after the carnage in Italy; it's just that I don't think anyone today would have the same impact. I don't know why, really, but Ayrton seemed different from everyone else. He had an aura around him that was truly difficult to define. I would have liked to have worked with him right through his career.

Although we were only really close to him on a day-by-day basis for one year, we were connected with him both before and after that time. When he came to see us at our motorhome, or when we met him in the McLaren hospitality area while visiting Bob and Shaune, it was clear that he had changed. He had started to become detached from reality and seemed to be in a world of his own. Although on the surface this seemed to suit him, it was perhaps a warning sign. I think Ayrton realised that he had made a big mistake when he left McLaren for Williams.

I wrote to his mother after his death and I have spoken to Bruno Senna, Ayrton's nephew, at Formula 1 tests. I told Bruno I remembered him from when he was two years old, coming to the Brazilian Grand Prix with his mum, Ayrton's sister. He was kind enough to sign my superb limited-edition book of photographs of Ayrton. The book was by a very famous Japanese photographer, Norio Koike. I believe he has never attended a Grand Prix since Ayrton died.

Ayrton gave me my lucky charm at Imola in 1986 and I wore it on every race day, year after year, until it shattered – so I wasn't wearing it on the day he was killed. During that time he won three Formula 1 World Championship titles. I'll never forget him, or that dreadful weekend.

My favourite memory of Ayrton dates back to his last race for McLaren, when he won the Adelaide GP in 1993. The after-race concert featured Tina Turner at the top of the bill; she called Ayrton on stage and sang 'Simply the Best' to him. He stood there, wreathed in smiles, wearing a pink Hugo Boss sweatshirt, pale blue jeans and the famous blue Nacional sponsored cap. I can't listen to that song now without remembering Ayrton.

Chapter 21

ANNUS HORRIBILIS – 1994

It's amazing how the bare facts in sports history books can make a team's season appear to be a major success and obliterate all the stories behind the statistics. On that basis 1994 was a triumph for Benetton. Michael Schumacher won the Drivers' World Championship for the first time and the team was runner-up in the Constructors' World Championship. However, behind the facts the season was plagued by controversy, injury and the ultimate disaster of Imola.

We almost weren't at Benetton to be part of all the ups and downs of that season, as Steve Madincea had asked us to join Ford and take over their hospitality coach. However, 1994 was the year I felt we would finally be with a team when it won the World Championship, but what a difficult season it was on both the global and domestic scale.

In the run-up to the season a whole series of technical changes had been made to the regulations, mainly aimed at reducing the number of 'driver aids' available on the cars, but when the pre-season testing started it was clear that nothing had been done to slow down the cars.

The year started badly for Benetton when JJ Lehto was injured at Silverstone in pre-season testing, missing the first two races with damaged vertebrae in his neck. He was replaced by Jos Verstappen as second driver to Michael Schumacher. The first race was in Brazil, where Jos had a massive accident but was fortunately uninjured, while Michael went on to win the race. The second race was the Pacific Grand Prix and Michael again won easily after a big first-lap accident had left him clear of the field. JJ Lehto replaced Jos for the next race.

Imola was the third race of the season and a hollow victory for Michael with the whole of Formula 1 reeling from the shock of the deaths of Roland and Ayrton. Following the Monaco Grand Prix, where Michael won his fourth consecutive race, there was growing unrest among the teams and the governing body, who were all convinced that Benetton was infringing the rules. This feeling was underlined after the fifth race in Spain, when Michael was able to pull away from his pit stops despite his gearbox being stuck in fifth gear, which helped him to a second-place finish behind his chief challenger Damon Hill, driving for Williams.

Michael was still haunted by the fact that Ayrton and Roland had died and he was bemused by the reaction to his brilliant start to the season. Although he was technically minded himself, he didn't want to be seen to be involved in any cheating allegations. The technical guys in the team called all the shots, and whether it was cheating, exploring the outer limits of the rules, or whether Benetton were just being pulled in line because they weren't the 'establishment' is a matter of conjecture. The traction control question never really went away. A lot of people thought Michael had it, but he just said that he was good at starting under pressure and he had the car set up so that it handled well. He felt it was 'Get-at-Michael year' and he was pretty fed up about it.

By the seventh race of the season, in France, Jos was back in the second car as a replacement for JJ Lehto, who had been demoted to third driver, and Michael had won six races out of seven. On the surface it couldn't have looked much better, but the simmering resentment of the other teams about the possibility that Benetton were using banned driver aids was coming to the boil.

The season saw a lot of changes at Benetton. The staff had

altered and success was going to everyone's head a bit; the workload was getting too much for us, even though Flavio had authorised us to hire a girl, Debbie Wall, to help over the Friday to Sunday period. By the middle of the season a group of about six of the team mechanics had started to get a bit 'too big for their boots' because the team had started winning races, so we called them the 'Golden Boys'. They became very demanding. They wanted everything to change in the motorhome; the type of food they had previously enjoyed suddenly became unacceptable and they asked for it to be more Italian, despite the fact they were all English. We already did a lot of pasta and other Italian food, but this little clique wanted to become more continental. As an example, the team regularly had sandwiches in the garage for lunch because it was a very busy time. The sandwiches had lots of different fillings and these guys took it in turns to come and complain that they didn't like one or other of them. In the end we found that these lads had just got together and agreed each one of them would complain about a different filling until none of them were acceptable. It didn't get us down too much because most of the boys were fine, but it started to cause divisions within the team, and that had never happened at Benetton before.

When the Formula 1 circus reached Silverstone the stage was set for a real showdown between Michael and Damon Hill, who were in a battle for the championship. During the race Michael was black-flagged for ignoring a stop-go penalty for passing Damon on the parade lap, much to the pleasure of the huge British contingent and the frustration of the Benetton hierarchy. The team told Michael to stay out on track while they tried to get the penalty overturned, but in the end Race Control didn't have much choice in the matter and showed him the black flag, which meant he was disqualified. As a result of this Michael was banned for two races, but the team appealed and he was allowed to race under appeal.

There were a lot of satisfied people in the pit lane when

the proposed ban was announced – everything seemed to be turning against Benetton for one reason or another. Everyone still thought the team was running an illegal car. When we got to Germany for the next race the whole team was very tense. With the prospect of a two-race ban Michael was in real danger of being overtaken in the championship points; the stress in the team camp was almost tangible. On the Saturday night before the race, as usual, I went into the garage to check that all the team had been for dinner. I was surprised to find that one person was still there and he was messing about with the fuel rig; in my naïveté I said, 'Well, what are you doing there then? It's a bit late to be messing about with that thing.' From the look I got I decided to go back to the motorhome.

The next day, during the race, I had just taken some drinks into the garage and was walking away; I had only gone about 20 feet when I heard a commotion. I hurried back to the motorhome and went into the kitchen, where I had a small TV – and I saw a pit crew engulfed in flames. In my head I screamed, 'My God, which team is that?' and then I just saw some blue-clad legs rolling on the floor and I knew it was our team. I couldn't believe my boys were caught up in that. They were burning; there was fuel everywhere and fiery rivulets of it ran across the paddock in one direction and towards the pit wall in the other. In the centre of the action was Jos Verstappen's car, engulfed in flames. Suddenly there was foam everywhere; on the TV I couldn't see beyond the mayhem to the pit wall, so I'd no idea whether Stuart was involved. I couldn't believe all that could happen in such a short space of time.

Stuart was on the pit wall, operating the pit board for Michael as usual, and the fire went across there and momentarily they were all trapped without any fireproof suits, which weren't required in those days. There was a wall of flame and Stuart and the others were beyond it, but we couldn't see them and had no idea if they were safe. Stuart had a different perspective on the whole thing; he was on the wall with his back to the refuelling activity, looking after Michael's pit board. The first thing he knew about it was a sudden surge of heat at his back, which made him turn round pretty quickly, to be faced with the pandemonium that had broken out behind him. He couldn't move and just had to watch events unfold. Fuel had sprayed all over the car during refuelling and had caught fire when it came into contact with the red-hot exhausts.

Jos eventually emerged from the flames and they got the fire under control. Most of the pit-wall crew came back into the garage but Stuart, Gordon Message and Pat Symonds had to stay put as Michael was still running. They were wet through and covered in foam from the extinguishers, but otherwise unharmed. The race continued, but of course the Benetton refuelling rig had been destroyed – and Michael didn't have enough fuel to finish the event and couldn't refuel. In the end the problem resolved itself when the engine developed a misfire that forced him out of the race.

It was fortunate that no one was more seriously injured, and it was very lucky that the flames didn't reach up to the Paddock Club, situated right above the action, because that would have caused a major incident. The horrific sight of our boys burning in the pit-lane fire and Jos Verstappen coming back to the motorhome with the skin peeling off his face will live with me forever; pictures of the incident are shown in the media every time accidents in racing are discussed. Simon Morley, the team's refueller, was detained in hospital with facial burns and never travelled with the race team again. It had been a dreadful weekend, but battle was taken up again in Hungary and, amazingly, Jos was fit to drive. Michael won the race and eased the championship pressure, but he was still racing under threat of suspension and we were still cooking under threat of rebellion.

There were further regulation changes in the aftermath of the fire, and from then on all the pit-stop crew had to wear full fire suits and full-face helmets. That is still the case today, despite there being no refuelling at pit stops. The crew all come out of the garage looking like spacemen, which certainly adds to the spectacle.

The Belgian Grand Prix was yet another in a long line of fiascos. I didn't really understand what had gone on at first, but one of the engineers explained to me what had happened. Michael won the race but, after being scrutinised, it was discovered that the 'plank' underneath his car had more than the allowed level of wear, so he was disqualified. The 'plank' was one of several safety measures introduced following the fatalities in Imola and was designed to regulate the ride height of the car; it had a maximum permitted wear rate over the duration of the race, and Michael's had exceeded that. That's how it was explained to me, anyway, so I pass it on word for word.

All the journalists were hanging around because the stewards were sitting late into the evening while they were deciding whether to disqualify Benetton or not. The rest of the team had left the circuit but we were still packing everything up, the only ones left in the motorhome, when suddenly the whole journalistic pack descended on us wanting comments on the fact that the team had indeed been disqualified. We were busy and they were pestering us and I just said, 'We can't comment, it's nothing to do with us. We have no idea what's going on, but everyone seems to have it in for Benetton.' It was just a throwaway remark, but it was published by Tony Dodgins. I should have been more careful, because he has caught me out more than once.

In an attempt to add injury to insult the motorhome was stoned by the public as we drove away from the circuit that night, because Michael's fanatical German fans believed that Benetton had got him disqualified – and of course we had the Benetton logo emblazoned all over the coach.

Michael's two-race ban was ratified and he was replaced by JJ Lehto for the Italian and Portuguese races, which were both won by Damon Hill to really ratchet up the pressure on Michael and the team. Nerves were all becoming a bit shredded and Benetton was still not free of suspicion from the rest of the pit lane. While Michael was on his way to becoming a superstar he wasn't universally popular, the fans' favourite being Damon Hill, the son of a famous father, who was driving for an iconic British team and had a 'Mr Clean' image.

The FIA finally held an investigation into the circumstances around the German pit-lane fire in October and decided there were no grounds for excluding Benetton from the World Championship. On his return to action after suspension Michael won the European Grand Prix, leaving him just five points in front of Damon with two races to go. It was all going to go down to the wire, and when Damon beat Michael into second place in the penultimate race in Japan Michael's lead was just one point. Game on!

If we thought the season had been marred by controversy up to that point, then the worst was yet to come. In the final race, in Australia, Michael was leading Damon until, with Damon waiting for any kind of slip-up, he went wide in a turn. Michael's car touched the wall and he slowed down. Damon was right behind him and it looked like he was going to overtake Michael – and then the two cars collided. The Formula 1 world was in uproar and Michael was accused of taking both cars out of the race, but there was no formal appeal from Williams and the result stood. Michael had won the Drivers' World Championship by just one point.

The whole season had been a mess but it ended well for Michael, although his incident with Damon Hill soured it all a little. I thought it was fantastic that he had won the World Championship, but even as his biggest fan I felt sorry for him because it had been surrounded by so much controversy which had continued right until the very end of the season. I have lots of photographs of Michael celebrating his World Championship with the team, but somehow they were spoiled by everything that had happened before. However, in my mind, he was disqualified from two races and banned for two more and still won the World Championship, so he had proved his point. He was there to race. I personally would find it hard to believe he knew anything about any possible cheating.

During 1994 Formula 1 had lost one superstar and discovered another, but for many people the sport would never be the same again. We also had a bit of a change. That season at Benetton was our last with the team. After what was eleven years in our minds, three with Toleman and eight with Benetton, it was on to pastures new. At the end of the 1994 season we were called to a meeting with Flavio at the Benetton technical centre to discuss the future. At the time we were unaware that Flavio was suffering from back problems and was actually living at the centre, as it was impossible for him to travel by car, even if he were chauffeur driven.

We entered his rather palatial office but as we couldn't see him anywhere we decided to take a seat and wait for him. As we sat down we noticed a pair of monogrammed slippers sticking out from the end of a sofa (it seemed that most of what Flavio wore was monogrammed). We then had the weirdest meeting ever, with us sitting down and Flavio flat on his back. We discussed a few things and agreed to differ on a few points. By the time the meeting was over it was decided that we would move on. We parted amicably and I think that, in Flavio's own way, he quite admired us for standing up to him on the issues we felt strongly about.

Flavio had decided that too much was being spent on providing for the boys in the team and that they should only have pasta and water; equally, he knew Ford had been unhappy with Luigi as he always served up the same food and had some rather slapdash ways, so the obvious solution was that we swapped. Luigi went from Ford to Benetton and we passed him going the other way. At that point we fully understood how Roberto Moreno felt on his way to Jordan, but we had agreed and it was time to move on. The only disappointment was that

Johnny Herbert had joined Benetton for the last two races of the season and would be staying with the team in 1995 and we would miss the opportunity of another season of his practical jokes. That chance would come again, however.

As Stu and I prepared to move over to Ford we reflected on our time with Benetton, and particularly with Flavio. There had been some interesting moments and we had the warm feeling that Flavio had trusted us with both finances and confidences (although there were lots of confidences we perhaps wished he hadn't shared). We have talked about Flav's generosity towards us and we always tried to repay that in whatever manner we could, although it has led to some interesting moments both at the track and elsewhere. He sometimes had some quite mysterious guests and on a number of occasions we received very odd phone messages to relay to him.

A regular message was 'Could you tell Flavio that his grandfather has died?' Initially we passed the message on to him as sympathetically as we could, saying how sorry we were to have to break the news and offering our condolences. When we took the same message at the next two or three Grands Prix we began to wonder how many grandfathers he had.

Flavio used to ask us to do all manner of things, including being on red alert to witness Michael's draft contract signing at Spa in 1991 at some ungodly hour of the morning; we didn't have to in the end, as mentioned earlier, because it happened at a hotel in Monza. We also had to go to Italy for the weekend to collect his expensive new car. In addition to his business life Flavio also entrusted me with his dietary requirements which at one time were 'Slim Fast' drinks, followed by laxatives, after each practice. He often left items in his office/our bedroom which he would claim after I'd mentioned I had kept them safe, items which don't need describing except to say they were monogrammed. His passport was one of the things he often left behind, and Stuart frequently had to chase after him with it before he left the circuit.

Flavio was often difficult, but I'd worked out ways of deciding if he was in a bad mood. His English wasn't too good at the best of times, but when he was in a mood he spoke so quickly we had no idea what he was saying. The other warning sign was a slight twitch in his cheek, and when that started we made ourselves scarce.

There were many meetings with Bernie and others in his office while Stu and I were working in the kitchenette below, and often when voices were raised I couldn't help overhearing what was going on, some of which wasn't for my ears. I'm sure Flav knew we had overheard, but he trusted us enough to know we wouldn't discuss it elsewhere – and the conversation never stopped when we took drinks into the room, so the others seemed to trust us too. Having the kitchenette directly under the office had another odd disadvantage, too. On one occasion after a Grand Prix when Debbie, who was working for us at the time, decided to clean the oven in the kitchenette, she sprayed a huge amount of oven cleaner into the oven, then left the oven door open to get rid of the fumes and came outside to help us pack up. Debbie didn't realise Flavio was still upstairs; the fumes rose and Flavio burst out of the door shouting, 'Di, Di, you try to kill me!'

There were times when we felt like it, but we have to say it was certainly an experience working for him over the years, and one that we wouldn't have missed. Now that Flavio is not involved in Formula 1 he seems to have found happiness in his life away from the track, but he probably misses all the wheeling and dealing. In a strange way I think Formula 1 is missing him and his controversial image at a time when most team bosses seem stereotyped and trained always to say the right thing.

Love him or hate him, he was different.

Chapter 22

THAT NICE CHAP MICHAEL

It is impossible to draw a line under our time with Benetton without saying a few more words about Michael Schumacher and his enchanting wife Corinna. We spent over three years with Michael and we got to know him very well. He is very sensitive, caring and extremely family oriented, which is quite different from the public's perception of him. We had a lot of good times with the two of them, particularly when Michael was testing because, as I have said before, it's a little more relaxed then. Testing is all 'hurry up' and 'stop', with the drivers sitting around a lot of the time with nothing to do. The four of us used to discuss all manner of things.

In his earlier days with the team Michael, Corinna and their West Highland Terrier Jenny came to the house where we were staying in the south of France and we have a picture of them sitting on the sofa with Stuart's mum and her friend Meg, whose daughter lives in Germany and has regularly impressed her friends with photos of this event. I have a great memory of Stu and me standing with Michael in the garden, near the pool; as he looked across the valley to the hills between us and the coast he said, 'One day I'll have a house like this.' I think it's fair to say that he has achieved that dream. After he had relaxed for a while we went out for a meal in La Napoule to a restaurant we used quite regularly. The people who owned and ran the restaurant vaguely knew we were involved in racing but didn't really know what we did or even if we were telling the truth. One of the waiters was obsessed with Formula 1 and he just couldn't believe it when we walked in with Michael. Service was pretty good that evening, if a little over-attentive.

Corinna used to come to a lot of the tests and she and Michael brought Jenny the dog to some of them, which of course was strictly not allowed. Corinna used to sit upstairs in the motorhome with the dog in the area that doubled as our bedroom and Flavio's office. Normally that wasn't a problem. However, Flavio decided to fly out to one particular test in Jerez and when he arrived at the motorhome he walked upstairs and put his foot straight into the dog's bowl, spilling dog food all over his expensive deck shoes. He wasn't impressed.

On another occasion in Jerez it was Stuart's turn to be unimpressed by Michael's fondness for animals. We had started feeding a stray kitten that was hanging around the circuit and, when the test was over, Michael said, 'Can you bring the kitten round to Estoril?' (It was the next race.) Stuart put his foot down firmly, because it was an overnight trip. 'What the hell am I going to do with a kitten?' he said. 'No, Michael, I am not bringing it.'

Michael argued back. 'Well, I will collect my plane in Germany and will have it at Estoril and I want to take the kitten home, so would you mind bringing it?'

Stuart was adamant, however, so Corinna asked what we could do for the moggy. I suggested we get it some food, so she came to the supermarket with me and we bought a carrier bag full of cat food and gave it to the slightly bemused gate attendant, asking him to feed the kitten after we'd left. I'm sure he probably took the food home for his own cat, but the thought was there.

When we weren't looking after animals and the motorhome was being used for its proper purpose we used to keep lots of videos in the rest area upstairs, to try to keep the drivers occupied when it was raining or they were waiting for the engineers to try some wacky modification to their car. Michael watched a lot of videos on his own in an attempt to get some time away from the scrum that usually followed him around the paddock. On one occasion, when we were at Silverstone, he had been watching *Mr Bean* and he had cracked up, lying on the floor with tears rolling down his face. Shortly afterwards there was a knock on the motorhome door and when I opened it who should be there but 'Mr Bean' himself, Rowan Atkinson; he'd been brought round by someone from McLaren, where he was a guest. Rowan said he was a fan of Michael's and asked if it would be possible to see him. I was completely amazed by yet another in a long line of coincidences in racing.

Michael wouldn't come down to meet many people, and I always had the job of working out who he would be prepared to see and who he wouldn't. This time I went upstairs and said, 'Michael, you'll never guess who's downstairs,' to which he looked at me a bit warily and responded 'Who?'

'It's all right,' I said, when I told him to come down and see. 'You'll enjoy this.'

He wasn't at all sure about it – he could be a little bit touchy sometimes – but in the end he said, 'Oh, OK if you say so.' Coming downstairs he looked at Rowan and exclaimed 'Mr Bean!' because he didn't know Rowan's real name. I just burst out laughing because there was Mr Bean in awe of Michael in awe of Mr Bean.

Their faces were a real picture, so I just said, 'I'll leave you two to it,' and disappeared.

If someone used Michael's name to gain an advantage of any sort it really annoyed him, even if it was his own brother. One particular incident emphasised his irritation with name-dropping and I felt quite sorry for his brother, Ralf. It happened at a race in Hockenheim, before Ralf was racing in Formula 1. Ralf was staying with Michael and made a bit of a late start one morning. Hockenheim was always crowded with fanatics and, of course, Michael was the local hero so he made sure he was in the paddock early. On the day in question I asked Michael, 'Isn't Ralf coming in today?'

He just said, 'He was late and I couldn't wait for him. He should be here soon.' A little later Stu and I went out shopping and, as we were coming back, there was Ralf at the main entrance, unable to get into the circuit. Stu and I stopped and asked him why he was standing there.

'I have left my pass in the hotel.'

The place was absolutely packed and there was no way he could travel back to the hotel against the tide of traffic, even if he'd had a car – he had got a lift in – so he was stuck. He said, 'I've told these people I am Michael Schumacher's brother, but it didn't make any difference.'

I told him that Michael probably had 150 'brothers' at every race and of course they wouldn't believe him. In those days the people who had paddock passes and permission to bring their car into the paddock to unload at certain times were designated a special road in and out of the circuit. Stuart pointed it out to Ralf and told him to walk up to it and around the corner and that we would be there shortly. When he was well and truly around the corner we drove up, stopped the car, shoved him in the boot and drove him into the circuit in that somewhat unglamorous fashion.

Later, Michael found out somehow that Ralf had forgotten his pass and really laid into him. It wasn't the first time we had heard Michael rollicking him for telling people he was his brother. He had told him quite clearly, 'Don't ever say you're my brother because I don't want any accusations of favouritism.' Ralf was still under 18 at that time and Michael had given him a hard time as an education, not a humiliation.

At another Silverstone test Michael used our car, a Honda Prelude with four-wheel steering, to check the condition of the track, and adopted a more conventional driving position than Ralf had when he had 'borrowed' our car. Michael thought the four-wheel steering was excellent, and he kept the car so long we never expected to see it again – he was thrashing it around the track lap after lap. We thought it might need an MoT by the time it came back.

George Harrison was at our last race with Benetton and he was in awe of Michael Schumacher. He asked if I would mind introducing him – of course I didn't mind, it was a pleasure to do so. At one point, in the garage I had to get George a chair so that he could stand on it to see over the crowd to take Michael's photo; it seemed incredible that anyone so famous could be such a fan but I caught him in the act with my camera. The picture is reproduced in this book.

George had been at our first Formula 1 race and then at what proved to be our final one with a race team, and he had remembered us all that time. We met him in Sydney a couple of days later, by accident. We had gone to stay with some friends and George had apparently gone there with his son, Dhani. We were walking along the street, across from the Opera House, and they were coming in the opposite direction. We stopped for a chat, then went for an impromptu coffee together in the Hyatt Hotel. George had become quite nervous and odd by that stage in his life; you only had to speak to him and he would jump. He had a rather large bodyguard with him for protection after an incident at his home. We were very sorry when he lost his battle with cancer in 2001.

After Michael had retired from racing he often attended tests in an advisory capacity with Ferrari. I was walking past the Ferrari kitchen one time when he saw me and shouted 'Mum!' He told me to come in and I sat chatting with him, surrounded by a full complement of Ferrari guys, all looking perplexed and obviously thinking, 'That can't be his Mum. She's English!'

When I saw Michael at the test in Valencia in 2010, when he came back into Formula 1 after his retirement, I asked him, 'How's the house in Geneva?'

He just smiled and replied, 'It's not a house, it's a ranch.

Every time I go back there are more animals than when I left. We have cats, dogs, horses, ducks – you name it and we have got it. There will be something else when I get back.'

Looking back to that kitten in Jerez I thought, 'Some things never change.'

I couldn't believe how happy he was when he came back. He was much more relaxed and enjoying every minute of his time at the track. He seemed to have a new perspective on life and racing. It wasn't always like that, though. When Johnny Herbert and Michael were driving together they didn't really hit it off, but if you ask any of his partners I am sure they will say the same thing. In his first spell in Formula 1 Michael was a lot like Ayrton, a completely different person on the track to the man we knew off it. Just like Ayrton, he always knew what he wanted and made sure he got it. I don't think that Ayrton showed the same level of aggression as Michael, but then again Alain Prost may disagree. Both Michael and Ayrton seemed to be changed into much more determined characters by the Formula 1 environment, which is probably why they were so successful.

Contrary to the impression he sometimes gives, Michael is a great person. Anyone who still talks to me like he does after all these years and seven World Championships is certainly OK by me. I've always said that it was necessary to work closely with a driver to really know him and I think it's appropriate to mention one last example of Michael's nature.

I said at the beginning of this book that one of the unexpected roles that came along with the job in the early days was sewing badges on drivers' overalls and equipment. By the mid-1990s that part of the job had largely disappeared because the drivers' uniforms usually arrived complete with all the decals for the season. However, occasionally a last-minute sponsor appeared and their logo needed to be added right away. One such occasion occurred about an hour before the start of the pivotal 1994 Adelaide Grand Prix when two Technogym badges were thrust at me with the request that I hurriedly sew them in a conspicuous position on the back of Michael's gloves, so that they would be prominently displayed on the TV coverage. I just managed to finish up, with Michael already in the car on the grid, hoping for his race gloves but with spares just in case. When I handed them over he winked at me and said, 'Mum, if I win the World Championship, I'll give you these.'

He won the World Championship and, true to his word, he gave me the gloves. I asked him to sign them, and they will always be a treasure.

Chapter 23

THE BIG BLUE OVAL

It had been a big decision to leave Benetton as we'd had some wonderful years with the team, watching it change and develop. Despite all the happy times and the good friends we'd made, though, it was the correct step – the downside being that we wouldn't be able to work with two of our favourite drivers, Michael and Johnny.

Ford had also left Benetton. The company had been supplying engines to the Benetton team through their association with Cosworth, and this also finished at the end of the 1994 season. Ford moved on to supply Sauber and Renault moved in to provide engines for Benetton. Ford never really capitalised on their part in the World Championship and some people describe it as one of Formula 1's best-kept secrets. We had got to know all the Ford hierarchy quite well over the years and we had decided it was a good time to go and work for them.

The move was a breath of fresh air for us, because we were working for a supplier rather than directly for a team. With the teams we had got into a routine, or some might call it a rut. Also our last team, Benetton, had changed; it had stopped being the happy-go-lucky family group, with the professionalism which had done so much for the race results doing little for the atmosphere.

With Ford we had a much more varied role. While our primary work was Formula 1 hospitality, we also covered things like PR days and dealer days in Cologne which were interesting and a complete change. We were hired to feed the international Ford hierarchy on special pre-launch days, too, which was very cloak and dagger. We were able to cover such a diverse range of activities because the Formula 1 part of our role had changed a lot. At Benetton we had been doing all the races and all the tests; it had become too much, as there was almost unlimited testing in those days, unlike now. We'd asked Flavio for help but when it came it was far too little and far too late. We didn't have to go testing with Ford because there were never any guests invited and the track support boys were fed by their allocated team.

Ford had bought a brand new Van Hool coach of its own and Stuart had helped with the specification from the ground up, so we were now completely divorced from our old relationships. (The previous coach had been the one that was going to make us rich, and while it had been successful as a facility it was singularly unsuccessful at getting us into the *Sunday Times* rich list!)

At the racetrack we had three groups of people to support: Prism, or Public Relations and International Sports Marketing, to give them their full title; American Ford top brass who came over from Detroit for most races; and the Ford Cosworth people, whom I called the workers, with no disrespect to the other guests. All the groups integrated well.

Prism were Ford's marketing company, based in Detroit too, and Rod Campbell was still in charge. He was the guy who had interviewed us for our first non-job in Formula 1 all those years ago, so it was like reacquainting ourselves with old friends. The rest of the Prism team were Rod's nephew Jason, our old friend Steve Madincea, who eventually became overall boss of the company, and Andrew Philpott, who later took over Prism Australia. Prism also had Cliff Peters, who was and is full of fun. Ford press officer Sophie Sicot, a lovely and efficient person who is now a firm friend, was also at all of the races.

Cliff was a real character and was always cracking jokes. One of the things we remember fondly about him was that he was put in charge of designing the team uniform. Uniforms were a really big thing in Formula 1 – McLaren had Hugo Boss race wear and most of the teams had clothing sponsors; huge amounts of time and energy were spent on dressing and presentation, throughout the paddock. Cliff, however, was probably the most unlikely person in the whole of the pit lane to be made responsible for clothing. He didn't have the least idea about clothes, or any interest in them; his own clothes sense was pretty clueless and it was a bit of an achievement if he arrived at the track wearing a matching pair of socks. As for remembering his spare shirts, well he didn't. In recognition of his new role he was nicknamed Bugo Hoss and that name has stuck with him ever since. Even when he phones us today we still call him Bugo.

Cliff's other main preoccupation at the track seemed to be running the competition for forecasting the first six places in the Grand Prix. When all the journalists called at the motorhome for the big Ford breakfast he used to fill in everyone's forecasts, collect the money and then present the prize on the Sunday evening. It's amazing how many journalists of all nationalities used to come around and enter that competition to see if they could outdo the other scribes. Cliff went on to become CEO of Prism Europe before moving on to Bangkok and finally full circle back to Detroit.

The season started with a good omen because, in those days, in addition to the permanent passes that all full-time team members had to wear to get into the circuit, it was only possible to get to the pit wall with what was called a 'signalling' pass. Each year the passes were designed differently to make sure no one was using the previous year's pass. When Stuart collected his pass at the beginning of the season he was amazed to see that a picture of him wielding his pit board was the logo for 1995. At first he thought he was being wound up by the people issuing the passes, but then he realised that everyone had an identical pass with his picture on it. He was delighted to think that people like Bernie, Ron Dennis and particularly Flavio would spend the year with his picture around their necks.

We relished our role with Ford, despite it being so different, but I suppose the thing I missed most in 1995 was not having a driver to look after directly – although a familiar face was to turn up like the usual bad penny the following year. Instead of being 'Mum and Dad' to the drivers in that transition year we were more like distant relatives. Stuart wasn't as involved, because he wasn't spending time with the mechanics like he had previously, and despite having his picture on the signalling pass he didn't do the pit board in either 1995 or 1996, although he was 'first reserve'. He did, however, make his mark in no uncertain terms in subsequent years. There were a lot of people whom we had met briefly while we were at Benetton that we now got to know a lot better, particularly the guys from Cosworth.

The Ford Cosworth heritage in racing attracted an awful lot of the Ford Motor Company hierarchy to the track and we always had guests from Detroit, some of whom were a little unexpected. One of our visitors was Jacques Nasser, who eventually became president and chief executive officer of the Ford Motor Company; Jacques had previously stated that he wouldn't get involved with Formula 1, but of course he did and he loved it. Peter Gillitzer was director of European motorsport in 1995 and he regularly attended the races, along with a number of senior people.

It was a relief that our large workload with Benetton would not have to continue. With the requirement to attend all test sessions and race venues, we were often away from home for over 280 days in a year, and it had become too much. However, there were a couple of downsides: firstly, we missed the daily interaction with the drivers and mechanics; secondly, we were not scheduled to attend any of the 'fly-away' races to some of those places we loved visiting. Luckily for us there was one exception – the Australian Grand Prix – because of Ford's strong presence there and the large number of executives who attended, and this meant we were at the last race at Adelaide and able to say 'goodbye' to friends, shopkeepers and other people who we had come to know well over the previous ten years.

Imola, which was the first European race of the season, was a bit of a choker. It was a really strange experience when the Benetton boys walked past; actually they didn't walk past, every one of them came to see us on the first day when they arrived at the track, fresh from the plane. They all trooped into the new Ford motorhome, which was the last of its kind in Formula 1, despite the connection between Ford and Benetton being severed. Even Flavio dropped in, and the 'Golden Boys' were so friendly that I think in a way they felt a bit responsible for the change. Just like in every other walk of life, you have to be careful what you wish for because, during the European leg of the season, they got pasta until it was coming out of their ears and they got sick of it!

Some journalists had found out through the grapevine that our transfer had taken place over the winter, but a lot of the foreign ones were pretty surprised to find we were no longer at Benetton. The Benetton hospitality had changed and was by invitation only, with a menu outside like an Italian restaurant. And it wasn't the only one, because the whole ethos of hospitality was moving progressively away from a place for the team to eat; in fact nowadays there are very few teams who allow their mechanics into the motorhome during the day as it's reserved entirely for guests. Sometimes we wondered whether we liked the direction the whole thing was taking and questioned if it was time to call it a day; by that stage we had done almost 20 years.

In reality, our motorhome situation worked really well as Sauber had its own facility for its staff and guests, and Ford had the same. One terrific innovation that Ford and Sauber introduced was the Saturday night dinner parties. Every

Saturday night during the race weekends we had team dinner parties and one week Ford would feed the Sauber guys and the following week Sauber would feed the Ford guys. I am not sure who initiated these get-togethers but they really got the team spirit going, and it built up a great relationship. At some of the dinners the drivers used to get up and say a few words. Heinz-Harald Frentzen was quite funny. We all joined together, too, so when Sauber were cooking we would be washing up in their motorhome, and they reciprocated when we were doing the cooking.

Peter Sauber was always a real gentleman. He and Dietrich Mateschitz, the owner of Red Bull, who was the primary sponsor of Sauber, used to come to the dinners on a Saturday evening. Because Sauber was a smallish team at the time, and some may argue still is, it didn't have the pretensions of some of its larger rivals. The Sauber guys wanted to go racing and everything else was just a mechanism to make that happen. I genuinely don't know what Peter's relationship was with Ford, but he did everything he could to be successful on the track for the company.

We got to know the Sauber hospitality people very well, particularly Arnold Graff who was in charge and rejoiced in the nickname of 'Naldi' for no reason anyone could recall; he had a young chef called Silvio who was always burning the pots and pans. If Silvio was cooking in our motorhome we always made him bring his own utensils as we weren't going to let him burn ours. He made a real name for himself one evening when he dropped all the plates down the motorhome steps just as he was about to serve dinner. Everyone was waiting expectantly, but after that huge crash there wasn't a plate intact. We had to go next door and get ours or all the guests would have been eating from (burnt) pans instead of our cold plates.

It became traditional for the gentlemen of the press to come round to join in after the meal and *Daily Mail* sports writer Ray

Matts used to play his guitar until about three in the morning. It helped the harmony of the team supplier/press relationship, although some of the musical harmony went a bit awry as the evening wore on. As well as the team dinners we also had dinners specifically for the journalists, predominantly British but sometimes there were French and other nationalities too. I have no idea what they made of it all.

The hospitality area was open house for the press, but the big Ford breakfast got out of hand, with people queuing at the door, until it came to the point where we had to issue times for them all to come. I had no problem with the journalists and photographers; quite the opposite. They weren't the only ones who turned up, either. Professor Sid Watkins, the world-famous neurosurgeon and FIA medical delegate, used to come by frequently. He would work his way through a full breakfast with four cups of espresso, each with four sweeteners, and then sit there surrounded by plates with a large cigar in his hand, looking extremely contented with the world.

Murray Walker always used to come to the motorhome for a black coffee when he arrived at the circuit, and he used to say, 'Right, sit down, Di. What's the gossip?' and sometimes I would tell him that this or that had happened. If there was nothing to talk about he'd say, 'Well, if there isn't anything, can you think of something?' and I would tell him to 'come back tomorrow'. Then, later that day, all the motorhomers would get together and decide on a 'scoop' for him. He always told us that he had to tell the public something. Obviously we never mentioned anything that was confidential, just stuff that we knew would be in the public domain shortly anyway.

Lots of the journalists also came at lunchtime, unless we had the Ford top brass at the race, and then the guys knew to stay away or at least to ask if they could come in. They always used to have a good time at the races and I learned to have a good supply of headache pills and 'Resolve' for their hangovers. That's why we instituted the 'Golden Resolve Award'.

We got through so much 'medication' that I used to keep a chart of the top British journalists' consumption of hangover cures and headache pills. Towards the end of the season Stuart used to take a box of 'Resolve' and spray it gold, and then there was a presentation ceremony for the 'Award'. It was always quite tight, if you'll excuse the pun, but the finalists were normally Ray Matts, Alan Henry (a freelance journalist and writer), Stan Piecha from the *Sun* and Bob McKenzie of the *Daily Express*. Bob always seemed to win it by a short head (or stomach). I am sure none of them were drunk when they came to the track the next day, but some of them looked decidedly second-hand. I think it's fair to say they enjoyed their jobs. Bob was destined to become even better known for another feat, when he promised to run round Silverstone naked if McLaren won a race in 2004. They did, and so did he, although I believe he was wearing a sporran. At least I think it was a sporran!

In return for our efforts the journalists always used to have a 'whip-round' at the end of the season and one year I was given a watch and Stuart was given record tokens, while on another occasion he had a radio and I received a bracelet. They were very appreciative of what we had tried to do for them.

In addition to our dealer days and other events we occasionally turned up at some SMMT (Society of Motor Manufacturers and Traders) days. We met Jeremy Clarkson a few times and he was much nicer than he seems on TV, although he was quite rude about some cars; fortunately not the Ford variety. If he had disliked them he would undoubtedly have been uncomplimentary about them, even though he'd been invited to lunch. At these SMMT days he went out in every car and I always remember he was very rude about the Porsche Cayenne.

One way in which we stayed close to the teams in 1995 was that we hired coaches from Van Hool for Sauber, Williams and Simtek and rented them out to each team. This generally worked out fine, although we did get our fingers burnt with Simtek. We had hired the coach for the full year and our names were on the agreement with Van Hool, but we sublet it to Simtek. However, Simtek had a limited budget: after we had done two races with little payment, things came to a head and we refused the management entry to the motorhome in Monaco. The day was saved when Barbara, a previous sponsor and resident of Monaco, paid for the food for the weekend. Then the Simtek team went pear-shaped after Monaco, leaving us with a hired coach and no income for it. Nick Wirth, the team owner, told us that he would settle up when all the dust had settled, but of course he never did.

We were also involved with other teams on the fringes because the Ford Cosworth guys also supplied 'customer' teams as well as Sauber, the official Ford 'works' team. The first year we were involved Cosworth had some pretty unsuccessful customer teams, including Larousse, Pacific, Forti Corse, Minardi and Simtek.

By the end of 1995 we realised that we had made exactly the right move. Although we still missed the boys, over the years we had been doing the job we had made lots of friends in the paddock and Ford didn't seem to mind who came under the canopy because they were there to publicise the Ford 'Blue Oval' as widely as possible. Prism did a good job of promoting Ford through their clever use of the motorhome facility.

Motor racing is a real leveller. We were there working and the guests were desperate to be there. It is not possible to buy a pass from Bernie – everyone has to be invited – and even then, if Bernie doesn't think they should be there then they don't get in. Accordingly, when people do get inside the hallowed paddock they tend to be grateful and not in the least bit arrogant, and that makes our job easier.

In 1996 there were a number of changes, the first of which we knew about while the other one had just been a rumour. We knew that Johnny Herbert was to be the team's new driver, replacing Karl Wendlinger, because one day when I was busy in the motorhome the Sauber PR girl came around and said: 'Johnny wants to see you.' I had to drop what I was doing and go along to the paddock to witness his signature on his driver's contract. The other major change was that Martin Whitaker turned up as Ford's new director of European communications, and later replaced Peter Gillitzer as director of European motorsport. Martin was well known in the paddock as he had previously worked for McLaren and the FIA, as well as being a journalist in his early years with *Motoring News*. We had heard rumours Martin was on his way, but weren't sure he was coming until he arrived. He carried on where his predecessor had left off and the Ford motorhome became even more of an 'open house' to the journalists; the one real difference Martin brought to the table was a fanatical interest in rugby and rallying, as well as four-cheese pasta and tea. The rugby and rallying were to feature in our lives to a greater or lesser extent in the future; pasta had already had an influence on our careers, of course.

A lot of people thought that Johnny Herbert and his team-mate Heinz-Harald Frentzen didn't get on, but they were actually pretty good together and there was quite a bit of banter between the two of them – although it's fair to say that Johnny banters with anyone! Peter Sauber really liked Johnny for all the reasons that Flavio hadn't. Flavio thought Johnny needed to present a more serious face to the public and be a more serious driver, but Peter enjoyed him as a breath of fresh air in the paddock.

Peter had an opportunity to revise his view on Johnny's sense of humour on one particular evening, though. Some of Johnny's antics would be censored if I tried to include them, but he was always one for a surprise, and Peter was particularly surprised at one of our regular press dinners in the motorhome. Johnny was sitting at the right-hand side of Peter with Heinz-Harald on the other side. Johnny got up to go for a pee and while he was out Peter stood up to make a speech to the scribblers. He had his back to the returning Herbert, who sneaked up on him like a pantomime villain. I almost expected the watching pressmen to shout 'He's behind you!' but that would have spoiled the fun. As Peter was getting to the point of his speech Johnny reached between his legs and grabbed his goolies. The look on Peter's face was a picture, although unfortunately none of the press contingent caught it on camera – or if they did they never published it! Johnny had been disappointed when he joined Benetton and we left two races later (nothing personal, John) but he was back among us with a vengeance.

Johnny and Heinz-Harald proved categorically how close they were at the start of the Spa race in 1996 when they crashed into each other at the hairpin at the start of the race. Both of them were out before completing a lap. The lads who had been working all weekend on the cars and deciding on strategy were less than impressed. H-H was quite quiet in his own way, although it's difficult to be quiet around Johnny, but I think they probably exchanged a few words on that occasion. Since the Sauber days the two of them have competed in a number of smaller series and they still get on well together.

Johnny used to come around to the Ford motorhome a lot, to the point that the team always knew where to find him if he was missing or late for anything. They just used to shout 'Is he there?' and nine times out of ten he was. I suppose it was because we were friends and we had the British sense of humour, which was sometimes missing in the Swiss camp. The team all loved him, particularly the tyre man Tom, who still works there. Whenever we saw him later on he always asked us to give Johnny his best wishes. Many years later, when we were working for Bridgestone, Johnny happened to ring me while Tom was there having his tyres fitted, and I just handed the phone to Tom and said, 'Here, somebody wants you.' He almost cried when he realised it was John. They had a special relationship; Tom thought the world of him.

Under Martin Whitaker we continued with the usual round

of dinners and normally Martin stayed at the motorhome to eat rather than going into the nearest city; on some occasions he invited the odd guest. This was usually done at short notice, so we tried to anticipate when it was going to happen and have something available that was quick to prepare. On one occasion we were preparing fajitas for our evening meal and Martin was still around. He was on the phone to someone and, being a polite chap, he invited the 'someone' to dinner. Obviously prompted by his potential guest Martin asked what we were cooking and I said, 'Well, we weren't sure you'd be staying, so we are knocking up a few fajitas.'

Martin proffered his phone and said, 'I have just invited this person to dinner. Can you tell him what it is?'

I didn't have any idea who was on the end of the phone so, in my best telephone manner, I said: 'It's just a simple meal; it's Mexican fajitas.'

To which this voice replied, 'What the hell are Mexican fajitas?'

I recognised the voice immediately and thought, 'Oh my God, it's Bernie!' so I rallied and quickly thought of an alternative. 'But I can offer you a plate of pasta!' He did come to dinner and settled on the pasta, but each time I passed him he looked at me with a slightly impish but reproving expression and said 'Bloody fajitas!'

During 1996 Martin Whitaker negotiated a deal with Malcolm Wilson, a former world-class rally driver and then owner of the Malcolm Wilson Motorsport rally team, which resulted in the team becoming the Ford-sponsored World Rally Championship entrant from 1997 onwards, renamed as M-Sport. Martin told us that he would like us to fit in a few rallies in the future, between Formula 1 events. He was determined to raise the profile of the Ford 'Blue Oval' and what better way of doing it than by being successful in a world championship in a car that looked like one we could all buy from a dealer. Well, vaguely.

As a bit of a dummy run to be ready for the 'occasional' rally trip we went to a rally sprint day at Goodwood, with Malcolm Wilson driving. We had the coach with us and we were well away from Goodwood House and all that's associated with it, out in the middle of nowhere – and a branch went through the window. The rally scene wasn't prepared for tall hospitality vehicles like ours at that time, so we felt like explorers.

Towards the end of the year we were asked to take the coach and awning to the Cheltenham leg of the RAC rally for two days, then to Builth Wells for just one meal! While we were in Cheltenham we had to prepare a meal for the touring New Zealand All Blacks rugby team; I guess this was where Martin Whitaker combined his two passions. Jonah Lomu was with the team then, and he was about 6ft 5in tall and 19 stone in weight, but he didn't look out of place among his team-mates. Ford had sent two Ford Galaxies to the hotel to collect the team, thinking that would be enough space for them all, but they each ended up making three journeys as the blokes were so big they could only get about three of them in each people carrier.

When the whole lot were finally assembled we offered them the menu and asked them to pick what they wanted. They just looked at us and said, 'Everything.' So that's what they had. After their starters they had pasta, a roast dinner, apple crumble and then ice cream. They were a bit uncomfortable eating all that, not because it was too much, just because they were too big for the chairs and had to perch where they could. After Cheltenham we had to pack the whole show up and drive it all the way to Builth Wells and set it up again for one meal, then break it down again and drive all the way home. I had a feeling I wasn't going to like this rally business.

Jackie Stewart was a regular visitor to the Ford motorhome and his relationship with the manufacturer right from his World Championship-winning days as a driver is well documented. Jackie was so close to some of the top brass in the Ford hierarchy that sometimes people thought that he was the head of Ford motorsport worldwide; equally, many of the Ford senior executives felt that Jackie was the go-to man to develop the Ford brand through racing. In late 1995 Jackie had put forward a business plan to start his own Formula 1 team with the backing of the Ford Motor Company. It was eventually rubber-stamped by the company and the team prepared throughout 1996 to start racing in 1997.

When we looked back on the changes that had occurred in our first two years with Ford it was amazing – new company, new coach, new boss, new driver, new experiences. Would 1997 have as much in store?

Oh yes.

Chapter 24

TULIPS, WHAT TULIPS?

Before we could get to grips with our new relationships in Formula 1 in 1997 we had another learning curve to negotiate. As we have already said, we had been 'asked' by European motorsport director Martin Whitaker to try our hand at providing hospitality for the World Rally team. Martin might have been a rally fanatic, but the nearest we had come to rallying was the odd trip to spectate in Sutton Park, Sutton Coldfield; that had summed it up for me as 'Cold fields!' We weren't desperately keen on the prospect, but of course we said 'Yes' and together with Graham and Tracey, our new staff members, we unwittingly embarked on what some time later was to become a three-year 'World Rally Experience'. We soon realised it was going to be very different from Formula 1.

The trial rally we were asked to attend was at Monte Carlo which, in our minds, conjured up all the usual glamour, atmosphere and razzmatazz of a Grand Prix, with us parked on the harbour wall in relative luxury. It was taking place in January, though, so we thought we might need to take jumpers. Prior to arriving for the event we had been asked to meet John Millington, the team/logistics manager, in Carros near Nice. He was down there checking on things prior to the start of the rally a couple of weeks later, and we were taking a break in the area before the season started. We agreed to meet him at his hotel.

Tulips, What Tulips?

John Millington, or Milly, as we later found out he was called, was a rally legend in the organisational field, but it was obvious when we met him that he had an awful lot to do and he didn't really want the hassle of sorting us out as well. It had been Martin and Malcolm Wilson who had discussed our arrival on the rally scene, Malcolm being pleased it would 'up the image' of his team and Martin loving the idea of having a presence on the rallying world stage with the Ford 'Oval' having such a prominent position.

During our meeting we gave the coach's footprint size to Milly and it became clear he had no idea of how big a vehicle we were going to arrive in; he just said, somewhat enigmatically, 'I think there will be some problems,' and handed us our instructions in the form of a booklet. He added, 'Study the booklet and be back here at the hotel in ten days.' We thanked him and went back home to study the 'book'. Even on first reading it became quite apparent we were stumbling blindly into a very different world.

The first major shock was that the Monte Carlo Rally was anywhere but in Monte Carlo.

And the second was that the 'book' said we had to attend a 'shakedown' prior to the actual start of the rally, and this would take place in Sospel, way up in the mountains behind Monaco. We took the Ford coach, and Tracey and Graham followed on in the Ford Transit kitchen. We travelled to the hotel where we had previously met Milly and he told us that Pam, who was the regular motorhome lady, was on the 'recce' with the 'recce' team and she would be talking to us later. While we were waiting to have a meal at the hotel there seemed to be all sorts of folk in rally uniforms popping in and out. It was very bewildering. Another thing which astonished us was that everyone seemed to come to the bar in the evening dressed in uniform, something unheard of in Formula 1, where 'going out' in team uniform was virtually a hanging offence. We were in civvies so the new arrivals at the hotel wouldn't have known we were involved in the rally anyway, and consequently no one spoke to us.

When Pam finally arrived Milly introduced us. She had been out on the 'recce' for the last couple of days, and she had been catering from her motorhome. We had to ask what a 'recce' was, which hardly endeared us to anyone, and so we learned that this was another aspect of rallying that we had never heard of, and it came with yet another set of people. Just so that no one else has to be embarrassed about asking the question, 'recce' is short for 'reconnaissance' and, apparently, before the rally starts, the driver is allowed to drive round the stages with his co-driver. The driver tells his co-driver over an in-car intercom system the best way to drive every stage, paying particular attention to hazards. The co-driver writes all the instructions down in his own peculiar brand of shorthand on what are called pace notes. On the rally proper the co-driver reads the pace notes back to the driver on each stage so the driver can concentrate on driving like a lunatic.

I found myself apologising to Pam for our presence, explaining that we had no intention of taking over and that we had been sent by those in charge of things at Ford who were obviously trying to boost the team image. In order to try to understand what was going on we got out the 'instruction book' we'd been given a couple of weeks earlier, and we had to admit to her that it seemed like Double Dutch; the maps looked as though we were actually entering the rally ourselves. Pam started referring to 'tulip routes' (then we really did think it was all Double Dutch as we had no idea what she was talking about). It transpired 'tulip routes' were the directions to the service park (the paddock in Formula 1) and were vitally important as without them you'd get very, very lost.

While we were being schooled by Pam, Stuart got a call to take the coach up the hill to the village. As it was too tall to go through a nearby tunnel, except right in the middle of the road, he had to meet up with another couple of Ford trucks and some vehicles from other teams so that they could all go through the tunnel in convoy, with Milly at the front stopping any unsuspecting villagers heading in from the other direction. When Stu got back to our hotel he said, 'I don't think they were expecting anything quite that big up there.'

We were getting a bad feeling about all of this and wondering what on earth we had let ourselves in for. We didn't know anyone in the team, and I could imagine all of them saying, 'That's those Formula 1 folk, guess they reckon they know it all.' No one really seemed to welcome us into the fold, so we were a little lost about what was actually going on, and everyone was buzzing around us. But this was rallying and we had arrived, whether we were wanted or not.

The next morning we were off early for the shakedown, but there was no room for the canopy at that first service park; it was in the village square, which was covered in snow, so no doubt we parked on the flower beds and left a lasting impression. Despite having gone to all the trouble of taking the entire infrastructure into such an inaccessible spot we cooked bacon butties and made tea and coffee from the kitchen in the Ford Transit van.

A shakedown is what would be called a test session in Formula 1, and this generally takes place on the day of scrutineering prior to the start of the actual rally. Having managed our first experience, we packed up and slithered back to the hotel. By now it was snowing heavily and I was feeling uneasy about the journey back down the mountain on narrow roads in the dark. Stuart, as previously mentioned, has always been an excellent driver, but rallying was to test all of his skills to the full. Pam was at the hotel when we got back and, in our relief, we told her with some degree of pride how such a difficult trip had been completed with nothing worse than frayed nerves, squashed flowers and some imaginative and comprehensive blasphemy from Stuart. She just said, 'There's worse to come. Look at the tulip route. It's Gap next.'

The next day saw us getting up at 4.15am ready to set off at five to travel to Gap, approximately four hours away. Now we had a vague idea of which way up the tulip routes were printed, and we could see the route to the airstrip where the service park was located. That's about all we could see, though, because the route just got snowier by the hour. Stuart was driving and I was shouting out directions from the tulip routes, feeling rather like a rally co-driver, until we finally got to the airstrip. We were already freezing when we arrived way up in the mountains and we then had to set up the full awning with all the bells and whistles. With the help of Graham and Tracey, we set to. I was glad I'd packed that jumper. By the time we were well into erecting the awning other teams were arriving, but none of the vehicles were as big as ours and, to add to the spectacle, our coach was still covered in Formula 1-style logos, so that raised a few eyebrows. Ford had definitely announced their presence, but we felt a little overdressed. One blessing was that we didn't have to sleep in the truck; we stayed in the Hotel Arizona that night (nothing to do with my map reading). It was pretty basic, with few bathrooms, but at least it was warm and had a good restaurant. Well, we were in France.

After the rally team had done what they had to do we dismantled the awning again, ready for the trip to Monte Carlo. This time we had to work in the pitch black with just truck lights and a temperature of minus ten; it was so cold that the awning roof actually stayed up without support poles. We were freezing too. Next time it would be two jumpers.

Our one moment of glory on the whole trip was when we found out that a lot of the more experienced rally fraternity had forecast that 'they will have trouble getting that massive thing on the harbour wall in Monte Carlo' – but obviously we had been there previously, on a number of occasions, and we knew the best route in. As it turned out, the other trucks were happy to follow us. Monaco is a daunting place for a large truck, or anything else for that matter. The harbour wall was the service park; we arrived in the dark at around 11pm and then had to rebuild the unit again ready for breakfast next day. We finally got to bed about 2.30 and were back up again at 5am. This first experience of World Rallying left us all shattered, bewildered by the logistics, and wondering if it could get any worse at other venues. At least it wasn't our full-time job – or so we thought at the time. We couldn't wait to be back in Formula 1 where we could set up, stay in one place for a few days enjoying the luxuries of running water, electricity, toilets and shops, and on top of that we'd actually see and hear some of the action.

One thing was certain. All the rules and regulations regarding a truck or motorhome driver's legal working hours didn't apply to rallying. The other certainty was that we had never made so much tea.

Chapter 25

TARTAN CHECKS AND RIGHT ROYAL HOWLERS

It was all change again for 1997. The Ford–Sauber relationship was at an end and Sauber had moved on to BMW engines. Ford's works team, and our next-door neighbour at the circuit, was now Stewart Grand Prix. Jan Magnussen and Rubens Barrichello were the Stewart team drivers in the team's first year and we had lost our daily contact with Johnny because he had stayed with Sauber for a second year.

When Stewart Grand Prix entered Formula 1 they had the big American Newell motorhome that had formerly belonged to Ron Dennis and had been driven by our friend Bob McMurray for so long. Ron and Jackie Stewart always seemed to be very friendly, but in reality perhaps they were not quite as friendly as it appeared on the surface. Ron was a bit perplexed when Jackie used to descend on his motorhome for breakfast; the reason he was there was that Bob and Shaune used to cook porridge, which was Jackie's staple race weekend fare. Anyway, Ron sold Jackie the motorhome but it didn't come with Bob, Shaune or hot and cold running porridge as far as I can remember. A lot of the lads who worked for Stewart were people we had known from other teams. Whenever a new team appears there is always a need to hire guys from elsewhere in the paddock to speed up the process of getting the team up and running.

MSL were contracted to supply the Stewart Grand Prix hospitality and we parked our vehicles in the paddock in such a way that the awnings were alongside each other, in between the two hospitality units. It was a good layout, particularly in nice weather when both canopies were open, and we all looked like a single team, which in fairness is what we were supposed to be. Jackie is a brilliant speaker and when I listen to him talking about motorsport I am always really impressed. He has done so much for safety over the years, and has been massively successful despite his self-confessed dyslexia; he is a real role model, but sometimes he loses the common touch and that's how I feel he approached the Formula 1 programme. The Saturday night dinners stopped after the Sauber days and there was a very clear divide between the people in the Stewart motorhome/awning and the Ford motorhome. Jackie always went for high-profile visitors, with royalty, political figures and as many sultans as you could 'sheikh' a stick at on the guest list; even the Ford CEO was asked to eat there rather than in the Ford facility. The three years we spent alongside Stewart Grand Prix were some of the funniest times we had in motor racing and quite often this was down to the royal connections.

On one occasion, in Barcelona, and unbeknown to Stuart and myself, King Juan Carlos of Spain was going to come to Jackie's hospitality on the Saturday night before the race. Before he was due to arrive the police went through our facility with their sniffer dogs because our canopies were adjacent. We weren't expecting any guests and so we were a bit surprised by this, until the situation was explained to us by one of the policemen. The king's security people asked if they could have a table by the doorway, under our canopy, so that they could keep an eye on events next door. It was a warm evening and the canopies were open, so it was quite possible to see from one to the other. We said that was fine and everything seemed in order.

We sat with Graham and Tracey at the end opposite the door

of our canopy, having our dinner, while all these people were milling around in Stewart's; King Juan Carlos duly arrived and was introduced to everyone and, with that, they all stood around their allocated tables waiting for the king to sit. He started to lower himself into his seat, with his backside almost down, so everyone else started to do the same. Then he looked across and saw us. At that, he got back up again and, with a big smile on his face, waved to us and said, 'Good evening.' Everyone else, seeing him stand back up, had to do the same, and it was just like a Mexican wave going through the canopy. Then, of course, we felt that we should stand up too and to cover our embarrassment we said, 'Have a good evening and a nice meal', smiling and bowing and standing around watching all the Stewart guests standing around watching us and waiting for the regal bottom to descend once more so they could have their dinner.

Jackie had quite a reputation for being close to royalty, and on the team's first visit to the Monaco Grand Prix in 1997 he was perplexed when he arrived at the circuit to find that there was no space allocated in the paddock for the Stewart Grand Prix support trucks; they had been located in the car park up the hill from the circuit. Feeling a bit put out by this turn of events Jackie complained bitterly, but to no avail, and the trucks had to stay there all weekend; all their pit equipment had to be ferried up and down the hill throughout the event. When Bernie Ecclestone was asked why the Stewart team had been located so far away from the paddock he is reputed to have said, with that slight smile of satisfaction that flits across his face on such occasions, 'Jackie is so fond of being close to royalty that we thought we would put him up near the palace.' Jackie wasn't put out for long, though, as Rubens Barrichello came second in the race, which was only the team's fifth event. Jan Magnussen came seventh so it was a really good result, although these were few and far between in that first year as their season was dogged by mechanical reliability problems.

Princess Anne's son Peter Phillips, a nice lad, had been hired by Stewart Grand Prix to work in the marketing department, and we got him out of a scrape or two. I had to help him one morning because he had been up all night and didn't dare go back to the Stewart motorhome; he came to us to sort him out. I asked him where he had been and he just shrugged and said, 'I don't know.' His shirt was all crumpled and he looked a real mess, so he asked me to get him a clean shirt before Jackie got to the track. It seemed they had started off taking some sponsors out and, after that, it had got a bit out of hand. Peter unwittingly got me into a scrape, though, and I wasn't quite so lucky.

As the Ford works team, Jackie and his boys were in and out of our area quite a lot and we got to know the group very well – and just like the rest of the pit lane, they could all spot a bargain. When Stu and I were equipping the kitchens for our various motorhome customers I used to get a good deal on some excellent espresso machines from Saeco, a former sponsor; the guys in the pit lane, as well as a number of the drivers, including Ayrton, Johnny and Nelson, were forever asking me to order one for them. The machines were usually delivered at the Imola Grand Prix as the Saeco factory was close to Bologna, and on one particular occasion I had got one for Peter Phillips. He came to collect his machine in the late afternoon while the motorhome was full of journalists. When I handed it over he suddenly said, 'Oh, Di, can you get me another, because my mother wants one as well?'

I was surprised, thinking they must have had a run on them at Harrods and I had cornered the market. I said, 'Of course I'll get her one. I'll see if I can get it organised on Monday and have it brought out for the next race.' As Peter walked away I made the mistake of saying 'His gran will want one next!' I thought I had said it under my breath but unfortunately one of the journalists, Tony Dodgins, heard me. I didn't realise that after we left the circuit and were en route to our overnight stop the quote was put on a website. Jackie Stewart saw it and went ballistic; apparently the website had claimed that Jackie was trying to secure his knighthood by supplying cut-price coffee machines to the royal family. He wasn't a happy man on that occasion, and in fairness I wasn't too happy with Tony either. You think these guys are your friends and then they drop you in it while still coming round for their meals every day.

We also met Zara Phillips, Peter's sister, through the Jackie Stewart connection. When we first met her Zara was going through a rebellious stage; she had a stud in her tongue and all that kind of thing. She came to quite a few Grands Prix and she seemed a very nice, ordinary, lively young girl. I remember her climbing up to the top of the perimeter fence in Hungary and her 'companion' looking at her in disdain before saying, in a very upmarket accent, 'That's not very royal, Zara.' She just smiled and stayed where she was.

On a later occasion I bumped into her at Stratford-upon-Avon races. I was there with my brother, Garry, who was a club member at the course; Zara was going out with the jockey Richard Johnson at that time. I said to Garry, 'Look who's there in the queue.'

'Where?' he said, with a completely blank look on his face. It finally dawned on him. 'Oh, it's Princess Anne's daughter.' He wasn't too clued up about celebrities or royalty. Zara was in the queue for pork baps, completely on her own. I waited until she had been served before saying hello. It took her a moment to put me in context and then she said, 'Hello, it's Di, isn't it?'

My brother was speechless. I tried to introduce him but he couldn't get any words out at all. So, to cover his embarrassment, I told her he was a member at the course and she said, 'Come along, are you going to have a bet on Richard?' My brother was, as it happened, so she said, 'Come and meet him.' She walked us all around the back of the stables and there was Richard getting ready to go out for the race. Garry was gobsmacked that he had spoken to Richard Johnson and Zara Phillips, even if he hadn't had much to say. It would be wonderful to report that we made a killing, but as it happened Richard came nowhere and our money went elsewhere. Zara has done her best to remain out of the public eye all her life, despite being the Queen's granddaughter and Eventing World Champion. She married Mike Tindall, the Gloucester and England rugby player, in 2011 and I wish them well.

In our more familiar racing environment the team found Stu plenty to do over the weekend, which helped to keep him occupied. It was probably a good job too, because he can be pretty disruptive when he's bored. With Sauber we had just been running the motorhome, but as soon as Stewart took over we started to readopt some of the additional jobs we had covered before. Dave Stubbs, the team manager of Stewart Grand Prix, asked Stuart if he would do the pit board for Rubens Barrichello, and although Stu wasn't too keen he agreed. In fairness, Stu has had quite a few 'incidents' while manning the board on the pit wall and, just like everyone else, he's dropped the numbers on to the track when they were not secured properly. He also has the dubious distinction of clouting Edsel Ford II, a director of Ford and the great-grandson of Henry Ford, on the head. It happened in Detroit, where the pit wall was low and the space behind it very narrow. Stu was in a hurry to get the board out so that the driver could receive his information and, as he turned round to get to the pit wall, there was someone in the way; Stuart had no time to mess about so he swung the board round a bit over-zealously and cracked Edsel on the back of the head, presumably making him head sore Ford. And Edsel apologised for getting in the way!

Despite these odd aberrations, Stuart thought that if he had been doing the pit-board duties well enough to satisfy Michael Schumacher and Nelson Piquet, among others, he must have had a grasp of the basics. However, Paul Stewart, Jackie's son, seemed to have different ideas and he kept saying, 'Put this on the board and put that on.' Stu knew that there was a limit to what the driver could absorb as he flashed past, so he continued to do the job in the same way he had always done. Paul eventually took exception to this and got his dad involved. Jackie then started to tell Stuart how he should be doing the job; in the end Stuart just said, 'If it's good enough for Michael Schumacher, then it's good enough for Stewart Grand Prix.' Rubens was fine with the information he was getting anyway, because all the driver really wants to know is their position and how far behind the guy in front they are (although in the very early days Stuart used to put jokey things on the board to make the driver laugh and brighten up their race). Stu stopped doing the pit board shortly after that. That was fine by me, because when he went off to do his board duties there wasn't enough cover at the motorhome so I always ended up on my own, trying to feed the guests and do everything else.

Although the Stewart team had an outwardly more serious air than many of our previous teams there were still plenty of pranks being played on one poor unsuspecting soul or another, and once Stuart was released from the pit wall he joined in the fun with gusto. One of his favourite tricks involved a Casio watch he'd bought in Japan. The watch had a calculator on it with little rubber buttons; the buttons were too small to see properly and too fiddly for his fingers. However, the watch had its uses because it had another function – as a television remote control.

As I mentioned earlier, the two coaches, one belonging to Ford and the other which was for the use of Stewart Grand Prix, were parked in the paddock side by side and we could see from our canopy into theirs. On Saturday nights when the team had their television on, Stu used to sit quietly under our canopy and play around with his watch until he had locked on to the Stewart TV. He would then turn it off. The lads spent ages messing around, trying unsuccessfully to work out what had happened, until he switched it back on again, leaving them a bit puzzled. That was just a rehearsal, of course. On Sunday the team always had a full house in their canopy when the race was about to start, and as he was no longer occupied with his board Stuart used to watch the TV for the moment the cars left the grid for the formation lap. He would then turn off their TV, causing havoc. It probably wasn't very kind to the guests but it certainly amused Stu, and he always put it back on again as soon as the race got going.

He's been known to walk up and down the paddock turning other teams' TVs on and off too. Unfortunately he didn't restrict his remote-control activities to the paddock. When we were at home and doing some shopping he used to go into Curry's or Comet and change the volume or switch off the sets. While I would make for the door as quickly as I could, Stuart stood around innocently watching the shop assistants' frantic efforts to turn their TVs back on or to reduce the volume to stop their other customers going deaf.

Throughout the period we were working with Stewart Grand Prix we continued to cover some rallies between our Formula 1 commitments, one of which was in Finland. M-Sport usually had a Finnish driver at that time and they wanted to have a high profile while they were there. The problem for us was that the rally was scheduled for the weekend after the Hungarian Grand Prix and that was quite a journey by road, requiring us to make a pretty nifty getaway from the GP to make it to Finland in time. Immediately the Grand Prix finished we had to tell our guests, 'Sorry, we have to pack up to go to Finland,' while gently easing them out of the hospitality area. We had drafted in extra staff to help with the driving as it would have been totally exhausting, not to mention illegal, to ask Stu and Graham to do the driving between them.

We needed to be in position in Finland by Wednesday morning so, after packing up in Hungary on Sunday, we had to get as far as the Austrian border that night. On Monday we travelled through Germany into Denmark, crossing into Sweden and then setting out on a 19-hour ferry trip from Stockholm to Turku in Finland. It was tough going, but at least we could relax on board; it was a wonderful trip that I should like to do in a more leisurely fashion some time in my life. From the port we had to drive straight to the rally and start a series of very early mornings and long days until the rally finished on Sunday night, when we had to reverse the process in an even bigger hurry in order to be in Spa for the Belgian Grand Prix by Tuesday night.

We also went to a few rally days at the Silverstone rally stage supporting the Ford Ka, which was fun – and particularly for Stuart on one occasion when he was awarded a Blue Peter badge. One of the television show's presenters, Katy Hill, was there to be filmed in a Ka and before she got into the car she changed in the truck and left her clothes there. After she'd finished her session she came back to the coach and started to get undressed, only then realising that her clothes were in the other vehicle. She shouted down the stairs to Stuart, dressed only in her bra and knickers, and he, very kindly, without a selfish thought in his head, helped her out. I was shopping at the time and when I got back I found a very happy-looking Stu standing there, proudly showing off his badge.

'Where have you got that from?' I asked.

'I just got Katy's clothes for her,' he said, smiling at the recollection. She'd apparently been very grateful and awarded him a Blue Peter badge for his trouble – which I'm sure was no trouble at all.

Things continued in the now familiar pattern at Stewart Grand Prix, with celebrities and royalty coming and going. On another memorable occasion we were parked in our regular format, canopy to canopy, and as usual Stewart had a lunch planned with a celebrity. It was Anthony Quinn, the famous film actor, who was the guest of honour. Anthony had been ensconced in the Paddock Club, which was and still is an expensive and exclusive area usually located directly above the Formula 1 pits to feed and water high-rollers. He was due to leave the Paddock Club at a specific time and he was a little late. The Stewart PR people were chasing around, asking if anyone had seen him, and there was a hint of panic in the air. Suddenly he appeared, in our canopy, and the first person he saw was me. He walked straight up to me, obviously thinking I was someone important, shook my hand, said 'hello' and asked how I was. He was so charming and asked me about my job and whether I went to all the Grands Prix. I could see the Stewart PR people over his shoulder, champing at the bit to take him where he should have been. I was a bit flustered and asked him if he would like a drink, thinking he would say, 'Sorry, but I have to be somewhere else,' but he just replied 'I would love a coffee!' I gave him his coffee and he then asked me if I lived in England. When I told him that I did he said he loved England.

'Where in England do you live?'

'Near Stratford-upon-Avon, actually.'

'My dear, do sit down a minute. I would love to talk to you about Stratford,' he said. By now I was feeling really uncomfortable; he shouldn't have been with us, he should have been next door where they had a special meal planned. I knew I shouldn't be sitting around talking to him, but I had no option. I couldn't be impolite. I could still see the Stewart PR people and they were getting redder and more furious by the minute.

'Could you just make me a little sandwich?' he asked, and he then carried on talking about Stratford for around half an hour before realising that he had to be back in the Paddock Club to meet someone. As he was getting up to go I said to him, 'I actually think you are due to be having lunch next door.'

He checked his watch and replied, 'I don't think I'll have time now,' and left. He never went to the Stewart area at all. What a charming man – but I'll never forget Jackie's face.

We never went out of our way to upset Jackie and we admired him a great deal, but things just seemed to happen and we always seemed to be somewhere in the middle of it. Perhaps it was just some kind of communication breakdown.

There was one occasion when Jackie came around to see us and told us that Princess Anne would be coming to their motorhome that day. 'She may want to use the toilet facilities. Could she use yours? Can I go and inspect it?'

I was puzzled and said, 'You can, but you have a toilet in your own motorhome. Why can't she use that?'

Oddly, he just said, 'Yes, but that's mine.' He went on to say that the princess usually brought her own seat, but we had to point out that motorhome toilets were different from ordinary toilets and it wouldn't fit. As luck would have it she never needed it all day, so another tricky situation was avoided, but I did wonder where her toilet seat was kept. I couldn't imagine someone wandering around the pit lane with it in their hand.

We didn't know it at the time, but 1999 was to be the Stewart Grand Prix team's last season in Formula 1. In retrospect it seemed appropriate that we should be teamed up with Johnny Herbert again. He was driving alongside Rubens and the two of them got on very well. They both used to come to our motorhome to eat, as they said they preferred our food, and there were times when Paul Stewart had to come to get them and take them back to their own facility for briefings or sponsor commitments. It wasn't our fault; they just used to come around and we couldn't and wouldn't turn them away. I did say to them one day, 'Look, you should really eat in the Stewart motorhome,' and they both looked up at me and said, 'Why?' and just carried on. I don't know if that created a problem.

One day Paul came rushing into the motorhome kitchen on a different mission. Tracey and I were preparing some food when he burst in, looked around in a panic and asked, 'Have you seen the Sultan?'

Without batting an eyelid Tracey replied, 'Yes, Paul, but he's finished the washing up and now he's gone.'

Paul shouted 'Has he?' and, turning quickly, he shot off. We cracked up because Paul's head was always somewhere else. When Stuart had been doing the pit board Paul would stand on the pit wall between Stu and Jackie, but he got into such a state that he didn't really seem to know what he was doing, and if his dad shouted at him he was a wreck. In a way I felt sorry for Paul as he was always in his dad's shadow and couldn't always cope with it.

Jackie had got into the habit of inviting as many royals of any country as he possibly could to the circuit, along with any other mover and shaker he could identify. It's easy to scoff, but the objective was to raise awareness of the brand. I'm sure Jackie did that for Ford, and in the process he didn't do his own brand any harm.

As usual, Johnny was a breath of fresh air and his antics kept everyone on their toes. On one particular trip we were on our toes quite literally. We were in the reception area of a Detroit hotel at the start of a visit to the Ford Motor Company. As we waited for our turn to check in we heard a noise and, when we looked out of the large plate-glass windows, Johnny, with Cliff Peters from Prism on board, almost crashed through the window to join us while trying to park the car. That's racing drivers for you.

Ford treated us very well. In addition to the trip to Detroit, Rod Campbell on behalf of Ford invited us on an all-expenses-paid trip to an Indy Car race in Fontana, California. The purpose of the outing was to take a look at their US hospitality operation and, needless to say, we didn't need asking twice.

We flew to Los Angeles and were met and taken to our hotel. We had expected to be staying close to the circuit, but we travelled out of the city to one of the only hotels actually on the beach side of Malibu, where we were enthralled by the views from our fabulous room. Rod picked us up and took us to the circuit the next day, which was quite a drive, and we were escorted into the Ford suite prior to going into the paddock. In the suite there were lots of familiar faces from the Ford hierarchy and we were made to feel very welcome, although it was strange to be waited on rather than doing the waiting.

When we visited the paddock it was very, very different from Formula 1, quite relaxed and friendly, and everyone seemed to be popping into each others' motorhomes which made for a lovely atmosphere. I have to admit to being a bit surprised by the Ford hospitality area. We had expected something quite grand but it was very simple, with plastic tables and folding camp chairs. Steve was front of house as well as driving the truck, and the food was provided by caterers. Later, when we became involved with Le Mans, we found this was pretty common in the States, with the food staying until the caterers took it away. It was all a bit low key and I should have loved to have spent a season in Indycar to try to improve it. I guess that might have been unpopular, though.

After we left the hospitality area Stu and I wandered off to take a look at the amazing American trucks, which to me were far better looking than the boring European ones. As we strolled around we suddenly heard a voice shouting, 'Mum! Dad! What are you doing here?' We turned around in amazement to find an ex-Benetton chap called Wayne striding towards us. Wayne had left Benetton and moved to the States to work for Honda. It seemed that within an hour the word had spread around the paddock that Mum and Dad were there and we caught up with several chaps from earlier years who had managed to find work in the States and, more importantly, get their 'green cards'.

We were told to visit the Honda engine truck and ask for Mike, which we did, and the very bemused engineer who met us there shouted into the truck, 'Mike, your Mom and Dad are here.' It was great to see a very surprised Mike Janes, one of our Cosworth old boys, who was working for Honda in the USA. Mike did the rounds and is now back in England working for Mercedes engines.

We spent a couple of days at the track, mainly in the Ford suite, but on race day one of the Visteon chief engineers said to Stuart, 'Come down to the grid and I will introduce you to some folk.' (Visteon were at the time the electronics arm of the Ford Motor Company.) I decided to stay in the suite as their tea wasn't bad and I could people-watch from above the crowd. After a very short space of time Jim, the Visteon engineer in question, reappeared in the suite and said, 'I've given up. Stuart knows more people than I do.' He was right, of course, because there were a lot of mechanics that we had worked with before, not to mention drivers like Stefan Johansson, Mark Blundell and Roberto Moreno.

We had a great weekend and returned to Malibu each night. Rod took us to his favourite Italian restaurant, which was often frequented by the rich and famous. When we arrived we were asked if we would like a screen; there were a number of people tucked away out of sight the night that we were there. Rod was having a house built in Malibu at the time, next door to the actress Jane Seymour, and we went to see it. It was hard to believe we had first met him in the front room of his house in Oxford in 1977.

We later found out that the Cosworth hierarchy, including a certain Bernard Ferguson, were staying at the Holiday Inn near the circuit and we felt a pang of guilt – but only for a moment. Our time with Ford Formula 1 was a very pleasant change from being with a team, the events were varied and the people were a combination of fun, focus and professionalism. This just made what was to come more difficult to take.

Chapter 26

STABBED THROUGH THE HEART

We had been aware of the changed circumstances of Stewart Grand Prix and the rebranding strategy from Ford to Jaguar in the second half of 1999 because we had been told by Neil Ressler. At the time Neil held the unlikely job title of 'Vice-President and Chief Technical Officer of Research and Vehicle Technology with responsibilities for Advanced Vehicle Technology, Scientific Research and Environmental and Safety Engineering for the Ford Motor Company'; what a mouthful. Ford owned Jaguar and the Ford management had decided to promote the Jaguar brand through Formula 1, so that was the name under which they wished the team to be known going forward. Jacques Nasser, the Ford chief executive, had been so impressed by the sea of red Ferrari hats at every Grand Prix that he was determined to match it with a 'sea of green', as the Jaguar brand was just as impressive as Ferrari.

Once the deal was done, Jackie was to assist Ford through the transition period. Obviously Stuart and I were pretty interested in how the whole change was going to affect our position, but our minds were put to rest at a large meeting at the German Grand Prix in August 1999 when we were told that we would be responsible for running the motorhome which would serve the Jaguar management and guests; someone else would be responsible for running the race team's catering facility. This made sense, as we knew most of the Ford senior management and a fair number of their likely guests. The Stewart Grand Prix team had previously been using the hospitality company MSL, who had also been around for years in various forms and often provided central catering for the teams which didn't have their own facilities. Present at the meeting were Neil Ressler, Martin Whitaker, who was Ford's director of motorsport in the UK, Paul Stewart, the Stewart GP team principal, and Dave Stubbs who was the Stewart GP team manager. In addition to deciding who would do what in terms of catering, we were also told that Stuart should get involved in the design of two new motorhome vehicles, which would be joined together at the track by a central atrium connecting them into one self-contained facility.

Safe in the knowledge that our future seemed secure we carried on happily through the winter, quite excited at the prospects for the new season. Stuart had been working with the truck suppliers, sorting all the floor plans out, and we were looking forward to seeing all our Ford management friends and the lads on the team again, all new and re-badged in Jaguar racing green. Imagine our feelings when, early in the year, out of the blue, we got a pre-printed four-line letter from Stewart Grand Prix saying 'Your application for the hospitality contract has been rejected, thanks for your interest.'

It felt like someone had stabbed us through our hearts. We were amazed and thought, 'We're doing it; we've been told by Ford that we are doing it. There must be some terrible mistake.' But deep down we had the uncomfortable feeling in the pits of our stomachs that it was real. We hadn't applied for anything; we had been given the job and we had been getting on with it, but the letter made it sound as if we were one of five hundred no-hope candidates that had applied and been rejected. I sent a text to Martin Whitaker, who happened to be at a PR day at Ford Cologne along with Tyrone Johnson, who was another Ford representative at the races, and various other members of the Ford hierarchy. I just asked Martin to ring me as we had received this strange letter telling us that we would not be doing the hospitality in the future. When he rang us back it was clear that neither he nor Neil Ressler knew anything about it. Apparently the whole PR event had come to a standstill because they were all so shocked and had no idea what was going on.

The story came back from the Stewart camp that Paul Stewart had been told that we didn't want to take the job. There was absolutely no reason for that message to get to him because it had never been discussed since the meeting at the German race. We felt that something very strange had gone on, and it became clear that while Stuart was working on the plans with one truck manufacturer, someone else was working with another one on a different layout. To this day we can't understand why no one rang us to ask why we didn't want the job any more, if they genuinely believed we weren't interested.

Eventually it emerged that MSL would be doing all the hospitality, not just catering for the team members. I felt very let down because I had asked in the original meeting how MSL would be affected by the plans and suggested they could perhaps run the hospitality at the tests – and that had been agreed, as far as we were aware.

We were absolutely gutted. We thought it was all over for us. It was almost the start of the new season, and we had no hope of securing an alternative team at that late stage. We thought, like most people, that if we were going to stop we would have liked to have done so at a time of our choice. It was very hard not to feel bitter. We thought back to a glorious farewell party after the European Grand Prix at the Nürburgring, held because the Ford 'Blue Oval' was leaving the team and the Jaguar brand was coming in. It was a memorable bash, especially as Johnny Herbert had won the race. What we didn't realise at the time was that it was us who were also leaving!

Life has a way of compensating for disappointments and we had no way of knowing that we were on the threshold of a whole new series of experiences which would eventually lead us back to Formula 1. Plainly we hadn't upset anyone; we loved being with Ford and they appeared to like us – a feeling which was reinforced when we found we had a brand-new role looking after hospitality for Ford's World Rally team. Martin Whitaker had been distraught at the way things had turned out for us in Formula 1 and he was even more determined to promote the Ford brand through the World Rally Championship now that Jaguar was the brand of choice in Formula 1. Fortunately, he also still believed that achieving his goal would be made much easier by having a real PR and hospitality presence in the service points at all the events. He was instrumental in securing us a full-time permanent position running the Ford WRC hospitality facility. We had had a few practice runs and now it was for real – bring on the mud and snow!

Chapter 27

MUD, SWEAT
AND TEARS

And so we went rallying. The mud and snow were duly brought on, and so was just about every other variation of weather, terrain and obstacle. We had realised our working life was going to be very different, but even after the practice runs we'd had we hadn't quite appreciated how different it would be now that rallying was to be our full-time job.

It came as quite a surprise to a lot of people that we weren't in Formula 1 any more and the news plainly hadn't percolated through the Ford organisation. As usual, the first event of the new season was the Monte Carlo Rally and we were parked in a familiar position on the Monaco harbour wall near the Yacht Club. The new Ford Focus rally car was due to be launched with Carlos Sainz and Colin McRae (or two stuntmen) sliding down ropes from a hovering helicopter amid a spectacular firework show. Our coach was forming the backdrop to the action and, as we waited inside for the action to start, we heard a voice say to Martin Whitaker, who was close by, 'Are Stuart and my girlie here?'

Martin shouted for us to go over to meet the 'new man at the very top', Nick Scheele, now Sir Nick Scheele, who was the chief operating officer of the Ford Motor Company. We had met him previously when he was the top man at Jaguar and he'd attended a Grand Prix as a guest of Tom Walkinshaw. Ironically, Nick Scheele lived near us and we often saw him around the high street of our small town. He seemed genuinely pleased to see us and was very friendly, which surprised a few people who didn't realise we already knew him. He said, 'Well, girlie, you will be seeing more of me; I won't be in Alcester (his new job necessitated a move to America) but I'll be at the Grands Prix.'

Stuart and I looked at each other and Stu said, 'Well, actually you won't, as we're not providing the hospitality at Formula 1 any more.'

Mr Scheele seemed taken aback and asked, 'Why? Don't you want to?'

Stuart, to the point as always, said, 'I think we have been stitched up as the contract has gone to someone else.'

'Who?'

'The company who were doing Stewart Grand Prix hospitality.'

Mr Scheele looked genuinely surprised. 'But you know everyone at Ford and we know you both. I will certainly look into it.' This man was the head of Ford operations and we felt he shouldn't be worrying himself about our affairs so we said, 'It's too late and although we are very disappointed at least we are staying with Ford. Martin Whitaker is keen to raise the level of hospitality in World Rally, so hopefully we'll be doing something useful.'

Despite our protestations Mr Scheele said he really would look into it, and after he'd done his investigations he announced that, in compensation, we were to be provided with a Ford vehicle for our own use for as long as we had a contract with the company. We were amazed by this turn of events because, after all, we were just there to make the tea and shouldn't even have been on his radar. But perhaps it's that kind of attention to detail that takes someone to the top of such a large organisation.

Later we took delivery of a Ford Maverick that we were able to keep until 2005, although even that wasn't without a bit of drama. At one point Ford's auditors pointed out that, as contractors, we weren't entitled to a car and demanded to see who had authorised it. After they were shown the signature by the relevant department it all went quiet and no more was said.

At another of the early rallies a journalist whom we knew from Formula 1 asked if he could interview us about the differences between World Rally and Formula 1 from our standpoint. 'How long have you got?' we said. Considering the subject again after all this time and after so many experiences, I thought I might now answer the question slightly differently and certainly more fully, but the fact remains that the sports couldn't be much less alike from every standpoint. However, the question provides an excellent framework for the story of our rallying experiences.

The main differences revolve around weather, terrain, working environment, viewing facilities, logistics, venues, drivers and co-drivers – in other words, just about everything. In the early days, while our coach was not in any way exceptional in terms of Formula 1, it was the longest and tallest in rallying which was another trial for us and also for John Millington (Milly), M-Sport's long-serving and long-suffering logistics manager. It simply wasn't really suitable for many venues and a number of the other teams took exception to its size.

The weather is a particularly important difference. In Formula 1 the venues and dates are selected in a manner which is intended to maximise the possibility of the weather being dry, and in rallying mastering all types of weather and terrain is part of the competition, so event dates are chosen to make the conditions as challenging as possible.

In the Formula 1 paddock at that time each motorhome space was on tarmac and was provided with water, electricity and pretty much everything required; once the motorhome was in place it stayed there for the weekend. Weather wasn't an issue. The World Rally (WRC) equivalent to the paddock was a service park, which at that time was generally in a field with no running water, electricity or toilets, and we often had to move on every day. We always hoped for fine weather, not mud or even snow; it was usually mud, though. At one of our first Monte Carlo Rallies we had to climb around hairpin bends to Levens where we parked on what looked like the village green. It had been raining and when we came to leave our 23-ton coach had sunk to the point where the doorstep was level with the grass, so we had to get tractors to pull us out.

Our first Swedish Rally filled us with trepidation as it was held in February, which meant cold, snow, icy roads and a logistical nightmare. Together with Graham and Tracey, our staff with the kitchen truck, we had survived the cold and fatigue of the Monte Carlo Rally, but that was child's play by comparison. We'd been advised to buy thermal clothes and snow boots so we visited our local outdoor shop and came away with what was necessary, and some fairly inelegant underwear too. To get to Sweden Stuart decided against the ferry to Gothenburg, preferring to go to Calais and drive north; he reasoned that driving would be less boring than spending time on the boat. We headed off through Belgium to northern Germany where we started to experience snow. We crossed on the ferry from Denmark to Sweden, by which time the snow had become a blizzard. It was late afternoon when the boat docked and we could hardly see anything.

Stuart said, 'Don't worry. The roads will be cleared because the Swedes are used to it.'

I thought about the chaos in England when one inch of snow fell and hoped he was right, but he was wrong, very wrong! Leaving the docks we found that the roads were completely blanketed in snow and the blizzard was still raging. I'd never seen snowflakes so large and snow was building up under the windscreen wipers. Cars were rocketing past as we crawled along, aware that a 23-ton coach takes a lot of stopping. It soon became apparent that the roads weren't cleared; everyone just changed to snow tyres and got on with it. We had a reality check when we came across a car on its roof and later a Coca Cola truck on its side, presumably because neither of them had snow tyres.

We needed to find a hotel and quickly. We knew there were Scandic hotels along the route and we were peering through the snow in the hope of seeing a hotel sign, despite the fact we couldn't even see the slip roads. I had a hotel guide with me and noticed that there was a hotel listed only 20km further on, so we rang to check out the room situation. They had two rooms left so we booked them in the hope that we could make it. We crawled along the road, which had become a single track by that point, with Graham and Tracey slithering around in the kitchen truck behind us. Spotting the exit sign we slowly turned up a slight slope to get off the road. After two or three attempts we made it and were relieved to see the hotel right in front of us. Graham pulled around us to find a suitable parking spot for our oversized coach, pointing to what looked like a suitable place. Finally we were safe, but we felt drained by the ordeal of trying to control the vehicle while peering through the gloom. At the reception desk Stuart asked if it was OK to park where we had. The receptionist peered through the window and said, 'Not really, you are on the flower beds, but I'm off duty now so don't worry.'

We awoke the next morning to brilliant sunshine but could hardly see the coach; the blizzard had almost covered it, despite its size. It was a while before we could make it safe to travel, and we felt really cold as we tried to clear the snow; later we discovered the temperature was −18 degrees. Luckily both vehicles fired up and we slipped and slid the 200km to the rally venue at Karlstad. We found the hotel OK, but couldn't initially get up the slope to the spot allocated for rally vehicles, until Milly spoke to the hotel manager who promptly arranged for some snow to be cleared. The hotel itself was wonderfully warm, with heated floors and all mod cons, but when we ventured outside the weather was colder than I could ever have imagined. It took our breath away and we felt the liquid in our eyes freezing. Stuart's beard was actually frozen. An interesting feature of the hotel was an area of the garden outside the restaurant windows where the locals, who had been in the hotel sauna, came outside to roll around naked in the snow. That's not exactly ideal entertainment when you're eating.

The following day just getting to the service park, situated on an airfield, was an adventure and we all had so many clothes on we could hardly move. When we tried to put up the canopy the poles were frozen together and the awning was so brittle we couldn't unpack it. The next problem was that it was impossible to fill the water tanks as the liquid would freeze and split the tanks, which meant visiting the nearest garage with containers to collect water (the taps at garages were in heated cabinets). We had to get back to the motorhome quickly because the water started to freeze on the way back.

It was a catering nightmare as we tried to work without the awning. We decided to keep it simple, with stews, soups and lots of hot tea and coffee. The milk started to freeze as we put it out but everyone was so cold and hungry that everything disappeared immediately.

The Scandinavians are really obsessed with rallying and turn out whatever the weather. Early one morning we heard voices and three people were standing outside dressed as wolves. At least they were warm in their fur. We were outside in very deep snow for four days as the blizzards came and went, but we actually did get used to it. The scenery was beautiful and we saw cars driving across frozen lakes, fishermen sitting on stools with their lines through the ice and all manner of odd things. Fortunately that first time in Sweden was the coldest we ever experienced and our subsequent trips were warmer, with slush on the roads, which was a headache for the tyre supplier and for George Black, M-Sport's tyre wizard, but not quite so bad for us

It wasn't just the snow and the cold that caused us problems, however. On one occasion in Corsica we experienced a mini-hurricane: the lads had to hold the awning down to stop it disappearing. We had seen the bad weather approaching from the sea while the guys were eating dinner; they never got their dessert as the storm hit and all hell broke loose. Other teams' awnings took off into the distance and some trucks were damaged. A similar thing happened in Greece when our E-Z ups spiralled away into the sky. An E-Z up was a folding cover or gazebo which was extremely portable and, as the name suggests, easy to erect. All the teams used them for fly-away events, but sometimes they flew away on their own.

So we suffered snow and wind, and naturally we came across quite a lot of rain as well, including one memorable time in a place called Vic in Spain. We were parked on a rugby pitch when the heavens opened, the whole area flooded and we were all marooned. There were other trips when the heat became a serious issue; it seemed like we only needed a plague of frogs to complete the full biblical set.

The terrain was a bit different in rallying from what we'd experienced in Formula 1, and that caused its own set of issues. In Formula 1 most events, other than Monaco, are held at permanent circuits and access has been planned for and improved over the years (although some are still not brilliant). Rallying, on the other hand, has no permanent sites and therefore uses the facilities and access that are available, and this has certainly created a few 'moments' for us over the years in our large coach. One time in Corsica we were supposed to park on a sports field, but the coach bottomed out as we turned through the gate, blocking the whole road. The teams and other vehicles following on behind couldn't get into the field either and the area was gridlocked. The police showed up, took one look and left. The problem was only resolved when one of the rally mechanics arrived an hour later, fetched his tools and cut through the tow bar, which was firmly entrenched in the ground. Things were a little late starting that day and we were not popular. We also blocked one village in northern Portugal completely when we couldn't negotiate a particular bend and a street sign became embedded in the side of the coach.

The differences between the two types of motorsport were very clear and influenced the working conditions with which everyone had to contend. The lack of water and electricity obviously affected what we could offer in the way of hospitality, but perhaps the lack of toilet facilities was the biggest inconvenience (pun intended). The men had a bit of an advantage, of course, and although there weren't many ladies around the few of us who were there were often put in embarrassing situations. We had a toilet in the coach, but that had to be kept for the drivers – and once it was full it couldn't be used any more. On one occasion I actually knocked on the door of a house and asked to use their facilities. They were very obliging. When I started rallying I was asked to keep any carrier bags I had finished with 'as we may need them', which bemused me for quite some time before I realised what they were probably used for.

The World Rally Championship has changed a little now, but when we started we had to move the whole hospitality facility every day, and sometimes twice or even three times, with breakfast being served in one place before dismantling everything, moving and setting up again somewhere else in time for lunch, and if we were lucky, dinner. There was never enough time to set everything up to Formula 1 standards and the demands of this constant setting up and breaking down could be soul-destroying. There were only four of us to do it all, and somehow find time in between driving and the set up and break down to do the shopping and prepare the food. There were many occasions when a pot of curry or a pie or something had to be left cooking in the oven while we moved on to the next venue.

We always prepared tea and coffee in Airpots (stainless steel vacuum-sealed drinks dispensers) at the venue we were leaving so that they would be ready on arrival at the next place; drinks were always in demand as soon as we arrived. We don't think that Martin Whitaker or M-Sport boss Malcolm Wilson ever realised the logistical nightmares that occurred in those early days. Milly was the only person in the team management who really understood and he lent us a mechanic to help with dismantling and building if one was available. After a while we started to have a small support truck carrying chairs, tables and other equipment as well as an additional small motorhome for drivers to use if the rally stages were too far away to allow them to get back to the service park.

The drivers and their co-drivers turned up at the service park three times a day, at the most, and when they did they generally had a maximum of around 20 minutes to be fed and watered. It was all a bit of a rush for us, particularly when the team were running three cars, as they sometimes did. Often all the drivers and co-drivers wanted different meals and that could stretch our sense of humour, although in fairness the drivers sometimes radioed their meal requests to Milly, who relayed them to us.

If we thought the working conditions weren't too good for us then the mechanics had a much more difficult set of problems to contend with, as well as a lifestyle very different from their counterparts in Formula 1. I really admire rally mechanics. I can't imagine Formula 1 lads under cars, rolling around on waterproof sheeting in all weathers – in the heat and dust of the Safari Rally, ice, snow and –20 degrees in Sweden, or on hot tarmac in Cyprus, where we've had to rig up a shower to keep everyone cool. I have seen lads trying to change components on cars in freezing temperatures, unable to wear gloves with fingers as they were unable to feel what they were doing, and when they were finished there was no cosy truck for them to sit in, or even heated garages, so they just hung around listening to rally times and waiting for their driver to arrive back at the service park. Then they only had 20 minutes, while the drivers ate, to solve any problems, repair any damage to the car and send it out again looking clean and businesslike.

In my opinion, those boys are real mechanics. I don't mean any disrespect to Formula 1 lads as they also do a grand job, but their working conditions are pristine and they moan if it's a bit too cold or hot in the garage. They work hard, too, but I don't think they would swap working at a Grand Prix for working in World Rally, and I am sure the opposite applies. Formula 1 lads used to turn up at the track in designer clothes, carrying designer briefcases; rally lads have a cloth toolbag and arrive in overalls. Their hotels are not always the best, but as they rarely spend any time in them it hardly matters. Rallies start incredibly early, as well. One year in New Zealand we were leaving the hotel at 3.30am for a 6am start as we had to drive two hours south to reach the service park, and we always needed to be there an hour before everyone else to start preparing breakfast.

Our role in rallying never allowed us to see or hear any of the action and that's something we really missed. It always made me tingle when I heard the Formula 1 cars, even after I had been around them for years. In rallying everything happened away from the service park, and unless there happened to be a radio close by there was no way to keep up with what was going on. It always seemed a bit hollow when we heard the team had won because the drivers were still miles away.

As a consequence of the increased requirements of the team our own infrastructure began to grow and change. A marketing company owned by Katja Heim had been hired by Martin Whitaker to develop Ford's image in World Rally.

Katja was well-known in Formula 1 circles and had done a lot of work for Bernie Ecclestone, occasionally being on the wrong end of his impish sense of humour. One particular example of this occurred when Katja went to see Bernie in his office and asked him if she could take two weeks' holiday; he asked her why she wanted the time off and she told him she was having a little 'cosmetic work' done. Bernie looked up from his desk, studied her for a second and then said, 'I think you had better take six months', before calmly returning to the job in hand. Katja obviously had a sense of humour as she told me the story herself. I think that sense of humour must have spread to the rest of the people in the marketing company as, in their infinite wisdom, they came up with the idea they would sell 'tours' to Ford customers.

Rallying has never been a sport for guests to follow or watch on more than one stage; the best way to see anything is to follow the action by helicopter, which of course wouldn't fly in bad weather. It was one of those decisions that are made without consulting the people who have to deliver the service. To cater for this influx of potential new guests we had to provide a larger awning and flooring. Flooring was commonplace in Formula 1 but would be new to WRC; the additional time required to fit it and take it up made moving during the day impossible without additional staff. There was also the sheer difficulty of feeding paying guests to the standard they expected in the conditions in which we were operating. Shopping was always an experience as we were often miles from a shop, which might or might not stock enough food for a team of around 60 people; the extra paying guests added to the nightmare.

By mid-2001 Graham had left to go back to Formula 1; Tracey stayed with us initially, as another partnership bit the dust. We employed two new chefs, Pete and Jamie, who happened to be cousins; Doug Denhart, who worked for the company that provided audio systems to Formula 1 teams, was Pete's dad. Pete had always been a little reluctant to leave the security of working as a chef in the City, but he had been on the fringe of motorsport through his dad's involvement with Formula 1; in the end he agreed to join us when Doug told him it would do him good! His cousin Jamie had recently ended a long-term relationship so we enticed him along by saying it would be good for him too. Jamie had dabbled in Formula 3 and, in fact, had previously worked for our old mate Briggsy.

It was as big a shock for the two of them to be on the road with World Rally as it had been for us initially. There were no huge kitchens, no one to do your shopping for you or empty the rubbish and, as often as not, no water or electricity. Pete and

Jamie had been trained to hand over some tasks, but it is a DIY job in motorsport. They certainly had to rethink their menus as it was impossible to buy some of the ingredients for their dishes in many spots we visited. However, we now had two chefs on board, plus Stuart, Tracey and myself, and we somehow managed the extra workload. The wage bill and the expenses were growing considerably faster than our income, however.

We established Pete and Jamie in a 7.5-ton truck that we had had built and, by careful menu planning, we were generally able to buy enough local produce wherever we were. If that wasn't the case, the new truck increased our kitchen and fridge space so we could carry more provisions with us to feed the staff and guests, despite the challenge of not being able to guarantee electricity. In an effort to improve the tables, chairs and other fittings the marketing company bought some new equipment, but unfortunately they were totally impracticable as they didn't dismantle for transportation. They also seemed to attract dust like a magnet, which made them look terrible, and to compound the problem they were finished in silver-coloured metal and burnt the arms of the guests when the weather was hot. We were amazed at the logistics of looking after the guests as we regularly had to wash up hundreds of plates, cutlery and wine glasses by hand, often without running water, which was pretty difficult.

The addition of all this new equipment meant that we had to have a larger support truck to carry everything, and then someone to drive it, so the costs were really starting to escalate and WRC was beginning to look more like Formula 1. The final piece of the transport jigsaw fell into place when we were asked to provide a vehicle with a catering service for the 'recce team'. While the recce team are out on the course they obviously needed feeding and watering, so the fact that we were to be responsible for that necessitated us having yet another vehicle built and another person joining our happy band: Alan Wright. Alan drove the vehicle, which was half-kitchen and half-lounge, and he would stop on the side of the road or wherever and magic up some food for the drivers. People from different teams who did not have their own facility would be welcomed in by the Ford drivers, so poor Alan often ended up cooking for considerably more people than he'd planned for.

Alan had been involved in rallying for many years, and prior to joining us had been working with one of M-Sport's contractors. He was a mine of information on every aspect of the rallying world and we learned an awful lot from him in our early days. His previous task was on the gravel crew, yet another set of people who are often experienced ex-rally drivers. Jimmy McRae, who was a former British rally champion as well as being Colin's dad, did the job for Colin and Nicky Grist when they were together at Ford. There was a co-driver in each gravel car whose job it was to go out at the crack of dawn on each day of the rally and check to see if any of the surface conditions had changed since the original recce.

It took us a long time to find out who all these crews were and when they expected to be fed, but eventually we got there. A bigger concern was where all this increase in staff and equipment was going to end. We had started our first season with a coach, owned by Ford, and a Transit van converted into a kitchen belonging to us, looked after by four of us. Besides the Ford coach our personal fleet had grown to a large support truck, a small motorhome, two 7.5-ton trucks (one designed as a kitchen and one formatted to provide a kitchen and a lounge) and we had significantly increased our staff, all at additional cost to ourselves. To add to our workload we had also secured a contract with Inmarsat, who were the World Rally Championship series title sponsor, to provide hospitality for their guests from 2002 onwards; we hired three more people to work on that.

Despite all this chasing around from one place to another, erecting and disassembling equipment, there was still plenty of opportunity for Stuart to get himself into trouble. On our way back from a rally in Spain we were stopped for a spot check at the French customs. We were fined €180 for carrying two packs of Red Bull into the country because it was illegal. The cans had been packed at the last minute and were just on the step inside the coach. We had forgotten to put them into the support truck that was following behind us. The rally support guys used to survive on Red Bull due to the early starts and late finishes so we always carried plenty. Our stock was confiscated by customs but fortunately the support truck, which was carrying crates of the stuff, was waved through.

The customs officers were pretty reasonable, but Stuart managed to upset them by opening every can and pouring the contents down a drain before handing over the empties. It was spraying all over the place and all over them. They told him to stop, but he replied, 'It's illegal, you can't drink it!' They didn't see the funny side of it and marched him off, leaving me with a coach I am not licensed to drive. When Stu finally reappeared with a written warning in his hand we asked for a receipt and the officers were not very pleased; we did eventually get a scrap of paper but it didn't look very official. They obviously just wanted the Red Bull; Stuart started to say they only wanted it to add to their vodka but I stopped him short, as I had no intention of learning to drive a motorhome.

We were stupid enough to tell the Ford administrator, Spencer Hall, about our experience and at the next rally emblazoned on the Ford website was the headline 'Ford hospitality couple stopped and fined for carrying illegal substances'. There was a huge hue and cry at Ford, because the daft devil hadn't mentioned Red Bull. It looked as if we'd been carrying drugs or something. His hospitality area was a bit less hospitable that weekend.

Chapter 28

RALLYING THE WORLD

We had become pretty familiar with all the usual Formula 1 circuits, so it was a real experience to travel to the venues where WRC events were held. Some rallies took place in countries we thought we knew well, like Australia, but being in a forest a few hours south of Perth was a completely different experience from being in Melbourne or Adelaide. Instead of avoiding traffic on the way to the circuit each day we had to avoid kangaroos on the way to the service park. As we were on the road very early there were always a lot of them about, although sadly some didn't survive the influx of strange visitors in odd-coloured vehicles. The surface of the service area in the forest was left in its natural state, which was small 'balls' similar to the ones for sale in a garden centre to put in the top of pots. It was incredibly difficult to walk on, let alone drive flat out over – and surrounded by trees. We had experienced some Formula 1 cars hitting deer, rabbits and groundhogs, but at this event in Australia it was all about drivers hitting kangaroos.

There were unfamiliar insects and spiders everywhere in Australia's forests, one of which was brave enough to bite Stuart on his earlobe. His ear became infected and swollen, forcing him to visit a clinic to have a piece of the lobe removed and eleven stitches inserted. What was really impressive was the fact that anyone could walk into one of these clinics, see someone, get sorted and be on their way, just like a dentist, with the laboratory report being forwarded on to the UK.

I didn't attend the Safari Rally as I had just undergone cartilage operations on both my knees at the same time, but Stuart, Graham and Tracey went. The wildlife naturally changed again and they encountered giraffe, antelope and zebra plus a few challenges that were a little unexpected, to say the least.

The Safari Rally is no longer on the calendar but it was certainly another experience. We flew out E-Z ups and barbecues for the catering, but the local food shopping was very difficult. The hotel base was in Nairobi and Milly had said the hotel would help with sourcing the food. Graham and Tracey ventured out and found a butcher of sorts, but as there were no cattle around it was difficult to imagine what the meat was – probably wildebeest. The hotel provided the bread, fruit and sundries, as Milly had promised, and a 'tab' was kept of the purchases; another chap who had been team helper for a few years obtained the drinks, so there was a catering plan of sorts.

Graham and Tracey drove their vehicle into the Masai Mara each day to the service park and Stuart travelled in a truck with one of the mechanics called 'Chopsy'. On their first journey Stuart spotted handles on the inside of the roof of the cab and asked what they were for. Chopsy replied simply, 'They're the Jesus handles!' When Stuart asked for an explanation he was told, 'When you see a pothole, grab a handle, lift your backside off the seat and shout "Jesus!" '

The service area was about a couple of hours away but locals would appear from nowhere, selling hand-made products. Stuart had no idea how they got there or where the village was, but he felt obliged to buy something as it helped them to survive. One Masai warrior regularly turned up on a bicycle, dressed in his full regalia, and just stood there, silently watching.

I was pleased I hadn't gone on the trip when I heard about the toilet facilities. There weren't any. The procedure was that the locals would dig a hole in the ground and put a screen around it – and that was it. When it was full they covered it over and moved on to another spot before repeating the process. Tracey was quite ill and the whole thing was pretty disgusting, but at least no one suffered food poisoning.

When Stuart checked out of the hotel at the end of the rally the hotel bill was astronomical. He queried it and discovered that all our provisions had been charged at room-service rate and were therefore ten times more expensive than normal; no wonder they volunteered to help. Similarly, the 'helper' tried it on with the drinks bill, charging for drinks no one had had. Once again, Milly was left to sort it all out.

It sometimes seemed that the rally organisers had a bit of an odd sense of humour, a trait which became particularly evident when they decided to arrange for a boat to take all the rally vehicles from Italy to Argentina. Fascinated by this unusual turn of events, everyone duly assembled with coaches, trucks and all the rest of their equipment on the quayside at Savona. A boat was spotted entering the harbour with a terrible list to one side, and no one thought that it could possibly be ours – but it was. As the captain started the loading procedure lots of team members were taking photographs of the boat's alarming list, in support of any future insurance claims.

Ford had initially been reluctant to let the coach sail due to the astronomical cost of marine insurance; however, Malcolm Wilson said he would put it on his insurance list, with his vehicles. It became apparent pretty quickly why they didn't want it to sail because, leaning as it did, the boat only looked capable of sailing round in circles. One member from each team had to travel on the boat and the nominated drivers, including Stuart, flew to Buenos Aires. They were then taken to the Ford factory where they were loaned cars, which they drove to a service area for a break, before travelling on to a hotel near the River Plate where the boat was due to dock. The next morning everyone was assembled on the dock wondering if they would ever see the boat again. It eventually arrived, still listing; it caused trouble with the unloading but nothing had been lost. When everyone was ready they were driven in convoy, with security guards, to Cordoba to set up for the rally.

Apart from the wonderful scenery, the magnificent sight of condors soaring and the gauchos working, an abiding memory is of the poor quality of the meat. Argentina is normally renowned for the excellence of its beef but apparently, at that time, all the best was being exported. It was a big disappointment.

Not all of our trips were quite so exotic, and of course lots of our European trips followed familiar routes, but Corsica was different because it included another boat trip, this time from Marseilles. It was surprising that such a simple journey always turned out to be so chaotic. We would travel overnight in a sleeper cabin and book the cabins in advance, but the shipping company never seemed to take any notice of our reservations. On one trip Tracey and I found we were booked into a dormitory room with a group of mechanics from other teams. It turned out the beds were allocated in alphabetical order. We soon put a stop to that.

Corsica seemed a strange island that didn't have a clear identity, unsure as to whether it wanted to be French, Italian or Greek. What was apparent was that Corsicans didn't like rally people, which became obvious when we were shopping; the shopkeepers ignored us until they had served all the locals, similar to Hungary in our early Formula 1 days. We used to park on the airstrip, then venture inland on a very hair-raising trip with ravines either side and hairpin bends. I was a very nervous passenger. It was incredibly dangerous for the rally drivers and I felt anxious for them, the countryside being extremely rugged and rocky. On one occasion Colin McRae, our driver, had a really big accident and rolled down a ravine, where Nicky Grist, his co-driver, managed to crawl free but Colin was trapped. The rally was stopped and Colin was cut out of the car and taken for treatment for facial and head injuries. He was injured but not too seriously, fortunately.

Corsica seemed intimidating, or maybe it was just in the area of Ajaccio, but Greece was very different and our trips there were always interesting. One time we were waiting to board the super-fast ferry from Ancona in Italy to Patras and there was a knock on the coach window. Outside was an Albanian family who wanted to thank us, as British people, for helping them in their troubled country. The father was a teacher and they had fled their country but were now going back; he asked if he could have a Union Jack sticker similar to those on the coach.

The initial stages of the rally required us to travel south of Athens and then move north for the later stages. Unfortunately, to accomplish this, we had to drive around the outskirts of Athens where the traffic was horrendous and it was very easy to get lost. Once several of us ended up at the docks after taking the wrong road and we had to hail a taxi so we could follow him to be shown the correct route. We saw parts of Greece no tourist would ever see and, in later years, when the rally moved away from Athens, we saw even more as the service parks were dust bowls, miles away from anywhere. As we approached one such service park we noticed a car in the spot where we were supposed to park. We pulled alongside and peered through the windscreen, and there was Martin Whitaker fast asleep. Apparently he had flown into Greece overnight, been collected from the airport and brought straight to the service park. The allocated Ford driver from Ford Greece had been confused and thought the rally was starting from there. Martin knew someone would come along eventually and just slept while he waited. When we woke him up the first thing he said was, 'I'd love a cup of tea'; he'd been there for hours.

At another isolated service park inland we found a small shop in a village where the owner spoke some English; he apparently had relatives in London. We bought water and looked around to see what else he had. There were a few chickens but we needed about 20, so we thought that wouldn't work, but he then told us to make a list of what we needed and he would telephone our order through to his cousin who lived two hours away, close to a big town, and could get whatever we needed from the market. The plan was that his cousin would do the shopping, bring it halfway and our friendly shopkeeper would drive out and meet him and collect it for us. We gave it a shot and it worked brilliantly. He probably made more in the five days we were there than in six months looking after his villagers – and if he did, good luck to him.

The return trip from the Greek port was also interesting because we had to keep a watch for Albanians who were intent on stowing away. We actually spotted three climbing under the tarpaulin of Mitsubishi's rally car transporter and felt obliged to tell the driver, despite feeling sorry for them. All they had was a carrier bag with their belongings in it.

One Greek Rally brought an unexpected bonus when a group of us were invited to attend the England versus Greece World Cup match at the Olympic Stadium in Athens as guests of Ford. David Beckham scored a fantastic goal – unfortunately I was looking the other way – but I've seen it on TV many times since.

This mini-tour of some of the memorable places we have visited in support of rallies takes us full circle back to the Antipodes, where we seem to experience more than our fair share of coincidences.

At Rally New Zealand one year the service park was close by Auckland harbour, where a magnificent ocean-going carbon-fibre yacht was moored. During a lull in proceedings Stu and I, together with a bunch of the rally lads, wandered over to take a closer look at the craft because it really was something special. As we stood around in awe a man's head appeared from below decks, followed by a pair of shoulders and shortly afterwards an arm waving us to go closer. We suddenly realised that we knew the chap as someone who was often in the Formula 1 paddock with McLaren, and sometimes came to see us because he knew we were friends of Bob and Shaune. We hadn't seen him for a while and we discovered that he'd undergone an operation for throat cancer, which was the reason he was waving rather than shouting to us. He was as amazed as we were and immediately invited the whole lot of us on board to take a look around; we found that everything below deck was carbon fibre too. Our host was obviously very wealthy and the lads didn't believe that we knew him until he called us by name. It massively increased our street cred.

At the Australian event the whole rally circus had to travel to a small town north-east of Perth and set up on the main street. We parked our hired camper and all our paraphernalia in front of a typical Aussie house with a porch. We were a little concerned that we were stopping the people who lived in the house from leaving if they needed to get out, but it wasn't just us, the whole street was blocked in. I had noticed a lady sitting on the porch watching the antics and later she came over and told us that, if we needed water or to use the outside toilet, to just go in through the gate. A gentleman visiting the house wearing sunglasses and a typical Aussie hat sat watching proceedings as well. After about 15 minutes, when the drivers had been and gone and I was taking it easy, I saw him heading in my direction.

Suddenly he said, 'Have you got a cup of tea, Mum?' I was astonished and thought at first he had heard some of the rally boys referring to me in that way. 'Long time since I've seen you, Mum. How's Dad?' (Stuart had just walked off to the shops.)

'He's fine,' I said, tentatively. The man must have sensed that I was confused so he took off his sunglasses and I recognised him immediately as a chap who used to work for Williams in Formula 1. Amazed, I asked him if he was following the rally and he just said, 'No, I own that house there' – pointing at the house we were parked in front of – 'and I came to collect the rent from the tenant.' We could have parked anywhere along that street but there we were, in a small town on the other side of the world, bumping into someone we knew.

Lots of the Formula 1 lads had formed relationships when they were in Australia which were forgotten the minute they stepped back on the plane, but this one had lasted. He had left the UK, come back to Australia and got married; his wife was the local doctor. Of course I gave him a cup of tea!

Chapter 29

DRIVEN MAD AND DRIVEN OUT

I'm not one to typecast people based on their job, nationality, or anything else for that matter, but I am prepared to make an exception in the case of rally drivers and say that, to a man, they are all crazy. This conclusion is based on my experience of working with quite a few driver and co-driver pairings over our years in rallying (some of which didn't make it through the year). There were French guys, the odd Italian, Scot or Belgian, not to mention quite a few Scandinavians. They might all have been from different countries, cultures, backgrounds and age groups, but they were all certifiably mad.

We had one young Finnish driver, Jari Matti Latvala, who was so young he had to find time to do his homework during the rally. Mikko Hirvonen also arrived as a young gun, and it's interesting to note that the services of both these youngsters were dispensed with and then they were rehired by M-Sport and went on to fight for the World Championship. Rehiring seems to happen a lot in rallying; well, at least at M-Sport.

Our relationships with rally drivers were significantly different from those with the guys in Formula 1, because it was difficult to get close to them. Formula 1 drivers tended to be around the motorhome all weekend, except for the few hours they were on the circuit or in debriefs, whereas rally drivers and co-drivers arrived at the service park as bleary-eyed as the rest of us; sometimes they'd have breakfast and sometimes not, and ten minutes later they would be gone, not to be seen again for several hours. Eventually they coasted back into the service park, the driver in the car and the co-driver on foot, because he had to check in at time control. Then they would have a relaxed chat to the engineers about tyres while the lads worked frantically on the car, have a bite to eat and disappear again. It was difficult to relate all that to the TV images of them flying through the air, driving on the edge of a ravine or plunging through water, usually sideways, and always at high speed. The driver's hands and feet are a blur while the co-driver sits head down, shouting instructions from the recce notes. As someone who finds it difficult to read while a car is in motion I have no idea how the co-driver isn't sick, particularly after he's eaten.

Having said that it's difficult to get close to rally drivers, I certainly got a bit too close to one of them. In 1999 a young driver called Petter Solberg joined the team. He was Norwegian and had come over at Malcolm Wilson's request to learn every aspect of World Rallying. He went to the factory every day and worked on the cars with the lads, as well as doing some testing to improve his skills. On several occasions he travelled to events with us in the coach, helping us out generally by setting up the awning or even washing up. He was a very willing helper and a lovely lad who just wanted to go rallying like his brother, Henning, who was a respected rally driver. As time progressed he was allocated a third car and entered in some rallies, and to help him further he was teamed with a very experienced co-driver, Phil Mills.

Petter's girlfriend Pernilla was also a well-known Swedish rally champion. We became friends with them and were invited to their wedding in Sweden, but we were never as close as we were on one particular day near the M-Sport headquarters in Cumbria.

M-Sport have their own test area in the Cumbrian forest near their base in Cockermouth, where they sometimes incorporated a test with a corporate guest day. These events gave the guests the option of going out in one of the rally cars with whichever driver was testing that day. Some took up the option; others were either too scared or too smart. Each guest who went for a ride had to sign an insurance waiver and that often put people off. The ones who did venture into the car were given a video recording of their adventure.

On the day in question it had started raining and all the guests had left, along with some team members. Stuart had popped into Cockermouth to get something or other. It was then decided to do one or two more runs as a wet-weather test. I was washing up at the time. Martin Whitaker, who had been there all day looking after Ford guests, came to me and said, 'The lads need someone to go out with Petter in the car on one more test run. Would you mind doing it?' For fairly obvious reasons I had never really fancied being a co-driver (or in this case, ballast), but Martin was quite insistent.

'Why don't you go?' I asked, to which he responded, 'I have to leave soon as I am travelling by helicopter and the weather is closing in.' So I was persuaded… Apparently it was me or a sack of potatoes – which didn't do much for my self-esteem – but unfortunately I had used them all up. Abandoning the washing up, I walked nervously to the car and, as I was being strapped in, Petter said, 'Shall we go at the slower guest speed, Mum, or shall we go normally?'

In my naïveté I replied, 'As it's a test we'd better go at what you would call normal.'

'You can talk to me if you want to,' he said, and with that we shot off like a rocket, shingle shooting in every direction. Before we got to the first bend I was convinced I was going to die. Despite the fact the co-driver's seat is so low I could see trees flashing past in a blur and banking ever so close. At one point I attempted to speak, but nothing came out, so I tried to watch his feet, but with the jolting and the speed he was using the pedals they were a blur as well. Eventually we made it back into the service area. I had felt quite secure in the seat, really, but I was very relieved to be back. Then, before we came to a halt, I heard the radio crackle and Petter was told to do one more run. Off we roared again, only this time we seemed to be going even quicker.

I thought, 'This really is it this time.' At one point there was a steep slope downwards, with a bend at the bottom; on the first run it had been very scary. Rally experts say if a driver isn't sideways he's not trying and Petter had been performing his sideways moves all around the test track. As we approached the slope for a second time I sensed that we were going straight and even I knew that, by that point, he should have been sideways for the bend that was coming towards us very quickly. Suddenly the air was full of Norwegian expletives as we careered straight on through a hedge, over a ditch and towards a small tree. Fortunately some of our speed was scrubbed off as we plunged through the undergrowth, but we still glanced off the tree and that turned the car on its side. It all seemed to happen in slow motion (although it certainly wasn't) and, as we finally came to a halt on our side, I found that I was the one against the ground with Petter suspended above me by his safety harness.

'Are you OK, Mum?' he shouted. I told him I wasn't sure, but I thought so.

'I'm dying for a pee!' was his response, and with that he unbuckled his harness, crawled out through his window and disappeared out of sight. I couldn't get out from my position and all I could see was a torrent of liquid. I'm sure it wasn't rain.

The radio had been smashed so Petter said, 'I'll go to get some help,' and he left me there, still buckled into my seat. I could hear the mechanics shouting 'Has Petter passed you yet?' to each other from their positions around the test route. The only other sound was a hissing noise from a damaged hose.

After lying there for a short time I decided that I must still be alive and started to wonder if any bits of me had been displaced. Everything seemed to be where it should be and I wasn't in serious pain so I made up my mind to try to get out of the car.

The safety harness seemed difficult to undo but I managed it eventually and, with a struggle, succeeded in climbing up and out the driver's door, which was up in the air, and then falling out of the car to land in a heap in the mud. I hadn't realised I was quite that agile, but it's amazing what can be done in an emergency. I heard a vehicle in the distance coming towards me and realised that Petter had found the lads and they were all coming to the rescue. They found me standing in the rain, next to the upturned car; they helped me gently into the van and took me back to base, with concerned looks on their faces.

By the time we got back Martin had left, as had most other people, so I assured everyone that I was all right except that I felt a bit stiff and had a sore neck. One of the lads said Stuart had radioed in on his way back from Cockermouth and told them, 'If you're looking for Petter, I can see his car from the road and it's on its side, but he must be OK because the car door's open!' He apparently had quite a shock when he was told, 'Yes, he is – and by the way, Di was in the car.' Stu had no idea that I'd gone rallying and certainly didn't believe it.

Petter was later summoned by Malcolm and accused of showing off, but following an investigation by the mechanics it came to light that the wheel had split after a hard day's running. He wasn't to blame, poor kid. I refused to go to hospital so we started the long drive back to the Midlands in the coach. Halfway home our mobile rang and it was Martin: a very concerned Malcolm had phoned to tell him I had a broken arm and injured leg and it was his fault for making me go in the car. Martin apologised and asked if there was anything he could do. At first I didn't understand what he was on about, until it dawned on me that Malcolm had wound him up. I told him I was OK and he rang off a very relieved man – although he rang me again the next day to make sure. I never got the in-car film, however, as the camera was damaged in the crash.

I hadn't signed the accident waiver, so it was lucky that I hadn't been injured or there would have been serious repercussions. When I had the knee operations which made me miss the Safari Rally in 2003 the specialist attending to me said my cartilage condition was similar to that found in people who had experienced a sudden jolt in a car accident, as both knees were damaged. I told him that I had never had an accident like that, although some time later, during a check-up, I told him that I had remembered that day in the forest a few years earlier.

'That explains it,' he said. 'You don't even have to bang your knees as the sheer force of a collision can tear a cartilage, particularly if you are strapped in.'

Petter left Ford under a bit of a cloud, as Ford and Malcolm had thought he was under contract to the team and he wasn't. He went on to become World Champion with Subaru and now drives for his own team. Good luck to him.

On a less dramatic note, one of our early drivers was Juha Kankkunen, who was a big rally star in Finland. On one particular occasion, when we were testing there, we had to park in a lay-by next to a lake. Testing is pretty informal and we had to pull up where we could, erecting our E-Z ups and getting on with it. There was a camper van parked in the lay-by and the occupants were asleep. All the people involved in the test erected E-Z ups around the camper, as this had been the nominated place to park, although the van's occupants weren't to know this because it was a public parking area. When they woke up they were pretty angry because there was no way they could leave until we had finished testing. However, Juha came back in the rally car and, when the campers saw who it was, all was forgiven. Juha was a nice chap; he signed autographs for them and I made them some tea while they sat happily watching the events of the day.

The driver pairings for 2000 were star drivers who had both been World Champions – Colin McRae, with his co-driver Nicky Grist, and Carlos Sainz with Luis Moya. It was quite a coup for Ford to secure both of them. Although, as I've mentioned, it was difficult to get close to rally drivers, it was easier to develop a rapport with Colin and Nicky because they were both British, although we probably got to know their families better than we knew them.

Colin was extremely talented, if a little crazy. He loved life and extremes and was very popular. Colin's father, Jimmy, came to all the rallies and his mother, Margaret, came occasionally; she always nervously supported her family in everything they did. She had lived her whole life in the rally world, with Jimmy being British champion on several occasions, and now her two sons, Colin and Alister, were competing in World Rally. Alison, Colin's wife, often came along and sometimes brought Holly, their little girl, as well as her own parents. We became part of the 'Scottish squad'. Nicky, on the other hand, was Welsh and a very experienced co-driver with the immense amount of concentration and dedication required to be a successful partner. His wife Sharon, or Shaz, came to every rally, so with all the waiting around the families had to endure it was an opportunity to form friendships. Colin and Nicky had been partners for some time so the families knew each other well.

Jimmy and Margaret also had a younger son, Stuart, who was not involved in rallying. They often talked about him, and worried what he would do with his life. We had met Stuart at a couple of rallies and he seemed quite interested in what we were doing as he was involved in catering. At that time, in addition to our rally commitments, we were operating a contract in Formula 3 and needed a chef, so one day I asked Jimmy, 'Do you think Stuart would be interested in working as a chef on our F3 contract?'

Jimmy seemed happy about it and said he'd have a word, and Stuart jumped at the chance and became one of our contracted employees. Colin sought us out a couple of rallies after Stuart had started working for us and thanked us very much for giving him the job, saying he really enjoyed it. That conversation seemed to break the ice with Colin who, strangely enough, seemed a little shy. Nicky was very friendly from the start and we formed a firm friendship with him and 'Shaz'.

In the rally world drivers can have a major accident at any time, whether due to driver error, mechanical failure or a wrong call from a co-driver. Colin and Nicky had quite a few major accidents in their time together, and every time the news crackled in over the radio our hearts would sink; all we could do was hope it wasn't serious. Rally cars, like Formula 1 cars, are very safe, but when some cars get back to the service park after an accident we often wondered how anyone got out uninjured. My experience with Petter gave me a clue.

Colin and Nicky stayed together until a misunderstanding between them in Rally New Zealand caused an accident and Colin dispensed with Nicky's services right there and then. Nicky came and sat with us in the hotel that night. Looking desperate, he quietly told us he'd been fired. It was one of those times when we felt he needed someone to talk to, and he chose us as people who were interested but impartial listeners. Nicky left the country as quickly as he could. Colin stayed with Ford until the end of 2002 when he joined Citroën. He eventually recalled Nicky and they made peace, bringing a pairing back together that should never have been separated. Colin and Nicky went on to feature in computer games for 'Codemasters' and on one early sleeve Stu and I were thanked for just being around.

Carlos Sainz was a different character altogether. He was a very experienced rally driver, a hero in Spain and a big Real Madrid supporter. Carlos could be quite aloof and at times abrupt and demanding; he had eyes that made ladies melt but often a slightly arrogant way about him. Within rally circles he was known as 'the King of Spain' and the Spanish paparazzi followed him everywhere. Carlos sometimes seemed quite unapproachable, even when all we wanted to ask him was what he'd like to eat, but when he smiled his whole demeanour changed. On one rally he upset the team because he hadn't obeyed team instructions, and he was given the cold shoulder when he arrived back in the service park. I felt sorry for him and went to ask if he needed anything. He seemed quite surprised and became quite chatty. I actually found him charming and was surprised he knew my name, as up until then we hadn't had any real conversations.

His co-driver, fellow Spaniard Luis Moya, was absolutely crazy, totally outgoing and very different from Carlos; they had been together for a few years, previously driving for Toyota, and they complemented each other really well, although Luis was easier to chat to. We didn't have quite the same rapport with the Spanish pairing and their crews, who were known as Juan A and Juan B, as we did with Colin and Nicky's group, but nevertheless it was an experience working with such professionals.

Markko Märtin, an Estonian, and Michael ('Beef') Park joined Ford in 2002; Beef knew Colin and Nicky well, so there was a nice atmosphere around the motorhome. Markko was quite a character, although he had strange eating habits – well, strange to us, but perhaps quite normal in Estonia. For breakfast he always had two hard fried eggs and two large gherkins, and this would often be repeated for lunch and again at dinner. He had a group of very patriotic supporters who followed him from rally to rally, singing their national anthem and waving the national flag because they were so proud of their countryman. When Markko won a rally in Finland, unbeknown to anyone, the prime minister of Estonia chose to fly in by helicopter to share in the celebrations. He arrived at the motorhome with a small entourage and draped himself in the national flag before going to the podium to congratulate Markko. I offered him a drink afterwards and he chose orange juice, which was tasted by a minder before he would drink it. It's a good job there were no bath salts in it. Unfortunately the visit caused an international incident as he arrived unannounced and hadn't been welcomed by the Finnish prime minister.

Beef was a quietly-spoken chap from Gloucestershire and, despite his nickname, quite small in stature; he was friendly and very easy company. He wasn't one for formality or sponsors' dinners and often asked us what we were doing in the evenings. Whenever possible Jamie, Pete, Stuart and I ate with him. Beef was very easy to please foodwise, just enjoying plain cooking and tea. He and Markko got along well, but as Markko often had friends with him they didn't spend much leisure time together. Markko was also known to like a good night out with the lads and often brought his mates from his home town to a rally with him; they were a good bunch, just enjoying themselves and their mate's success.

Rally drivers were more likely to be friends with each other than Formula 1 drivers are, and a lot of friendly banter would go on between them while they waited around at time checks. One friendly rival was Richard Burns, who was driving for Subaru with a friend and fellow Scot of Colin's, Robert Reid, as his co-driver. Richard and Robert often stopped and ate with our drivers on the recce. During 2003 Richard was taken ill while giving Markko Märtin a lift to Rally GB in his private car. Richard pulled over on the hard shoulder and apparently said he felt strange. Markko wasn't familiar with our road network and was unsure where they were or what to do, so he phoned the team for help. A rescue operation was soon under way and Richard was taken to hospital for tests, where he was diagnosed with some form of brain tumour. That was his last year in World Rally and after a long and painful battle he finally succumbed to the tumour in 2005.

At the end of 2003 Ford imposed budgetary restrictions and reduced their commitment to developing hospitality in rallying. Although they have continued to be very successful in the WRC it was without the help of either Martin Whitaker or us. Martin returned to the world of Formula 1 when Bernie asked him to help set up the Bahrain circuit; he lived in Bahrain with his family for seven years before moving to Australia to become CEO of the Australian V8 Supercar series.

Malcolm Wilson decided to take the Ford rally hospitality

operation 'in house', using staff he already had within his company. We had been contracted to Ford so he had no responsibilities towards us. He thanked us for our time and effort and said he realised we had done far more work than was originally intended, which was nice of him, but it didn't help to cushion the blow of having five vehicles that had been flat out supporting WRC now surplus to requirements. Through 2004 we moved over to personally supervise the contract with Inmarsat, but it was on a completely different scale from what we had been used to at Ford; Inmarsat were series organisers, not a team, and they only really needed our articulated hospitality truck. All the rest of the equipment we had bought to support the Ford WRC programme was left standing idle. The problem grew when Inmarsat announced that they would be withdrawing their sponsorship from the end of the 2004 season. At their final rally the company sent us up in a helicopter on the last day to watch the closing stages, which was a fine gesture and a fitting finale to our time in WRC.

Gruelling as it was, the opportunity to visit areas of the world we would never otherwise have seen – some beautiful villages in Portugal and Spain, Scandinavian forests, the Corinth canal, and all manner of places where the roads were unsuitable for large vehicles – made rallying exciting and very different from pulling off the motorway into a Formula 1 paddock. However, there is a dark side to rallying and injury is never far away.

Beef was killed instantly on 18 September 2005 during Rally GB when the car Markko was driving hit a tree. We attended his funeral in Ledbury, along with Pete and Jamie; it was a very sad day. Photos of Beef were shown on a big screen and it felt as though he was in the congregation with us, but the most poignant moment was when Markko came into the church arm in arm with Beef's wife, followed by his two children. He was buried to one of his favourite songs by The Jam, 'Going Underground', which said everything there was to say about Beef.

Markko virtually withdrew from the rally world after that. Beef's family didn't blame him at all; they knew it was the risk involved in going rallying. Quite a few World Champions were at the funeral, as were most of the people who had been connected with Ford over the years. Despite the circumstances it was good to catch up with rallying people and we chatted to Colin and caught up on his news.

Colin was killed, together with his five-year-old son Johnny, Johnny's six-year-old friend and one of Colin's friends, when he crashed while trying to land his helicopter near his home on 15 September 2007. The accident shocked the rally world, and Colin is sorely missed by everyone who ever met him. We are proud that we had the pleasure of working with him.

So there lies the difference between rallying and Formula 1. I think that, given the challenges, rally drivers are the more skilful but, on balance, I preferred Formula 1. Most importantly, I am delighted we had the opportunity to compare the two. For us it was back to worrying about what the future held. Was retirement looming?

Not yet!

Chapter 30

JOHNNY HERBERT

When we saw Johnny Herbert at Silverstone in July 1988 he had just signed his first Formula 1 contract with Benetton. Peter Collins was in charge of the Benetton team at that time and he was a big fan of Johnny's. Johnny came bounding up the steps into the large office space at the rear of the motorhome, all blond and pink, and looking for Peter. We knew then he was going to be trouble because he had lost his car keys in the mud somewhere, as mentioned earlier. Stuart said Johnny was so baby-faced that, unless you knew him, you wouldn't put him in charge of a tricycle. Fortunately we did know him.

We got to know Johnny socially originally because he lived quite locally, and then professionally when he started driving for Eddie Jordan's junior team. Johnny, Becky and the family were living in rented accommodation close to where we lived because, although Johnny was an Essex lad, Becky came from the Sutton Coldfield area and wanted to be closer to her parents as John was spending so much time away. They had asked us what would be a nice area near to Birmingham and we helped them to find a rented place quite close by. We used to go round to their house, sometimes for a social evening and sometimes we were on babysitting duty looking after their daughters, Chloe and Aimelia.

An earlier chapter described the aftermath of Johnny's big accident in September 1988 and the subsequent test in Brazil. He drove through a pain barrier that most of us couldn't stand for a second, but he was able to take his place with Benetton due to his heroics at that test and the faith Peter Collins showed in him. He really shouldn't have been driving, but it was his big chance and he was determined to grab it with both hands. Unfortunately he was in permanent pain and he introduced us to Nurofen, which was not freely available in England at that time. He got them from somewhere, however, and was taking them in massive numbers, which wasn't really sustainable.

Although we were a generation apart we became firm friends; he seemed to like having us around. A lot of his cockiness was (and is) just a front. When we first got to know him he was quite shy and I think he developed that outward bravado to cover up his shyness; after his accident it was to cover up the pain he was suffering, because he didn't want anyone to be aware of just how bad it was. Unfortunately his happy-go-lucky persona rubbed Flavio up the wrong way and got him into trouble on a number of occasions. Flavio insisted he become more serious, telling him that he would never succeed in Formula 1 if he didn't. Johnny had worked hard at presenting his carefree exterior and it was difficult to switch it off in public, although he changed as soon as he came into the motorhome and could be himself. Over that first six months he was at Benetton the pain slowly changed him; I don't know how he even drove the car. He was also worn out because he couldn't sleep with the discomfort.

Johnny came back into Formula 1 after he was rested by Benetton in 1989, but his career thereafter was a bit chequered, moving from one team to another. He always came to see us, though, whoever he was driving for. John was with Lotus in the early 1990s, when Peter Collins was there, and he used to come and eat with us at the track. He would bring Mika Häkkinen with him, who at that time was quite shy. There was no money around at Lotus then and Johnny and Mika had to share a room when they were travelling. Johnny used to tell us that Mika wouldn't go down to the restaurant for breakfast or dinner without him because he was too shy; talk about opposites attracting. He may have been shy but Mika seemed to relax at our motorhome without too much trouble.

Things looked up for Johnny when he got the drive with Benetton for 1994 and 1995, and he stayed with Benetton when we left to go to Ford. When she came to the track Becky always spent her time with us in the Ford motorhome rather than at Benetton and there was a particularly memorable incident at the 1995 British Grand Prix. Michael Schumacher was leading Damon Hill in the race when Damon tried to overtake Michael, trying to keep the racing line, turned into him and they both ended up in the gravel trap. Now where have we heard of that kind of thing happening before? Johnny inherited the race lead, closely followed by David Coulthard, and they almost came together when David tried to overtake Johnny at the same corner where Michael and Damon had crashed. David had to serve a stop-go penalty that left Johnny with a clear lead, and a win if he could make it to the finish.

Becky was in our motorhome as the race ran towards its climax. None of us could watch as Johnny nursed the car home, and we were in tears as the chequered flag came out. Becky was interviewed immediately after the race had ended and she was asked where she had watched the race. Quick as a flash she said, 'With Mum and Dad of course!'

The perplexed interviewer then asked, 'Where were Mum and Dad, then?'

'At Ford, as usual,' she responded, which caused a great deal of confusion in the press.

Johnny dedicated his win to Becky and said she had 'supported him throughout his career, particularly through some difficult times since his crash in 1988'. As for Stu and I – well, his real mum and dad couldn't have been more proud.

John and Becky always lived relatively close to us during his early Formula 1 career and we have so many happy memories of spending time with the family, both at home and at the racetrack. I particularly recall Becky and the girls visiting Spa while Johnny was driving for Sauber. Becky went off to the pits and the girls were watching the start of the race on TV with us in the motorhome. Aimelia was on my knee and Chloe by my side as the race got under way and there was a huge pile-up at the hairpin immediately after the start, with cars cannoning into each other and wreckage everywhere. Chloe spotted her dad's car and said, 'That's dad's car. Is he all right?' I was concerned and at an immediate loss as to what to say, but we saw Johnny extricating himself from the broken chassis and start plodding up the hill, which was quite difficult for him as his feet were, even then, a long way from perfect. Being so close to a driver is great but it has its downsides; I just don't know what I would have said to the girls if he had been injured.

We stopped being close, geographically at least, when, in common with most drivers at the time, the family moved to Monaco as Johnny's career progressed. The Herberts made the commitment to live in Monaco as a family, with the girls attending the International School, unlike a number of other drivers who just took a small studio for tax purposes and never actually lived in the principality. The rules are tighter now.

Stu and I spend time in France when we can, in an area we became very familiar with – a number of us motorhomers used to park our American motorhomes on a campsite at a place called La Napoule. Over the years, while in the area, which is less than an hour from Monaco, we have visited quite a few drivers in their apartments, so of course we used to visit Johnny and Becky frequently.

On one of our Monaco get-togethers, when Johnny was driving for Sauber, Becky asked me if I would be godmother to the girls. I thought about it and said, 'I'm sorry Becky, I can't do it because I am not religious in any way.' She told me that she wasn't really either, but they would be moving back to England and when they were settled they would like the girls to be christened.

'Where are you going to get them christened, Becky?' I asked. 'Apparently it's not quite that simple.' She said she had an idea, but nothing was finalised at that point. Thinking it was another Herbert flash in the pan, I forgot all about it.

Becky and the girls came back to England before Johnny, and we then probably saw more of him in France than we did in England. He had a life in England but he was quite lonely in France. We still kept a washbag for him at the place where we stayed, because when he arrived in France he sometimes dropped in unexpectedly. Often we would arrive back from a shopping trip, or even arrive in France from England, and find Johnny sitting by the pool in a deckchair waiting for the 'motorhome' to open.

Eventually the whole family did move back to our local area and later that summer Becky announced, 'The christening is booked so you must be there.'

I was shocked and told her, 'Becky, I can't be a godparent. You know that if anything happened to you and the girls were still young we would look after them, but I can't stand up in a church and say all those words. I'd feel like a hypocrite.'

'It's all right,' she said. 'I've had a word with the vicar, and you can be a guardian.'

So it was arranged that we would go to the church near her gran's in one of the Birmingham suburbs. Apparently there wasn't much parking close to the church, so it was decided that Becky would travel with the girls and pick up her gran and John would pick us up. He turned up an hour late as he hadn't been able to find his car keys (there is a pattern forming here); also the church was an hour's drive away, we were supposed to arrive by 3pm and it was already 2.30pm; and the plan had plainly gone wrong completely because Becky was in the car, as were the girls. We decided we needed to get our car out and were in the process of sorting that when Becky said, 'Do you know, I can't remember where the church is.'

I realised this was turning into a typical Johnny saga and said to Becky, 'What's the name of the church?' I knew what was coming next.

'I haven't got it with me; all I can remember is going to Sunday school there all those years ago.' She had met the vicar to discuss the christening at her gran's house and she knew the church was somewhere nearby. And so we set off, with them in front and us following. The next thing that happened was that they pulled into the side of the road because they were running out of fuel, so we had to set off and get some to bring back to their stricken car; at this stage we were already late for the christening and we were only halfway there.

Eventually we arrived at the church and, as it was a perfect summer's day, everyone was waiting outside. The word had obviously got out that Johnny Herbert was going to be there and suspicion fell on a proud gran, who had been collected by Becky's sister Michelle. Michelle was going to be a godmother and Allard Kalff, who was a Dutch Sky TV presenter and sometime driver, would be a godfather; and then there were Stu and me.

In we went. I didn't feel too bad as it was a pretty modern church, but I had to sit near the front while the vicar was saying his piece. Becky, Johnny and the girls were in the front pew and Michelle, Allard and me in the one behind, which was reserved for godparents. Stuart was sitting there too, because Becky had told him to sit next to me in case I felt uncomfortable. When the vicar got to the bit where he said, 'Would the godparents stand up, including the one we won't call a godparent,' the three of us stood but Stuart remained seated.

Becky turned to him and said urgently, 'Stuart, stand up!' to which he replied, 'Well, I'm not a godfather.' This discussion was going on in the middle of the service. A horrified Stuart looked at Becky and blurted out, 'You never told me,' at which point Johnny turned round and said, 'Well, we wouldn't have Di without you, would we?'

Throughout this exchange the rest of the congregation was watching the conversation go back and forth like a Wimbledon rally. In the end Stuart stood up and suddenly he was a godfather. Despite my reservations the ceremony was very moving, and at the end of it we all had to go into the vestry to be given godparent certificates – well, all except me, of course. If anyone had ever told us in our early days, when all we'd wanted to do was go racing, that we were going to be godparents to a Formula 1 driver's children we would have had them certified. And now Stuart was certified.

Having been close to a number of racing drivers' lives we are always astonished by the contrast between their public life and their private life. One example occurred during British Grand Prix week, before Johnny and Becky had returned to live in the UK. Johnny would shun staying at posh hotels, choosing to stay the early part of the week at his gran's or with us. On one occasion we returned from Silverstone, where we had been setting up, to find that Johnny had let himself into the house and taken himself off to bed, as he felt under the weather. We hadn't noticed his car parked down the road and had been home for about an hour when we heard the lavatory flush – we looked at each other thinking we had imagined it. Then we heard a little voice saying 'I'm not very well', and there he was tucked up in our spare bed! The next day we took him to Silverstone, where he was much better!

In the next chapter I'll describe the fans at Le Mans chanting for Johnny until he eventually realised they were chanting for him and went out to see them. On the other side of the coin, only the other evening I was in Morrisons supermarket and Johnny was also there, doing the family shopping. We had a chat and went to different tills, and then I heard this man behind me saying to his son, who was about 14, 'That's Johnny Herbert over there, standing by the till.'

His lad looked at him oddly and replied, 'Johnny Herbert, the racing driver?'

'Yes, I think he lives around here somewhere.'

'Oh Dad, don't be stupid,' the lad said, plainly unconvinced.

I just wanted to turn round and put him right, but I held my tongue. It's sometimes easy to forget that extraordinary people still do ordinary things – and in their house John does the shopping. Why shouldn't he?

Whenever we have been in each other's company and Stuart has gone to the bar, someone will inevitably ask: 'Is that Johnny Herbert?' Oddly, however, although we have been out together often, there have only been a couple of times when people have come up and asked for his autograph. Most people are polite enough not to bother him. That's one of the reasons lots of drivers like to live in Monaco – no one bothers them because well-known people are ten a penny. The tax situation isn't bad either.

Ever since 1998 Johnny has organised a charity karting event in November each year and he loves to get in there and race; particularly against the kids, because, after all, he is still a big kid himself. Johnny has never been particularly good on the formal side of self-promotion and to an extent that reticence has hampered some opportunities throughout his career. Although he has been loved by thousands over the years, he has not always had the backing of the big corporations. I am amazed that John isn't on TV more often, promoting the sport, as his personality would make him a firm favourite with the viewing public. Maybe he isn't such a good public speaker as David Coulthard or Martin Brundle, but he is terrific fun.

Perhaps it's not surprising that the big corporations haven't appreciated Johnny because it's only in the last few years that his daughters have really recognised what he's achieved. They were too young, really; they knew he was a driver, but that was it. At Silverstone in 2007, when Stu and I were getting ready to do the catering for the evening rock concert, Chloe and Aimelia were around with their boyfriends. During a break I was standing on an embankment with Chloe, watching the start of the Formula 1 race. As the cars went past she looked at me in amazement and said, 'Did Dad used to go that fast?' Her eyes were almost standing out on stalks.

I said, 'Yes, of course he did.'

She looked at me and admitted, 'You know, I never really appreciated what he did.'

The girls didn't see their dad in that light; he was just their dad. I sometimes think that perhaps even Johnny didn't understand it either. With the accident and all the time and effort he went through to make his mark, he almost has the mindset that the success happened to someone else and not to him. As an example of this, I told his girls about one day when we were down at their house and Johnny was sorting his crash helmets out from his cabinet. He pulled three out and then picked one of those up, saying, 'I'm going to give Allard this one.'

I said to him, 'John, if I remember correctly, weren't those three helmets the ones you were wearing when you won your three Formula 1 races? I really don't think you should give those away, they are very special.' I felt that one day the girls might marry and have children and he should keep them in the family. It was typical of him; he never thought things through like that and was a bit impulsive. He had lots of other helmets he could give away, which would have been equally well received. He keeps promising us one, but he hasn't got round to it yet!

We have stayed friends with Johnny and Becky through all the good times and the bad times we've experienced in our careers in racing. We have been on holiday together and we've stayed with them at their place in Monaco. We have had some special times and we feel part of his extended family, although we would never try to compete with his real mum and dad, Jane and Bob, who did so much to help him develop his career. I still feel I should take him under my wing sometimes, when he goes off on one of his tangents.

When Johnny won the European Grand Prix at the Nürburgring for Stewart GP in September 1999 it was a very special moment for us in lots of respects. Johnny had had a pretty torrid season up to that point and he had qualified badly for this race too, starting in 14th. Fortunately for him there were a number of problems in store for the early leaders and Johnny managed to work his way up the field. When he was due to come in for tyres he saw a big black cloud in the distance and decided the circuit was in for some pretty wet weather, so he called his pit and told them to get the rain tyres out. It was a race-winning call, because when the rain arrived the rest of the runners were on the grooved dry-weather tyres that were in use at the time and Johnny was on wets. He had guessed, and he had guessed correctly. He said at the time, 'Sometimes you have to be lucky, but you have to make your own luck, and we made all the right decisions.'

Once again we were delighted for him, but as the team celebrated into the night we weren't to know that it would be Johnny's last Formula 1 win and our last Formula 1 event. What a high to finish on, though.

Chapter 31

LE MANS – IS IT ONLY 24 HOURS?

We thought we had seen all that racing could offer after all those years in Formula 1 and World Rally, not to mention the junior series we had covered in our early days. We had even had a stint in powerboat racing. Nothing we had ever done before, however, prepared us for the Le Mans 24-hour event.

At the end of 2002 we were approached by Kaye Wilson, who has her own marketing company based in Windsor. She was the press and PR person for the American Champion ADT team, which was racing in the American Le Mans Series, or ALMS. The actual Le Mans 24-hour race wasn't part of the ALMS championship season, but all the teams wanted to take part. Kaye travelled backwards and forwards to the States to look after the team's representation at the races over there, and then when she was back in Europe she was responsible for the logistics of the Le Mans trip, which was quite an undertaking. Kaye thought we might be interested in working with the team at Le Mans and tracked us down through Johnny Herbert, who was racing in ALMS at the time. We had met her before but she had lost touch with us after we left Formula 1.

ADT was owned by Dave Maraj, who was the biggest Porsche and Audi dealer in America. He wanted a more

European feel to the team, and he particularly wanted something to stand out from all the big American motorhomes in the paddock which, despite their size, had kitchens which were far too small to cater for large numbers of guests. Most teams therefore had to have their food bought in from outside caterers or they used a central catering facility in the paddock. Dave liked the idea of using a 'coach' with an awning where he could have food prepared by his own people to suit himself and the team. Johnny Herbert was driving for ADT and, during a chat with Kaye, he suggested she contact Stuart to see what was available on the market.

Johnny was aware that the Arrows Formula 1 team had failed during 2002 and was being liquidated. All their equipment was due to be sold off to recover as much money as possible to appease the team's creditors. Johnny knew that Stuart had previously organised for a Van Hool coach to be supplied on a lease to Arrows, which was then owned by Tom Walkinshaw; it was stored in one of Tom's facilities near Bedford and was due to be handed over to the receiver. Jan Van Hool clearly took a dim view of the possibility of losing his property and contacted Stuart to ask him to retrieve any leased Van Hool equipment to avoid it being sold off to cover the team's debts. Without going into too much detail as to what happened next, we basically took the coach to a storage barn near our house. Jan was pretty happy about this development and asked us to find customers for the equipment on his behalf.

We arranged to meet up with Kaye at the *Autosport* show in January 2003 and she had the ADT team manager, Brad Kettler, with her. The idea was to go from there to take a look at the vehicle. Brad was a bit nonplussed when we got there, as all he could see was a bus. It was a stretch for him to imagine the coach in all its glory, with the awnings out and people enjoying all the hospitality on offer, when he was in a barn in Warwickshire on a cold, foggy January day, but he managed it somehow and Mr Maraj bought the coach along with two race trucks. What happened next was the kind of thing that only happens in racing. The coach was shipped to the States with a 240-volt electrical system and had to be completely rewired over there. Perhaps that doesn't seem too odd, but hold that thought. The coach then spent the 2003 ALMS season travelling backwards and forwards across the USA on hospitality duties.

Kaye asked us if we could provide the catering for the 2003 Le Mans 24-hour endurance race with our own large truck, but unfortunately our rally commitments didn't allow us to take her up on the offer. We were pretty intrigued, though, and we arranged to stay in touch. Just before the 2004 season started Kaye called again to tell us that ADT were going to ship a coach back to Europe for Le Mans, and she asked if we would provide the hospitality and back up their coach with our small kitchen truck. We found that, with a bit of juggling, we could fit Le Mans between our rally events. In those days there was testing in early April for the 24-hour event and that fell between Rally New Zealand and the Cyprus Rally, but the Greek Rally was the week before Le Mans so we wouldn't be able to get to France until the Monday before the race – which was too late, really. We struck a good old British compromise, agreeing to cover the test and the race and promising we would send a very capable replacement to provide the hospitality during the pre-race weekend period, until we arrived. We were confident that Gary Timms, who'd worked for us on previous motorsport projects, would be able to manage just fine with the help of three staff.

It all looked a bit hectic but, having got the timing sorted out, we had to get down to the operating details – and that's when the second part of the coach electricity saga unfolded. Needless to say, when the coach was shipped back to Le Mans the electrics weren't compatible with the European power supply, having previously been modified to US standard; we had to re-equip the unit with generators so we could use it in France. After the race the generators were jettisoned and the coach was shipped back to the States. To add a little extra pressure on the budget, a second awning had to be manufactured to fit the coach. We were beginning to think this was a 'money no object' effort.

We should have had some inkling by this stage that Le Mans was not going to be any ordinary race, but fortunately Kaye was one of the best organisers to be found anywhere. When we realised what an intricate logistical nightmare it was, we had no idea how she managed it. Before we arrived at Le Mans we had, just like everyone else who hasn't worked there, some really glamorous ideas as to what the event entailed. The truth is a little different, and the whole thing nearly killed us. The timescale has changed now, but in 2004/5 the whole thing seemed to take forever with testing, day qualifying, testing and night qualifying, testing … and then it all starts again, so everyone is totally exhausted by the time the race actually starts.

We had the most fantastic set-up. When we arrived for the test we found the team were constructing the awning and flooring and it was a hive of activity; we were amazed because we had always had to struggle through, erecting all that stuff ourselves, in every other formula we had been in. Additional awnings were fitted on to the back and the front of the coach and a small hospitality area was placed to the rear of the coach because we didn't just have the drivers, their families and the team to cater for – there were lots of guests as well, particularly from Germany. The team were allocated one side of the hospitality area and the guests the other.

When we were introduced to the team we found they were quite a mixed bag, drawn mainly from the ALMS team and supplemented by contractors. A lot of them were American, but not all. There was a Haitian guy called Jackie, who conferred on himself the brilliant title of 'Head of Detail'. He worked in the showroom over in the States, but here he was basically a gopher and he cleaned and tidied things up. Some of the contractors were English, and some were Austrians; one or two of the guys had obviously had a bit of a chequered past and remained pretty quiet. Another chap who had worked for BAR had somehow managed to get an American visa and had gone to work as a truckie over in the States. Just at the point when we thought we understood who everyone was, several Germans arrived from Audi. It was a magnificent experience looking after so many different nationalities and stood us in good stead for some of our future contracts but, most importantly, it was a good introduction to the diversity of the world of Le Mans. We thought we were looking after an awful lot of people during the testing period until we were warned that the numbers would double for the race weekend!

If Jackie was Head of Detail then I guess I was Head of Laundry. The whole rear awning was used as a storage and laundry area, and with three drivers there was a never-ending supply of dirty kit. I had to do all the laundry myself, and I had two washing machines and two driers going continuously in a space which also accommodated two large fridges and a clothes hanging area. The weather was incredibly hot and the cars were hot and enclosed so the drivers were coming in to get changed as fast as I could wash and dry their kit. That was one trip when I didn't just make the tea. The back of the coach was like a Chinese laundry, with overalls and all the paraphernalia hanging everywhere. The only relief I got from laundry duty was when we were in Greece and Gary had to become the laundryman. He became affectionately known as 'Fluff and Fold'. He later regretted his kind offer of becoming my understudy, as he seemed to have made a rod for his own back.

We were at the test for about 12 days and, despite the workload, it all went smoothly on and off the track. At the end of the test everything was secured in the paddock until everyone came back in June to take up where they had left off.

The lads went back to America and various points in Europe, and we went off to Greece for the World Rally.

When we got back to Le Mans the Monday before the race weekend, as planned, the pace had really speeded up and we were plunged into the surreal world of endurance racing, a completely new experience. We were off to a good start, though, because, as expected, Gary together with Sophie, who had also been a chef in Formula 1, and hostess Gerry, who had worked at Prodrive and Subaru in WRC, had done a fine job holding the fort in our absence and they'd got the internal layout of the coach spot on. We were expected to cater for around 100 people at each meal prior to the actual race weekend, when it was planned to grow to around 150. To supplement the facilities in the coach we had sent our 7.5-ton kitchen truck over and Gary had set it up adjacent to the coach, with a small garden area at the rear. We really needed every inch of space as the number of people around the team grew as each day passed. We had two chefs at the track, but they struggled to feed those masses of people each day, particularly as the whole thing was very multicultural and stretched their culinary imagination. To compound the problem, we had lots of people turn up from other teams.

The drivers in 2004 were JJ Lehto, Marco Werner and Emanuele Pirro. We had worked with both JJ and 'Manwelli' at Benetton so it was quite a reunion, with Manwelli bouncing into the canopy saying, 'Hello Mum! Where's Dad?' JJ just said, 'Can I have a cup of tea?' Johnny Herbert and Allan McNish were both driving for Audi Sport UK Team Veloqx, but they were very frequent visitors for meals and cups of tea and, as word quickly got around, whenever the drivers were all off duty for a while they all used to descend on our garden. At one time we had nine drivers from Formula 1 and similar high-profile series all sitting around and calling us Mum and Dad; even Colin McRae, our Ford rally driver, was there contesting Le Mans for the first time in a Prodrive Ferrari. Johnny, JJ,

David Brabham, Emanuele Pirro, Marco Werner, Alex Caffi, Tom Kristensen and even Oliver Gavin, who we knew from when he won the British Formula 3 Championship (we had also been at his wedding), were all just hanging out together. They were all very friendly and there was lots of banter – it was really nice to see them laughing and joking and taking the mickey out of each other, unlike the way drivers isolate themselves in Formula 1 these days.

We were delighted that Johnny was about at the circuit, as he was such an asset to the paddock, but he always needed someone around who was friends with him for himself, rather than for being a well-known racing driver. I guess we fitted the bill, but we fitted it to such an extent that we used to forget he was famous, so it came as something of a shock when all the fans began chanting his name. At one point we were in the motorhome and there was this large group outside – they had been standing around for ages – and eventually I went into the coach and told him that he really should go out and talk to them, or at least give them a wave. There must have been at least 50 of them, chanting 'Johnny! Johnny!' and when he finally realised they were chanting for him he quickly went out and spoke to lots of them. It made their day.

Our Greek trip didn't cause us to miss the downside of qualifying; we were back in time. The daytime qualifying process was tolerable, but the night qualifying was a nightmare. It didn't finish until after midnight and it would be followed by endless debriefs before everyone finally came to the coach to eat dinner, which made for some pretty late nights. By the Friday everyone was already feeling pretty shattered and the race hadn't even started, but there was a bit of light relief when all the cars went into Le Mans for the grand parade of entrants. In addition to all our guests, extra drivers and the odd unexpected last-minute arrival, we had also been the headquarters all week for the US-based Speed TV channel broadcasters and, needless to say, just like all our other guests, their numbers swelled for the weekend. In fairness they were very appreciative of everything we did for them, but the hospitality numbers were getting out of hand. By Saturday lunchtime, just before the race started, we were on a shift system for guests who seemed to emerge out of the woodwork.

The actual Le Mans organisation was mind blowing. By the time the race began we had learned that it might have been called the Le Mans 24-hour race but, for the people who work there, it was more like 48 hours. We had to get up at 5.30am on race Saturday and it was clear that no one would get to bed much before 11pm on the Sunday!

Finally, at 3pm on Saturday 12 June, the race actually started.

All the previous week we had been operating a pit service, running food and drink to the garage to keep the team going, and this in itself had fully occupied one staff member. When the race got under way this wasn't sufficient, so we had to set up a mini-kitchen area in the garage to make sure hot and cold food was available at all times during the race. Unfortunately, due to the size of the team and the inevitable guests appearing in the garage at all times, the food disappeared as quickly as it was made. The weather had been incredibly hot all week and even in the late evening it was stifling; we were only just able to keep up with the demand for cold water and other drinks. By about 10pm increasing tiredness was sapping our strength. The team had chairs in the garage where they took turns to doze off until there was a pit stop or driver change. Guests were either in the suite above the pits or in the awning, trying to pretend they were awake, and despite incessant coffee consumption they still looked pretty sleepy to me.

I've never wanted any team we have worked with to break down, but on that Saturday evening I was so tired I just thought, 'If you're going to break down, would you mind doing it before midnight instead of two or three o'clock in the morning, so we can go to bed?' It was a strange feeling. We were very busy all the time as we were working with one of the top teams; it was a massive experience, but very wearing.

With each pit stop there was a real flurry of activity followed by a slight lull, which let us get our second wind. We had brought chairs so we could take it in turns to have a nap, but that's not too easy with those noisy beasts droning around. As it was the first time we were there I thought, 'I'll go and sit in the grandstand to sample the atmosphere.' It's supposed to be a memorable experience, watching from there in the dead of night. Dead was the word – only me and about 20 other sad souls sitting there. By midnight the grandstands were empty, but the funfair with the big wheel and the bungee jumping was going full tilt, as was all the other stuff that goes on around the race, but nobody was watching the cars. I was trying to stay awake but it was so boring it was sending me to sleep, so I just went back to the paddock and waited for the next burst of activity.

I sat down, feeling dazed, but fortunately another couple who ran the hospitality for Pacific Grand Prix in Formula 1 were parked close by, so Stu and I joined them. By 4am we were practically suicidal, just talking about anything that came into our heads to keep awake. By about 5am, when the cars were still going round and the sun was coming up, I thought, 'I am so tired I have no idea how I'm going to get through the day.'

The drivers changed periodically during the night, and they were just as shattered as we were. They would finish their stint, come into the motor coach and strip off and I would have fresh overalls ready for them. They used to ask for strange things to eat in the middle of the night, just to keep them going. We had made a pavlova for lunch and JJ Lehto said to us, 'Keep me some of that. I'll have it about two o'clock in the morning' – because he wanted the sugar content to keep him going. Allan McNish just wanted to drink tea. Johnny Herbert used to ask for chocolate and pasta (not together) and Manwelli had salty pasta at some Godforsaken hour. We never knew what would take the drivers' fancy next, so we had to have all sorts of combinations available just in case.

By dawn we began to get our second wind in the sure and certain knowledge that the race would finish later that day, and by that time we had gone past the stage of hoping the cars would stop. We wanted our cars to finish after all the effort everyone had put into the event. Slowly the realisation that 3pm was still a long way away crept up on me and I began to feel tired again. The advantage we hospitality staff had over some of the team was that we could pop back to the hotel in rotation, as it was so close, to take a shower and freshen up. The only problem was that we daren't sit on the bed or it would have been all over. The lads in the garage were looking totally shattered, and although they had dozed where possible there is no substitute for a bed.

Sunday saw a constant flow of people coming through the awning and food being churned out as incessantly as it had been all week. I was so proud of our workforce of Gary, Gerry, Alan (known as 'Global' because he had worked everywhere), Claire and Sophie as they deserved a medal, but the trophy went to ADT for coming home third. Mr Maraj and the team were all very appreciative and thanked us for our efforts in keeping them all going. He said he hoped to see us in 2005, but we were far from sure he would see us again.

That first time we worked at the race there were eight of us and we'd really needed 12. I thought that if we ever did it again we would have someone who never actually came into the circuit but just stayed outside, doing the shopping. The idea would be that they would come to the outside gate and we would meet them there, because the amount of food we had to have for the month was just phenomenal and the logistics of getting in and out of the facility were an absolute nightmare. Just like all the rest of the teams we did a deal with the 'Metro' cash-and-carry warehouse. We were able to order stuff by phone but getting out, collecting it and then coming back into the circuit past very officious gatemen was a hopeless waste of time.

I found the whole Le Mans experience too dangerous: looking at the state the drivers were in at 2 or 3am when the race had been going about 12 hours and they were only halfway through convinced me that they should never have been on the track for so long. They looked dreadful when they came in. Their only rest was in a little cabin where they could go to sleep, but it wasn't a proper sleep as they were all hyped up. It's impossible to go from driving at almost 200 miles per hour to then just stop and go to sleep. If we were driving around the roads in that state we would be a menace to everyone around us. Maybe there should be two 12-hour races on consecutive weekends, although the logistics of that wouldn't work. One of the drivers actually admitted that he shouldn't have been out there as he could hardly keep his eyes open. The pit crew were in the same state; they just sat on chairs in the garage. We had all the tea and coffee set up, together with energy bars and drinks for them, but we had to keep going over to make sure they hadn't run out of anything, including steam. Their mealtimes consisted of a quick bite during the night, sitting at their station in the garage. At that time the drink of choice was Gatorade, but I suppose it's all Red Bull now. We did have some Red Bull even then, because we were with Ford, but the Americans weren't used to it so they stuck with Gatorade.

As we'd expected, the call came from Kaye again for the 2005 season and, despite our reservations, we were keen to take the job as we had dropped out of rallying and were doing a number of lower-level disparate jobs at that stage. The bad news was that Mr Maraj, who had been spending a fortune on his racing, was determined to win and was fielding two cars, which meant twice the number of drivers, guests, team members, hangers-on and meals. In the full and certain knowledge that we shouldn't agree to do it, we did.

It was just as busy the second year, but we managed to increase the staffing level to 12. I still ended up doing most of the washing, though, because there weren't too many volunteers for handling the drivers' sweaty fireproof underwear. That second time we supported the race we had a better idea of what was needed, and if we had done it a third time we would definitely have had someone to do the washing other than me. In 2005 the drivers were Frank Biela, Tom Kristensen, Emanuele Pirro, Marco Werner, Allan McNish and JJ Lehto, so we were not short of names again, or banter for that matter. Sadly Johnny wasn't entered this time, but he was running in the Historic Le Mans race so he made ADT his base for that event.

It wasn't only Stu and I who had obviously forgotten how hard the 2004 race had been. All the former members of our team had come back for a second helping and, as I've said, we had increased the numbers. We must all have had short-term memory problems. Gary 'Fluffed and Folded' until the race weekend started and then he took charge of one awning with his nephew, Peter, who also serviced the pits. Sophie cooked again, along with Jamie our rally chef, while Gerry returned as hostess and controlled awning number two in fine style. Alan, our rally buddy, also returned and he shopped till he dropped. Stuart and I did a bit of everything. Incidentally, Gary and I did get a bit of help on the fluffing and folding front because Gerry thought Tom was wonderful and her knees would go weak when he was in the awning. Funnily enough, she always volunteered to wash his overalls so that she could hold them to her cheek when he took them off; it's difficult to imagine that being an attractive proposition after a stint in a very hot Le Mans car.

Mr Maraj got his wish and the team were first and third in 2005. We didn't have a big celebration; we were too shattered. After the race we had to rush straight back to England to be at

Goodwood for the Monday after the race. To be honest, I don't know how we made it. We had to fly a driver out because there was no way Stuart could have driven – it wouldn't have been safe. We had had to pack up our kitchen truck before packing the Van Hool coach for the return trip to the States. They were both full of the paraphernalia we had accumulated during the event. I don't know how we survived it.

The Goodwood event was a Ford PR day and we were working with Laurel and Hardy lookalikes, among others, which said it all really. Every Ford car that had been in a film or in a television series was there – like Lady Penelope's pink car and the Starsky and Hutch car.

We didn't have time to think about the Le Mans affair for several days and then we were able to consider it in retrospect. It would have all fallen apart if it hadn't been for Kaye Wilson's amazing organisational talent. She managed to have everything under control: all our equipment had to be hired, the fridges, cookers, everything, because the event is so vast. We noticed one other girl called Vanessa who seemed to be pretty close to being brilliant as well. She used to be in Formula 1 hospitality with West and Zakspeed. She went on to marry an American guy and, as far as we know, she still does hospitality as a central function in the States, but she comes over from America to Le Mans each year and feeds about four teams. The lads in the garages worked really hard too, and they didn't get up to much mischief because they had to work non-stop. They had about three days off afterwards and went to Versailles, although they were still half asleep – and when they got there the palace was closed.

So we had 'done' Le Mans and we wouldn't have missed it. It exhausted us, but what an experience. We had massaged each other's aching bones, and tried to keep each other awake when we were flagging. We'd experienced Gary setting fire to the barbecue when he forgot to remove the cardboard boxes being stored underneath it; Gary falling in the bushes at the hotel; Gary dancing with a bride on her wedding night at the Green Hotel when he had had a drop too much; Sophie falling in love with an American mechanic and later marrying him; Stuart and Alan nearly coming to blows with officials at the paddock gate; and Stuart contracting severe shingles when he arrived home. Apparently they are caused by overtiredness!

We all do silly things when we are tired, but at Le Mans we were able to laugh about them because we were with such an excellent bunch of people.

Despite everything we nearly did it for a third consecutive year, but a bit of a change of plan meant we didn't. It was probably a good job because, if I had continued to think of new staff roles, we would have needed a cast of thousands.

Chapter 32

TESTING TIMES

A recurring feature of our lives has been the fact that when things are looking a bit bleak on the working front a single message can completely turn everything around. This was the case in 2006 when we received an email from Peter Grzelinski, the motorsport service manager for the Bridgestone Corporation, asking us if we were interested in a role supporting the Bridgestone tyre-testing programme in Formula 1 from 2007 onwards. Peter had approached us previously about supplying hospitality for tests during 2006, but as Bridgestone was only supplying five teams that season the Japanese management were reluctant to sanction the budget. Bridgestone had never provided hospitality at Formula 1 testing until they secured the contract to become the single tyre supplier to Formula 1 from 2007, and then the company felt it really needed to step up its game.

We had seen Peter in the paddock before and had said hello, but we didn't really know anything about him. Needing a bit of background on him we rang Bob Warren of Travel Places, the company which organised most of the Formula 1 travel, and also several other people who were likely to know something about Peter. Everyone we spoke to said exactly the same thing: 'He's probably the straightest guy in Formula 1.' That was good enough for us. Peter was a contractor to Bridgestone and had been for around 30 years; he was supplied with an overall budget by Bridgestone Japan to provide all the support trucks, equipment and tyre fitters for their Formula 1 programme through a company called PG Motorsports which he ran jointly with logistics manager James Gresham. It was based in Langley, near Heathrow. The tyre engineers were employed by Bridgestone Japan but the two operations worked together seamlessly; the Japanese engineers based in the UK lived around Ealing and worked from Langley.

We got back to Peter pretty promptly to tell him we were interested and would like to be considered for the post. The job was originally due to start in January 2007 and we were quite optimistic that we were in with a chance, so we decided to take a last-minute break in late 2006 in case we were hired. We were in St Tropez, holidaying with some Australian visitors, and we'd just sat down at a pavement café to do some people-watching when our mobile phone rang. It was Peter Grzelinski on the line, and he simply said, 'OK, the job's yours – but I forgot to say there are two tests before the end of the year. Can you do them or do I have to find someone else?' We didn't want to lose the job before we'd even started it so we said, 'Of course we can do them.' We abandoned our friends – not exactly in the pavement café, but almost – and flew straight back to the UK to get ourselves organised. We later found that Peter had rung us on his way to Brazil for the last race of the season.

The deal was for us to supply a complete package, using our truck and equipment and hiring the additional support we needed to cater for both the Bridgestone staff and any visitors. Stu and I initially employed Kevin Charles ('Gerbil'), who had been a truckie with the M-Sport rally team, and then Steve Merry, who had been our driver on our Williams contract. With a chef called Nick Taylor, whom we had previously met at Le Mans, we were ready to go.

The first test we did was in Barcelona and at that stage our truck hadn't been painted in Bridgestone colours; it was still black and silver. Gerbil drove it to the circuit while Stu and I flew over to Spain to catch it up. On the way from the airport Stuart turned to me and said, 'Jesus, are we doing the right thing by getting involved with Formula 1 again? Am I going to be the oldest and the fattest there?' Within a few minutes of arriving at the track it became clear that everyone else had grown up with F1, just like us. Lots of the test teams consisted of former race team personnel who had stepped back a little from the full-on grind and commitment of the racing season and were now concentrating their energies on testing. It was amazing how many people we had known for years had followed this route, and they all came to see us at that first test because we were 'old school'. It even got a bit out of hand: one day we counted 11 different team race shirts in our awning at the same time, but it was very moving that, after all those years, the friendships were as strong as ever.

Peter Grzelinski was at that first event. I think he had turned up just to make sure we would be OK and that he could safely leave us to it. I had to apologise that so many people were milling around. I was afraid we would blow the whole season's budget first time out, but he just said, 'It's fantastic. We have never had so many people come to Bridgestone. Keep it up.' When the test was over he came to us and said, 'Get the truck painted and send me the bill as soon as possible.' So we did and he never bothered to come again that year.

During that first full year, in 2007, all kinds of people we hadn't seen for ages used to come along to say 'hello'. A few lads who had started as mechanics had risen through the ranks and become test team managers. One was Gerd Pfeiffer, or 'Pepper' as we knew him, who had previously been with the Toyota World Rally team as an engineer to Carlos Sainz. When Toyota withdrew from World Rally, 'Pepper' came with Carlos to Ford Motorsport again as his engineer. When Carlos retired 'Pepper' left and became Toyota's Formula 1 test team manager. It was great to see him again. At the last test of the year the race teams turned up instead of the test teams and the whole reunion process started again.

The Bridgestone tyre fitters would look bemusedly at us and wonder how we knew so many people. I could understand their confusion, as most were quite young and to them we were 'new kids on the block'. There was a Bridgestone engineer and a

Bridgestone fitter in every garage and they were used to seeing these race team people who never spoke to them and always appeared very serious. When they got to the motorhome they would see the same people come into the awning and they'd be laughing and joking with us. It was fantastic for us because Bridgestone were the sole tyre supplier, which meant we were part of every team. We were allowed to go in any of the garages and stand on any pit wall during the tests. I never took advantage of it, but Stuart did. It was another complete change, just like when we stopped being part of a race team and joined Ford, a car manufacturer with a works team to support. Now we were with a component manufacturer and were associated with everyone.

Occasionally some of our old friends from the driving fraternity used to drop by to see us. We went testing to Bahrain and Gerhard Berger was there with BMW. In the evening we had all been invited to a gathering in the prince's suite and Gerhard looked at us and said, 'Where have you two been all these years? You were at Ford and then you disappeared.' We really wouldn't have expected him to notice we were no longer there, so the fact that he had, and that he commented on it, was a really special moment. We said, 'We've been World Rallying,' to which he replied, 'I wish I had known you were there, I love rallying.'

Some people say Formula 1 shouldn't go to some of the new circuits and forsake the traditional old iconic tracks, but the facilities that are available in these new places are absolutely fantastic. When we went to Bahrain our old friend Martin Whitaker did us proud. He was the chief executive officer of the Bahrain International Circuit, a job he took on after leaving the Ford Motor Company. When we arrived at the airport he had a guy waiting for us who escorted us straight through the police checkpoint, then got our bags from the baggage hall and our hire car. Later that evening Stu and I went round to Martin's house for dinner, after which he led us to our hotel. His wife Nicky met us the next morning to take us to her regular shops. The area she drove us to sold pork, bacon, sausages and all manner of foodstuffs we never expected to find in a Muslim country; then she took us to another area where we could buy alcohol. Martin and Nicky looked after us, and their son Ben spent almost every day with us. He used to 'help' the lads in the garage and then come to the motorhome for his meals. Martin would come to us for breakfast; I'm not sure what Nicky thought of that. At one point he embarrassed us by introducing the prince to us, not us to the prince. Martin told him we were two people he should really meet as we were the longest-serving hospitality providers in Formula 1 – it was quite embarrassing, but the prince did take time to have a chat with us.

On another occasion, while Nelson Piquet Jnr was driving for Benetton, his father Nelson turned up at a test. One of the Benetton boys said, 'Hey, Nelson, Mum and Dad are over there' and 'Lippy' Lee brought him across to the canopy. Lippy came in first and then, with pomp and ceremony, he unzipped the canopy door and there was Nelson. Nelson just shouted 'Mum, what the hell are you doing here?' and sprinted the length of the canopy full of Bridgestone lads, most of whom didn't know him because they were quite young. They looked in astonishment from Nelson to me, and then back to Nelson, doing a bit of mental arithmetic and they obviously thought, 'Pardon?' He hugged and kissed both Stuart and me and then just burst out crying. He said, 'I thought I'd never see you again.' Nelson is a fabulous person and I still don't know why he was so attached to us. He'd often mentioned that he would like us to travel up the Amazon with him for a holiday on his boat, and when he saw us again he still remembered, after all that time: 'We haven't been up the Amazon yet.' We smiled and said, 'No, but we will one day,' and I believe we will.

Keke Rosberg often came to see us during testing as his son Nico was now driving for Mercedes. We enjoyed reminiscing with Keke about his time at Williams when we used to help our friends Tim and Maureen child-mind Nico.

Kenny Szymanski turned up at one test. He was still in touch with a few of the older Formula 1 reprobates, and one of them must have told him their team was testing in Barcelona. As usual, he came in on an American Airways flight and neither of us knew the other was there because he hadn't realised we were back in Formula 1. Kenny used to call me 'Lady Di' and Stuart was 'Fleetwood' after Mick Fleetwood of Fleetwood Mac, because they looked pretty alike when Stu had longer hair. Apparently Kenny had spent the whole day at the track before one of our old colleagues suddenly realised we had all been together at Lotus; unfortunately it was just as Kenny was due to go back to the airport. I was in the kitchen of our motorhome and I suddenly heard, 'Fleetwood, Lady Di!' and I thought, 'That can't be Kenny Szymanski' – but it was, and he came bounding into the motorhome, a glorious mixture of excitement and disappointment. 'I've been here all day and didn't know you were here,' he said, 'and now I've found you I have to leave for the airport.'

We catered for 16 tests each season during 2007 and 2008 and the highlight was Silverstone on both occasions, because all the Bridgestone employees were allowed to bring their families along for a day out and to let them see what their partners did at the track. Even the Japanese families were there, including small children interested in what their dad did when he was away from home. We had to put an awning on each side of the truck and enlist Maxine, Nick's partner, as an extra chef to cater for so many people, because Bridgestone didn't just feed their own staff: there were always guests to be entertained and one interesting group were junior kart racers, mainly French and Italian, often with their parents. They were always a pleasure to serve, despite being quite overwhelmed by everything.

As tyres are such a vital part of the racing car's performance, all the engineers and some of the drivers from the teams used to come to our truck to have meetings with their Bridgestone counterparts, who were Japanese or European. We were astonished at just how polite the Japanese were; they were always thankful for anything we did for them. We hadn't had any experience of dealing with Japanese culinary requirements before and we were a bit concerned, needlessly as it happened, because they loved their full English breakfasts. We had asked if there was anything specifically Japanese they wanted us to prepare, but it wasn't really a problem because we traditionally cooked a lot of stir fries and curries anyway. Strangely, they didn't like the other staple of race-team fare: pasta. Noodles were fine, but not pasta!

It was interesting that quite a few of the Japanese guys wouldn't eat potatoes but loved chips – they never quite understood that they were the same thing. Most of the Japanese engineers lived in the UK, but about four flew in from Japan for each test. The ones that were based in Europe full time were very accustomed to a European diet, but the guys who flew in from Tokyo were initially a bit bemused by the food. They soon caught on, though. It was odd to watch the UK-resident Japanese laughing at their Tokyo-based colleagues, because at breakfast time the travelling group would put everything on the same plate – bacon, egg, sausage, fruit salad, croissant and a dollop of porridge, but they ate it all and I never complained because it saved on the washing up!

We used those large self-service heated dishes with lift-up lids and quite often the Japanese guys would lift the lid and just stare at the contents uncomprehendingly. I had a brainwave. I started putting a funny picture next to each dish to explain what was in it. Things like swordfish were pretty straightforward, but Yorkshire pudding was a bit of a challenge to draw. It was a bit of a challenge for the Japanese lads, too – they were mystified because they knew pudding was a dessert and there were English people putting gravy on them. What was all that about? They also failed to get the hang of apple sauce with pork, but they loved sweets; they called custard 'yellow stuff' but they liked it. Sometimes they had sushi and we always did one dish with oriental leanings; we also kept green tea especially for the lads, but they liked the tea we made in the Brown Betty teapot that has been my constant travel companion. Good job, really, as I don't think I would have had time for the tea ceremony.

I think they considered me an eccentric English lady, and in retrospect perhaps they thought I was a bit too familiar because Japanese society is much more formal than ours. When the English boys arrived I would give them a kiss, and often there were Japanese lads mingled in with them and so I did just the same – maybe I should have shaken hands instead, but no one seemed to mind. I always made a point of trying to remember everyone's name, and if I couldn't get it right I gave them a nickname which would make them chuckle. We would have a list of names and the guys that came from Tokyo would look at it and point and say, 'That's me!' 'I can't pronounce that,' I used to think, so I gave them a nickname and after a day we would all remember the name. There was one we called Mr Marmite because his wife got a taste for it while he had been based in the UK. He had since been relocated to Japan, but when he turned up for tests he would look at the breakfast table and say, 'Ah, Marmite!', so that's how he got his name – and some Marmite to take home. I always kept three jars of the stuff in the cupboard for when he next turned up. He was pleased I remembered him and, although it was tricky, I remembered all 30 of the guys eventually. I also tried to remember if there was something they didn't particularly like on their plate.

Some of the nicknames I gave our Japanese engineers actually stuck and even their colleagues started adopting them. There was one really quiet engineer who looked about 18 but was actually in his late twenties – but then all Japanese tend to look younger than they are, lucky people. I christened this one MM because of his initials, and within a short time his colleagues were calling him that. He didn't always like what we had to eat but we always tried to accommodate him. Eventually he began to understand me and became far chattier. Early in the year he told me he would be 30 in December, so I wrote down the date and, on his birthday, while we were in Jerez, we gave him a card and a badge. He was actually quite amazed I had remembered. Sadly, he was transferred back to Tokyo at the end of 2009 and I wasn't able to say goodbye.

We always tried to cook a Christmas dinner at the last Jerez test, and while the Europeans thoroughly enjoyed it, our Japanese friends were a little bemused by what was on their plate. Some of them thought that sprouts were young cabbages, and as for stuffing, we had a terrible job explaining what it was. The Japanese lads thought the Christmas crackers were great and those who had arrived from Tokyo for just that one test took some home. I have no idea whether they ever got them through security. Everyone had paper hats in their crackers and we told them to put them on. The Japanese lads must have thought we were crazy, but they joined in enthusiastically. There was an 'end of term' feeling and everyone was allowed a couple of glasses of wine; they were certainly well received and led to everyone being quite 'relaxed'. Unfortunately some of them were so relaxed they went off to their respective team debriefs still wearing their paper hats. Goodness knows what the teams thought about it, but everyone took it in good part.

Tyre fitting is a tough job and a lot of people are not aware of the logistics involved. Tyres have travelled a pretty long way before they get anywhere near a wheel. Bridgestone tyres were produced in Japan and then sent to the UK by jumbo jet for trans-shipment to Langley, where they were sorted and stored. The tyre engineers nominated the tyres for each circuit and the appropriate tyres, along with back-up wet tyres, were shipped from Langley to the racetrack where they were to be used. The tyres were then mounted on the teams' wheels or rims and a lot of care had to be taken to make sure the rims weren't damaged. At the end of the race the tyres had to be stripped back off the rims and sorted; some then went back to Japan for evaluation and the rest were shipped to a recognised disposal facility by articulated lorry. The fitter's job is not always appreciated and sometimes a team would go all season without getting to know their fitter's name. However tough it was, there was one feisty lady called Tina who kept pace with the lads, which was pretty impressive.

Whenever a new person joined the group I always asked them if they had any allergies and one guy called Rick had obviously slipped through the HR screening net because he just said, 'I don't eat foreign food and I don't like foreign travel.' I felt perhaps working for a Japanese company in a job which took him around the world for a living wasn't his ideal vocation. It transpired that even English food cooked anywhere other than in England counted as foreign food, so we were a bit stuck. We tried everything we could to give him something he would eat but he just pushed it away with a few expletives to emphasise his displeasure. One of the other English fitters, Pikey, took Rick to one side and pointed out in no uncertain terms that he was being rude and it wasn't acceptable; they almost came to blows and Rick lasted two tests before he disappeared. He may have gone on hunger strike for all I know, but he wasn't greatly missed.

One engineer, Kevin Hunt, joined us straight from university. He was the palest person I have ever seen and so thin that I felt sorry for him. When I asked him about allergies and the like he said he only ever ate roast dinners. The English lads called him 'Luke' as in leukaemia, because he was so pale, and he answered to it because the alternative was 'Ann', as in anaemia. We changed his eating habits and when he left he looked a lot healthier and quite a bit heavier.

Despite these odd exceptions, the group were generally easy to please. Although new guys came and went, the nucleus of the group stayed the same throughout the year and then there would be an influx of graduate engineers at the start of each succeeding year. They seemed to be getting younger and we were beginning to wonder when 'Mum and Dad' would change to 'Grandma and Grandad'. It never did, but we sometimes got called 'Mother and Father' in mock formality. The boys all worked together brilliantly and, although the Japanese engineers tended to stick together in their free time, there were a few who happily joined in the beery nights out without it doing them much harm, Zen – who I will mention later – being one of them. A couple of British engineers, Jonathan and Richard, lovely lads who always liked to entwine the two cultures, often led the way. But although they sometimes looked a bit second-hand the next day, they carried out their duties admirably. There was also a young engineer called Anna, who, after a difficult start, was well able to hold her own work-wise, and in 2011 was retained by Pirelli and continued to work with Toro Rosso. Good for her.

We were relishing our role at Bridgestone, but nothing stays the same in motor racing and for 2009 the FIA vastly reduced the amount of testing time allowed to each team and banned in-season testing as a cost-reduction measure, so effectively our job just ran from November until April. That made it seem as though it was all over before we had properly got back into the swing of the thing again.

We had a champagne party atmosphere at the end of each year's testing spell because it seemed like we were never going back again. At the end of the run of tests there were always big speeches, and all the Japanese used to gather together and present us with a gift. At the end of the 2009 test period they presented us with champagne, a photo and a number of other small trinkets. Our staff guys, Kevin and Nick, weren't left out either. Hirohide Hamashima, the assistant to the director of Bridgestone's Motorsport Tyre Development Division, was there and he thanked us too. The atmosphere was not entirely happy, though, because all the staff had been told in Abu Dhabi that Bridgestone would be pulling out of Formula 1 at the end of the 2010 season.

Our Japanese friends are delightful people and are always scrupulously polite, despite finding just about everything in life funny. They loved Formula 1, and they were disappointed that it was all coming to an end and they would have to continue their careers in Japan. The English guys were even more disappointed as they had no secure jobs to go back to, so they would be looking for new jobs when the contract expired. The guys had no time to worry about how tough the job was, however, because there were another 12 months of hard graft in front of them before the end of the 2010 season and they just had to get on with it.

All too soon it was all over again and it was time for another farewell party. Our Japanese colleagues loved photographs and we all had to pose for each other over and over again at our almost final goodbye. At the end of it Stu, Kevin, Nick and I were all presented with red sweatshirts with all the boys' signatures and little comments on them, some of which were in Japanese so I hope they weren't too rude. Chief Japanese engineer Jun Matsuzaki was so polite and had thanked us every night of every test for looking after his staff, and now he made a real point of thanking us again, as did Zen, who was a Japanese guy who had been educated in America. Zen made us laugh by saying his wife had only just realised, after quite a few years, that she liked being in the UK, just at the point when they both had to go home to Japan, a prospect to which neither of them were looking forward. In the end Jun stayed in England, working for Force India, because his wife and two sons wanted to stay here and he wanted to follow his Formula 1 career, leaving behind a secure future at Bridgestone.

We followed the Silverstone tradition of getting everyone together, although in 2010 it was at James Gresham's house for a pig roast; we were honoured that Mr Yasukawa, the Bridgestone director of motorsport tyre development, came along. It felt nostalgic to see everyone there, but it really was the end of the line. There was one last test in Abu Dhabi, but we weren't needed as the race team hospitality staff were already there for the Grand Prix.

We are still in touch with some of the English lads and I contacted Zen after the 2011 tsunami. He was still making a joke of everything, but he told us that everyone was safe and well. It's sad to think we will probably never see our Japanese friends again.

We realised that, after over 30 years in the paddock, this would be our last Formula 1 contract, and it felt quite sad, but Bridgestone had been such a worthwhile job for a couple of old codgers it was perhaps fitting that we ended on that note. Pirelli were due to arrive for 2011, bringing their own hospitality staff, so sadly there was no opportunity to continue. The testing atmosphere was just like the race paddock had been 15 years earlier – we had met dozens of our old friends and made lots of new ones.

Even when we are back in Alcester there is no getting away from racing because, just inside our porch, we have that great photograph of Steve McQueen from the film *Le Mans*, the one where he is raising two fingers. It's signed, not by Steve, but by the photographer Nigel Snowdon. Nigel was employed as an extra on the film, as a photographer surprisingly enough. One year, when we arrived at Nice airport for the Monaco Grand Prix, the old GT car that was used in the film was on display alongside lots of still photographs. When I saw Nigel in the paddock I asked him if he had seen the display, but he'd driven down to Monaco rather than taken a flight. I told him that the two-fingered salute was my favourite photograph, because I loved that film almost as much as I loved Steve McQueen. Nigel promised to get me a copy of the picture, which surprised me a little because, until that point, I hadn't realised he had taken it; he signed it and Stu hung it in the most conspicuous place in the house. Oddly, we met Chad McQueen, Steve's son, at a Ford PR day and I told him about the photo and he said to post it to him and he would sign it too. He gave us his address on Sunset Strip in Los Angeles, but I couldn't bring myself to send it in case it got lost in transit.

I love it when people come to the door and see it. It's typical of Stuart's humour. I have no idea how he survived in hospitality all those years!

Racing has been our life and we wouldn't have changed it for the world.

Chapter 33

PADDOCK
CHARACTERS

The Spires family hailed from Alcester and Stuart was born locally, a few hundred yards from where we have lived for over 30 years. Most of Stuart's family lived close by; his dad was the one who moved furthest away – all of eight miles. The building where Stuart was born is now a retirement complex and there is a strong possibility we will end up there! On the surface we don't seem to have travelled far, but alongside all the Grand Prix and World Rally venues we've visited we have taken time out, where possible, to visit other places. We've been to Australia 34 times and New Zealand eight; we've been on safari with the McLaren boys in Kruger National Park, and visited Fiji several times after the Australian Grand Prix, as well as Tonga and parts of Asia. We've toured South Africa after testing, been confronted by a bear in the Rockies after the Mexican GP, and called in at Dubai and visited a desert resort before most people discovered it. We've visited America several times, and stopped off in Argentina and Kenya as well as touring most of Europe. We have travelled enough to fill two lifetimes, all due to following a dream, and we haven't regretted one minute of it.

We have worked with some of the biggest names in motorsport and also with lots of unsung paddock heroes. Many of the people we have come across have had their own peculiar superstitions and quirks. When we worked with Michael

Schumacher, for instance, he always wanted the same knife and fork saving for him; the fact that we washed it up with all the others didn't seem to bother him, although it might have done if we'd told him. When Riccardo Patrese drove for Benetton he had a superstition about giving me his watch to look after before every race. He wouldn't let anyone else have it then, only me, although as he drove for many other teams in his career he must have had a lot of other watch watchers. On one occasion he had forgotten to give me his watch and, when he realised, he came running back from the grid with it, just before the start. We have fed vegetarians who always wanted vegetarian sausages and didn't actually realise they were cooked alongside the regular sausages, but in fairness neither did I until Stuart admitted it quite recently. We have catered for all manner of culinary quirks, like the Senna sandwich and the nocturnal pavlova. Our life has been filled with characters, many of whom have already been mentioned in these pages, but there are one or two I should like to acknowledge because, without people like them, the racing world wouldn't be quite the same.

Tetsu Tsugawa

We have already explained how much Tetsuo – or 'Tetsu' as we called him – helped us when we were racing in Japan, but he is such an interesting character that we have to tell you more about him. Tetsu was a student of mechanical engineering in 1974, and a massive racing fan who was determined enough to find himself a temporary job as a gopher and general all-round assistant at the Fuji Raceway. During the course of the race weekend he was lucky enough to meet John Surtees and Peter Briggs, the Surtees team manager, which was an amazing and unexpected experience for him. Tetsu shook John's hand and didn't wash it again for three days he was so excited! It was a Formula 2 race, and the Surtees team won with their TS15.

Tetsu's dream was to move to Europe and find a role in motorsport. Fired up by his meeting with Surtees, he threw himself into his studies and, by 1976, he had secured a job with Bellco Racing in Japan as a mechanical design engineer. That was also the year he saw his first Formula 1 race and was blown away by it. Team Surtees was struggling along in Formula 1 and, by chance, Tetsu knew a mechanic called Sho Fujiiki who was working with the team. Sho talked to Peter Briggs, who remembered Tetsu from their previous meeting, and Tetsu got some temporary work with the team at the Japanese Grand Prix that year, sweeping the garage floor, polishing things and being generally useful.

At the end of the race weekend, when the team were packing up, Tetsu, who had very limited English at that stage, managed to communicate to Peter that he would like to come to the UK. Peter being Peter said if you make it over to England I would give you a job. Obviously Peter had these conversations all over the world and didn't expect to hear anything further. Five months later Tetsu arrived at Heathrow, with one suitcase and £1,000 to start his new life. Still a bit 'challenged' by the English language, Tetsu somehow managed to find his way from Japan to the race factory in Edenbridge, Kent.

Peter was quite shocked to find this linguistically challenged Japanese chap standing in front of his desk with a suitcase, a few English pounds and a firm conviction that he had a job waiting for him in Formula 1, but he was impressed that Tetsu had the drive and initiative to get there. In May 1977 Tetsu's career in Formula 1 started with a job as a fabricator in Team Surtees and he had his first step on the ladder. Sho had left the team by then, but Peter and his wife Theresa took Tetsu into their own home until they could find him accommodation with another team member. His skills quickly became apparent and he was promoted to mechanic, the role he held when we joined the team in 1978. Tetsu's English was still limited but he had bonded well with the team and we became firm friends. When Team Surtees closed he joined Maurice Nunn and his Team Ensign, who in turn eventually joined forces with Theodore Racing.

We seemed to have had a parallel career in many respects because, in 1983, Tetsu joined Toleman, and there we were together again. Tetsu felt very honoured to have worked on Ayrton Senna's car in 1984. In 1985 Benetton bought the Toleman team and Tetsu's future seemed to be much more secure than it had been since he came to England to build his career in motor racing; he married his long-term girlfriend Natsuo in the April of that year. However, their marriage was destined to be far too short. Tetsu's life was turned upside-down when Natsuo became terminally ill. He had to spend more time at home with her, and his only option was to leave Benetton, but he helped out when he could with the new Beatrice Haas team until he returned to Japan with Natsuo so she could be with her family at the end.

Tetsu vowed to come back one day and in 1986, following Natsuo's death, he returned to Benetton greatly saddened but back among friends. He stayed with the team for four more years before leaving to become a full-time freelance journalist and television commentator. He still attends Grands Prix and writes for a variety of Japanese motorsport magazines. He has also written a number of books on life in Formula 1 and is quite famous in Japan.

Once we boarded one of Japan's super-efficient, always punctual, trains with Tetsu and, to everyone's amazement, it failed to leave the platform on time. This was unthinkable and it was plain that the locals all felt there must have been some kind of incident. Then we noticed the driver walking along the platform, peering into each carriage. He did a double take at our carriage and, with a shout of glee, he came in and thrust his flag at Tetsu, for him to sign. Apparently the driver had been at Suzuka for the Grand Prix. We wondered how he had spotted him among all those people but Tetsu, in his modest manner, said that it was probably because he was with us, and we stood out as the only Europeans; Stuart, being quite tall, was head and shoulders above everyone else and had a beard so perhaps

Tetsu was right. Tetsu signed the flag, he and the guard bowed to each other and the train moved off. Then, when we were in Tokyo, girls came screaming after him and this time we knew it wasn't Stuart they had spotted!

When we went to Suzuka people came to ask us for our autographs because Tetsu had written about us in one of his books. The only problem is that it's written in Japanese and nobody will tell us what it says. We have seen his books in Japan but never found an English translation.

We became firm friends with Tetsu's family and enjoyed a wonderful two-week holiday in Japan, going places tourists wouldn't normally visit and experiencing the Japanese culture first hand. Tetsu's dad was fluent in French, so we were able to converse after a fashion. Tetsu is a legend, and was one of the few Japanese mechanics of the early days who persevered with his dream. We are proud to have him as our friend – and he still lives in Witney in England, close to where the old Benetton factory was, with his second wife, Motoko.

Professor Sid Watkins

We have previously mentioned Sid Watkins on a number of occasions, and it's unlikely that anyone reading this will be unaware of the debt that motor racing owes the 'Prof', as he is known. Sid campaigned tirelessly to improve the standards of safety in motor racing, both during his period as the chief medical delegate to the FIA and since his retirement. He is responsible for many of the initiatives that have saved the lives of drivers and trackside workers over the years.

There are many references to Sid's friendship with Ayrton Senna in books, articles and films, and his suggestion that he and Ayrton should retire and go fishing, shortly before Ayrton's fatal crash at Imola, is the stuff of legend. The events of Imola redoubled his determination to see that the deaths of Roland Ratzenberger and Senna himself were the catalyst for further safety improvements.

The outward face of Sid is well known and has passed into folklore, but little has been said about his kindness to everyone in the paddock, irrespective of their status. Whenever anyone was feeling ill they knew they could seek out the Prof and he would see them as soon as he had finished his circuit and driver duties. He often listened while team members discussed the medical issues of their family or friends, knowing that they had a sympathetic ear, although Sid could be quite blunt if his time was being wasted. He also prescribed an aspirin and a shot of whisky to cure quite a lot of non-life-threatening ailments. It was particularly comforting for us motorhomers to know Sid would be at the next Grand Prix, as we were often on the road for many weeks in succession and it was reassuring that, unless it was a dire emergency, we didn't have to throw ourselves on the mercy of doctors in Brazil or Hungary or wherever we may have felt off colour. We weren't really allowed to be ill in any case, as we had a job to perform and people to look after, come what may.

Stu and I had a personal experience of Sid's kindness regarding a friend and neighbour of ours and, although we know of many other good deeds he carried out, we feel it sums the guy up perfectly. Our neighbour Pete had experienced what was later found to be an unusual form of stroke which had gone unrecognised by doctors and specialists alike, and although he was definitely suffering serious after-effects he couldn't get anyone's attention; it seemed like he was being dismissed and that no one was actually interested. We were concerned for him, so just before leaving for a Grand Prix we asked Pete to write down all his symptoms and what he could remember of the day he had the stroke – we knew that over the weekend Sid would be arriving for his usual high-caffeine high-cholesterol breakfast and that I might have a chance to give him the notes.

After Sid had finished his usual 'fry up' and was relaxing with his cigar, I asked him if I could give him something to read about our friend's condition. Sid asked me one or two questions, then asked for the notes. I thought perhaps he would be able to take them home and read them before the next Grand Prix, because I knew how busy he always was at a race weekend. I gave them to him on Saturday and was amazed when he passed me a note with a phone number on it at breakfast the following morning. 'This is my direct line,' he said. 'Get him to ring me early next week; I want him to make an appointment to see me as soon as possible.' Sid was a top neurosurgeon and not many people got to see him for an initial consultation. I was amazed that he had read the notes so quickly and was on the case the very next day. We were out of the UK and not due to see our neighbour for a while so we telephoned him with the news: he was ecstatic to think someone was going to listen to him at long last. When we got back to England we found that Pete had been to see Sid at his London clinic and had an excellent consultation with him. Sid had explained everything that was happening to him and had given him some tablets which were never offered by any of his previous doctors or consultants.

Pete recovered totally, which we believe was totally due to Professor Sid. Pete and his wife were determined to pay for the consultation and asked us to check on the amount owing. Sid would hear nothing of it and said, 'Any friend of yours or Stuart doesn't need to pay me.' We pointed out that our friends were nothing to do with motorsport, to which he just replied, 'It makes no difference. You look after me in many ways at the track and this is my way of paying you back.'

Tom Walkinshaw

We were first asked to quote for a job for Tom personally when he was running his Rover saloon car racing programme. We were subcontracting the programme because we were working in Formula 1, so we planned to hire a couple to manage the motorhome for us. Roger Silman was working for Tom and it was he who had asked us to quote. We worked out the numbers, came up with an offer letter and took it to Tom. He just threw it back at us and said, 'Is that what it's going to cost?'

'It's as close as we can get, based on the calendar you've given us.'

'Are you making any money?'

'A bit,' we admitted, because we had cut the quote to the bone to get our motorhome into use rather than standing idle. He totally amazed us by saying, 'Go back and put £10,000 on the quote. Look, if you are not happy with the deal, the people you are employing won't be happy and consequently our guests won't be happy.'

Stu and I walked out of his office and looked at each other in amazement. 'Did I just hear that right?' I said but, true enough, Stuart had heard the same thing. How many people would do that? Instead of rubbing his hands at the prospect of getting a steal of a deal, he sent us away to make sure we were making a decent return! He paid us on the nail every time we had to raise an invoice, as well. We always considered him to be a real gentleman after that, and he certainly restored my faith in human nature.

We knew him when he was with Benetton, of course, and it was really strange that he and John Barnard used to come back to the motorhome in the evenings. They both had enough money to go anywhere, but they would always say, 'Are you eating here tonight?' We were because we generally did, but when the two of them arrived we had to scrape together another couple of meals. I think they just enjoyed the peace and quiet of the motorhome when the press and guests had left. Sometimes it was a bit inconvenient, particularly early in the weekend when we were trying to get everything together, but looking back it was a real compliment because most people just wanted to get away.

We were both really upset when Tom lost his long fight against cancer at the end of 2010.

Maureen Magee, photographer

Anyone who was a pits or paddock regular at any time during the late 1970s to the mid-1990s will remember Maureen Magee. Maureen was a really eccentric character and totally dedicated to the art of photography. Unfortunately, from the 1990s onwards it became increasingly difficult to qualify for the credentials that allowed photographers Formula 1 paddock access without either contracts with a particular publication or a provable number of photographs published each year in the media. So Maureen disappeared from the pit lane.

Maureen used to travel to each GP in a very small, ageing motorhome. She lived in it for the whole of the European season, with the darkroom she had created inside. She often had no money and relied on sales of her pictures, which she developed overnight and tried to sell to the drivers, teams and anyone else with a few pounds. Everyone knew Maureen in the paddock – teams allowed her in their garages, drivers posed for her; even Bernie tolerated her and teased her whenever he saw her. Her favourite driver was Nelson Piquet, and we all know what he was like; he used to get up to his tricks when she was around and he tormented her terribly.

In those days, like now, all paddock passes had to have a photograph of the holder on it. Unlike nowadays, they were really easy to 'doctor'. A certain Kenny Szymanski changed his pass photo to one of Maureen topless; we were never quite sure how he got hold of the photo, but he was admitted to the track at every race with it around his neck. It certainly had his name on it, but a blind man in the dark could tell it wasn't his picture. Paddock access has tightened up considerably since then.

Another of Maureen's characteristics was that she always dressed in red; she was a rather large lady, so she became affectionately known as 'the Fire Engine'. At the end of each race weekend she used to come around to see if any of us Brit motorhomers had any food left, which we quite often had, and she would try to cram as much into her tiny motorhome fridge as was humanly possible, so that she would have enough to last until the next Grand Prix. She also tried to park her motorhome close to the paddock so she could commandeer goodies from us to take back for dinner after her working day was done. We always gave her cups of tea, which being British she loved. If a motorhomer had some food left over from dinner they always looked for her to make sure she had eaten during the day.

After the race was over Maureen left on the Monday, just like the rest of us, and we often saw her en route to the next race. We always stopped to make sure she hadn't broken down (she often did) or was in need of any help. Sometimes we used to give her some small financial help, but she always paid it back, either in cash or in photographic form. Maureen was just one of those Formula 1 characters; we have seen her a couple of times more recently at other motorsport events, taking her photographs in the lower formulae. Hopefully she is still healthy and living in Dunstable with her precious photographs.

Bob Warren, Travel Places

Bob Warren must be a saint or a total lunatic; I'm not sure which. Most people, given the choice between herding cats and trying to make the travel arrangements to get just about every Formula 1 team member to each Grand Prix around the world, would get out a tin of 'Whiskas' and start shouting 'Here kitty, kitty!' Bob mustn't like cats, however, because he is the one that accepted the challenge of getting all those extremely demanding people to the right part of the world, preferably at the right time. Needless to say, half the teams change their arrangements several times during the run-up to a Grand Prix and Bob's team of people have their work cut out trying to keep up.

A number of companies have made attempts to handle the Formula 1 business over the years, but few have succeeded. Bob's first step towards taking on the challenge was in 1974 when he joined a company called Special Events, which was providing a service for Formula 1 teams only. Bob was young and ambitious, and in 1980 he made the big decision to start his own business, which is now called Travel Places. He was then summoned to Chessington to see a certain Mr Ecclestone who wanted to know if Bob was interested in handling the FOCA (Formula 1 Constructors' Association) business. Naturally he said 'of course' and the relationship endures to this day, although it hasn't been completely without incident – and he has seen many teams come and go, some of them with his money.

Just like everyone else in the business Bob is an enthusiast as well as a businessman and, if pushed, he will admit that his all-time driving hero was Ronnie Peterson, who we mentioned earlier. He will also admit that his longevity in the business is down to the lessons he has learned from some of the main movers and shakers in Formula 1, chiefly people like Frank Williams, Ron Dennis and, in particular, Mr E himself.

Being an extremely amiable bloke, Bob has a huge number of friends in the pit lane but he is particularly close to many of the 'old school' chaps like Alan Woollard and Herbie Blash, both of whom have spent a long time as Bernie Ecclestone's trusted lieutenants. Bob is also close friends with many of the gentlemen of the great British press, the very men whose travel arrangements give him the biggest headache.

The Formula 1 teams seem to think that Bob and his team have a pretty easy life and therefore do everything they can to make it more difficult. They imagine that Bob can sort out anything they want and just steamroller his way through schedules, bad weather, full flights and any other circumstance that they feel is a personal inconvenience. Bob actually has a great record of responding to the constantly changing needs of his customers, but sometimes even he is beaten by events and it is usually when he has the high flyers, or would-be high flyers on board, because when things start to go wrong they really do go wrong. A good example was a trip from Sao Paulo to London, which eventually took 27 hours due to refuelling problems and all manner of mishaps. Needless to say Bernie, Flavio and most of the other Formula 1 hierarchy were on the trip and they weren't amused. Initially everyone blamed Bob, but after a few hours they all calmed down and took it in their stride, which may have had something to do with the in-flight service.

Bob always gets the flak initially, because it's naturally his fault if the plane breaks down; the Formula 1 guys just say, 'Get another one,' which isn't always that easy. Bob takes everything in his stride and gets on with it, with his trademark smile. Most of us wouldn't go within a mile of the job, but he loves it. We have become friends with Bob and his wife Chris over the years, and every time we see them we always tell them that he deserves a medal. Their two sons are now in the business and have learned their trade from the best; it will be in good hands when Bob finally hangs up his 'wings'.

Bernard Ferguson

Bernard and I have been doing this book together and he has made it plain that he didn't really want any of his exploits published as he didn't care to have his boss reading about them – but he is retired now, so I think he's fair game. Bernard was the head of motorsport for Cosworth and responsible for all the contracts between Cosworth and race teams in an awful lot of formulae, but particularly Formula 1. He was also the engine manufacturer's representative to the Formula 1 commission so he was kept pretty busy, particularly trying to get the money out of some of the more reluctant payers. Bernard's way of relaxing from the stress of all this was to have a sense of humour, a thick skin and the occasional glass of wine or beer or, if pushed, that lunatic Brazilian drink Caipirinha.

There are so many stories surrounding Bernard's travels that he could probably write his own book – except that he can't remember a lot of them. There seems to be a regular French theme to many of his 'misfortunes' as three of them happened in Magny-Cours at various French Grands Prix. On one occasion he was doing his rounds debt-collecting when the heavens opened and he got soaked; it was particularly wet underfoot and his deck shoes and socks were saturated. Stuart offered a spare pair of Timberlands and said he would dry Bernard's socks on the water boiler and his shoes in our hot water cupboard next to the generator. It was only when, two days later, Stuart asked for his shoes back that we remembered Bernard's shoes were in the cupboard. When we opened it up the shoes were done to a crisp; they were so stiff they wouldn't bend at all and Bernard had to travel back to England with his feet giving every indication they were wearing divers' boots.

On the next trip to Magny-Cours Stewart Grand Prix had booked Bernard into a château somewhere in the middle of nowhere. He had the attic room, which was minute and had been squeezed in where there was no space for a room at all; when he opened the corner cupboard to put his stuff in he found it was the en suite bathroom and toilet – and this was the background to the 'baguette story'. Bernard is often asked to tell this story at gatherings of his old cronies, and the time it takes to tell can vary from a couple of minutes to half an hour, depending on who is in the audience and how inebriated they all are. In short, on the Saturday evening before the French Grand Prix, Tyrrell, who were using Cosworth engines that year, decided to have a dinner for British journalists (we had stopped these during the Stewart era). There was to be a 'personality' at each table and Ken Tyrrell, Harvey Postlethwaite, the Tyrrell managing director, and Mike Gascoyne, Tyrrell's chief designer, were all set to perform, but they needed a fourth personality. Bernard was co-opted in.

To cut what can be an extremely long story short, each personality had to move table after each course and meet a new set of journalists, which presented four interview opportunities and four tables full of wine. Bernard concentrated his attention on the wine instead of the food, and the final course with all the *Autosport* journalists became a bit riotous. He finally left the dinner a bit merry (!) and pretty hungry, so he came and asked me for a large sandwich to take back to the hotel. I made him up a full baguette with ham and cheese, wrapped it in tinfoil, and off he went holding what he described as his 'light sabre' in front of him, at which point he was approached by two security men who asked him where he was going. He said he was going to get his car. It then dawned on him that he didn't know where it was, so he tried to ask the security staff where the media car park was; the security men did that famous Gallic shrug where the shoulders go up and the corners of the mouth come down. Being resourceful as well as half-cut, Bernard decided to ring his wife Sue, who speaks fluent French, to ask her to ask the officials where his car was. She obliged, but not without giving him an earful first. Eventually Bernard tracked it down and somehow also found his way back to the hotel but, as he describes it, he 'fell among thieves' in the hotel bar on his way to the bedroom, which was incidentally in the other direction. He finally set off to bed up the narrow, winding staircase to the top of the hotel, which unfortunately had old-fashioned timer switches on the lights; they are pressed at the bottom of the stairs, allowing some illumination, but they then go out when the hapless climber arrives halfway between floors. The 'light sabre' not being much use on the light front, Bernard tried holding the switch with the baguette as he mounted the stairs and then suddenly swinging it round in an attempt to press the next switch in front of him when he was halfway up the stairs, all with very predictable results.

Eventually he arrived at the door of his attic, but even though it had got bent on the way home the baguette wouldn't fit through the opening sideways. Not having the forethought to try the vertical approach instead of the horizontal, Bernard sat down on the step outside the room to devise a plan. A brilliant idea formed – all those years with the top engineers in the world had not been wasted – and he held the baguette so that the centreline of the loaf was in line with the centreline of the door. He pushed the baguette against the door jambs so they made a mark just in from each end of the baguette, and he then proceeded to eat one end of the baguette to its mark before turning it round and doing the same at the other side. Delighted with his engineering solution, he made it into the room and both he and the remains of the baguette fell into a self-satisfied if slightly crumby sleep.

It seems incredible that, on his final trip to Magny-Cours, he was in trouble again. The French police didn't like people speeding and they didn't like people using their mobile phones while driving; some people say that they didn't much like the English either, so when a long-haired Englishman went through a speed trap while talking on his mobile it follows that there was about to be a problem. Bernard was pulled over and told to hand them his licence and then follow a police motorcycle to a lay-by. The police bike was going far quicker than Bernard had been when he was stopped, but that didn't seem to count. He was fined on the spot, an amount that conveniently coincided with the Euros he had in his wallet, and he was told his licence would be sent back to him in England. Grumbling, Bernard went back to his hire car and was told he couldn't drive it.

'Why not?'

'Because you have no licence.'

'But you've got it.'

Another Gallic shrug with the shoulders and mouth and he was left at the side of the motorway, with no visible means of support. Bernard rang the track and got David McMillan, the Cosworth truckie, to pick him up, but of course the news reached the track before he did; the Formula 1 humorists constantly stopped him for 'speeding in the pit lane'. The bad news was that he had to go to a meeting in the centre of Paris on the Monday following the race with Tony Purnell, the Jaguar team principal, and as Tony was preparing a presentation in the back seat of the car Bernard had to drive all the way into the Place de la Concorde while officially banned from driving. He was not impressed.

Bernard's French troubles didn't even go away when

he retired. He was staying in the south of France with his family and after they had dinner in town one night he was breathalysed; fortunately it proved negative.

There are so many more stories, but I think I'd better save those for a sequel.

Gastone

Gastone has had a mention before, when he replaced Gaetano as the Benetton driver, but he is such an interesting guy he can't get away with it that easily. Gastone appeared in the paddock in the 1980s, and on the surface of it he worked for Fiamm, a battery company, which at that time supplied a lot of the Formula 1 teams. As an accredited supplier Fiamm were allowed to advertise around each racetrack at Formula 1 events and Gastone used to arrive early in the week before each race, as we all did. He drove a yellow Fiamm van carrying the company banners and it was his job to go around the track and display these banners where the TV would pick them up. Gastone carried a bicycle in the back of the van to help him get around. Once coverage started he would watch the television avidly from the nearest available Italian team motorhome and then, during the night, he would pedal off to adjust the position of his advertisements to make sure they had the best possible TV exposure. During the race weekend he appeared to sleep in the van and he had his meals with any Italian team that would supply them, often popping into Benetton for a coffee.

This became more regular when he was employed by Flavio to drive the truck from Italy. We were never quite sure how he seemed to know Flavio so well. He couldn't speak any English, but with our limited Italian we managed to communicate, and he always helped us to construct and dismantle the truck awnings when he had time between his Fiamm duties. When we raced in Monza Fiamm always held a large function on Saturday evening and Gastone used to invite Stu and I, Bob and Shaune from McLaren, and Tim and Maureen from Williams.

Although we often arrived late, because we had to feed the lads, there was always a fine Italian meal awaiting us as well as a gift; we were often seated with some high-ranking Fiamm bosses and Gastone always appeared to be on the door.

Gastone had an amazing photograph album that was passed around the guests and we always stared in amazement at the pictures it contained. The photos showed Gastone with some of the most famous people imaginable. There were pictures of him meeting the Pope (but we did think perhaps the Pope was being introduced to Gastone); he was shown at the shoulder of Prince Rainier at Monaco, and also with Enzo Ferrari and Gianni Agnelli, the head of Fiat. He was photographed with dozens of drivers, footballers from Juventus and AC Milan as well as famous film stars. It was an astonishing album; he seemed to be able to appear in photos with anyone he wanted. We often discussed just how he got so many photo opportunities and, for that matter, how he managed to get the six of us invited to the Fiamm dinners for high rollers.

We'd always thought Gastone had a lowly paid manual job at Fiamm and we tried to help him out because he was a terrific guy – to the extent that, at the end of the Grand Prix weekend, we often gave him food to take to his home, which he always accepted gracefully. It wasn't until the early 1990s we found out the truth and it was quite a shock. Just prior to our arrival at Monza we had been watching the TV news and there was some coverage of a mini-hurricane which had hit the Milan area; a huge tree had fallen on a very lovely, very large house in the suburbs. When Gastone arrived at the circuit he came to see us, as normal, and although neither of us had progressed much on the language front we guessed from conversation he was referring to the hurricane in Milan. We made all the appropriately sympathetic noises and told him we had seen it on TV. Then, like pulling a rabbit from a hat, he produced the exact photo we had seen on TV with the tree lying across the roof of a house, with its branches across a Mercedes, a Porsche and some Ferraris. He said 'Mia casa' and pointed to himself. In total amazement, we fetched his friend from Minardi who spoke some English and he explained this was Gastone's house and his car collection. It became apparent that he was not the gopher we'd thought he was but an important executive at Fiamm, which accounted for our dinner invitations; he just loved to be at the track doing his advertising banners. For years he had driven our truck and helped us build our hospitality facility without a word of complaint, and to add insult to injury we had been giving him food parcels that he had been too polite to refuse. We were mortified. He had befriended us all and not given any hint of the chap he really was. What a star.

Pasquale Lattuneddu,
paddock parking warden and policeman

Generally we have tried to describe all the people with whom we have had a positive experience in the paddock, but not everyone was a great person. I thought I might mention someone who became the most unpopular chap in Formula 1 with the motorhomers, although my writing partner gets on with him just fine, as do various other people.

I should explain. Each team was allocated an area in the paddock where they had to park their trucks and coaches. In principle, the garages are allocated in the order in which the team finished the previous season's championship, so the champions are at one end of the pit lane and the wooden-spoon team at the other. The teams' trucks park behind their allocated garage areas and the hospitality vehicles, where possible, are behind them on the opposite side of a designated main walkway through the paddock. The team personnel need to be close to both vehicles and to the garage, a very sensible arrangement that continues to this day.

In the early years, when we motorhomers arrived at a paddock, we generally had an idea where to park. However, we were not admitted until the Wednesday before the race as the circuit officials were not allowed to 'park us up' until the parking plan arrived. For some years Alan Woollard, who worked for the Formula 1 Constructors' Association, had the job of organising the parking and it generally worked admirably. Alan treated us all like sensible people and if he knew he was going to be late arriving at the circuit, and realising that this would cause us problems with our setting-up schedule, he used to send the plan through on a fax to one of us. Alan started arriving late on a regular basis so Stuart and Bob McMurray took charge of parking, when necessary, and it worked well because Alan trusted us all not to exceed our allocated area (although some foreign teams did sometimes pinch a bit extra).

It was all going well and then one season this guy called Pasquale arrived on the scene. Rumours were that Bernie's wife, Slavica, had met him when he was working in a bar she frequented and had got Bernie to offer him a job. He was to be the new parking warden, and he also became the new paddock policeman. He treated us all like idiots and, to compound the problem, he usually arrived late so we couldn't park and get ourselves set up before the team arrived. He had no concept of our jobs and was completely uninterested in our difficulties. Despite the fact quite a few of the motorhomers had been in Formula 1 for many years, he was quite obnoxious to us all.

Pasquale's other job was to issue passes to team personnel, and he revelled in his power to keep people waiting, with even team managers queuing for their respective passes. It was humiliating for everyone concerned. If a team asked for guest passes it was as though they were asking for the crown jewels. On the odd occasion Pasquale authorised Stuart to park everyone up, and Stu tried to do this as well as he could in order to help everyone out. However, Pasquale would often turn up on Thursday and tell a team their hospitality unit was two inches over their allocated area and then make them move everything – awning, chairs, tables, the whole lot – which was a mammoth task.

Pasquale is still in Formula 1, but I hope for everyone's sake he's mellowed.

Parking attendant at Imola

Notwithstanding our parking difficulties at other venues, there was one circuit where we all loved going because it was so well organised for our arrival. The officials had always asked for the plan in advance and we were admitted on arrival, which was generally a Tuesday evening. The first night we used to park in any space, then on Wednesday morning two young men would arrive with a copy of the plan and shepherd us into our areas. They were very pleasant young chaps and we became quite friendly with them, to the point where we used to have dinner with them in Imola town when we were all able to get away. Imola was excellent because not only could we walk into town from the motorhome, but we were also trusted to the extent that we were given a key to the paddock to let ourselves back in after a night out.

These young men welcomed us for about three years; it was their part-time job while they were at Bologna University. One of them found out we were trying to make time to look for some bathroom tiles from Imola Ceramica to take back to the UK. Imola Ceramica was a cooperative and residents of Imola received good discounts, so one of the chaps took Stu and me to the tile factory where we bought our tiles with his family discount card. He also told us his dream one day was to work at Ferrari and that was what he was studying for.

What was the name on the discount card? Domenicali! And his first name was Stefano, the future team principal of Scuderia Ferrari. It was a pleasure to meet him then, and it still is because he has always been a genuinely nice chap.

David Gambs, Alfred Bull Awnings

Everyone who has visited a paddock, particularly in the earlier days, will have noticed awnings attached to trucks and motorhomes. Most of these awnings came from a company called Alfred Bull Awnings, based near Guildford. The company was bought in the 1930s by David Gambs's grandmother and run by David's father. The company's original business was to hire out marquees for private and corporate events. David had joined the RAF, but after leaving he joined the company and decided to start manufacturing awnings that could be attached to the sides of vehicles, with bespoke fittings.

David first visited a paddock in 1958 in Germany and met Mike Hawthorn, and was instantly bitten by the racing bug. He decided that it was an area in which he could develop his business. Ten years later he received a call from Rob Walker Racing, asking if he had any method of keeping the team dry at events. David was always good with cryptic comments and immediately said 'Wear a hat,' but as he was not in the hat business he decided it would be better for his company if he developed a wooden frame covered by a cotton fabric that attached to the motorhome and did the job instead.

This first attempt was seen by none other than Bruce McLaren, the legendary racing car driver and constructor who founded the McLaren organisation, who asked for something similar to the awning Rob Walker was using. David had progressed to using a synthetic material and steel frame for his awnings and that's what Bruce was to receive. Ken Tyrrell, in turn, saw Bruce's awning and it went on from there. In 1976 Ron Dennis asked David to do a rush job for a race in Hockenheim and said if he did it within a week he could go as a guest to the race. This was an opportunity not to be missed and David hit the deadline, but his joy was to be short lived when the German police swept in and all the team's equipment was impounded, including the new awnings. Apparently the team's current engine builder had not been paid and he wanted the trucks and all the equipment seized to cover the debt. David had plunged into the murky waters of Formula 1 big time. Ron sorted it, though, and all was resolved reasonably amicably.

By 1976 the Americans had heard of Alfred Bull Awnings and David received a visit from a member of an American IMSA (International Motor Sports Association) team which was the start of a marathon flying and measuring episode: he flew half a million miles, taking measurements of motorhomes in order to supply awnings to a number of American race teams who, apparently, had a job understanding the quaint Englishman's accent and sense of humour. Fortunately the teams had a few Aussie and Kiwi staff and they helped out. The same thing then happened with a Japanese team owner, so David spent time in Japan making awnings, in between spending hours enjoying himself in Tokyo sushi bars – and why not!

His final job before retiring was making a large percentage of the latest Ferrari motorhome construction and while he was at the Ferrari factory, working on the project, the Ferrari management let him ride a motorcycle around Fiorano. In his time David had dealings with most Formula 1 teams and they always gave him a hard time wanting awnings 'yesterday'. He has had experiences with Paul Newman's race team, and a Porsche team at Sebring who were raided by the drug squad, as the programme was being run on drug money; he water skied at Watkins Glen after fitting an awning for March Racing, and he has had a lifetime of escapades. He sounds like Action Man, but David preferred the title of 'Mr Awning Man', a name conferred on him by former Formula 1 driver Eddie Cheever.

We had many dealings with David in our time in motorsport and we always found him amusing – sometimes infuriating, because we didn't always know exactly where we stood with him – but generally Stuart and I think we got on well with 'Gambsy', as he was known in the paddock. Whenever the season was about to start everyone was always chasing him for completion, each team thinking they were the most important one he had to deal with, even if their order had been placed very late. David always said, 'Can't possibly do it by then.' But he always did.

Other companies used to come and go in competition with Alfred Bull, but there was never anything as good as 'a Gambsy awning'. I used to marvel at his skills, considering I can't even sew a pocket handkerchief. Where would race teams have been without Gambsy? Wet, I suppose.

Fred della Noce

Fred della Noce was Rubens Barrichello's manager, and he used to spend a lot of time with us when Rubens was driving for Stewart Grand Prix. At one particular race weekend in 1999 Fred was looking pretty troubled – all through Friday, and again on Saturday morning, he looked as though he wanted to say something to me but couldn't get around to saying it. Eventually he came to see me just as I was up to my eyes in washing up and said, 'Di, do you think I could have a word with you?'

I had to tell him that I'd be happy to have a chat but asked if he could come back later, as I was really busy just then. A few hours later he knocked on the motorhome door as I was preparing the evening meal, and again I was busy, but he looked so agitated that I couldn't turn him down. We went to the awning and sat at a corner table, and I asked him what on earth was the matter. He looked me straight in the eye and said, in a really solemn tone, 'Rubens has been offered a drive by Ferrari, starting next year, but do you think he will be able to cope with being in the same team as Michael Schumacher?'

I looked at him in amazement. Why on earth, of all the people in the paddock he could have spoken to, had he asked me? I just made the tea!

EPILOGUE

In the early chapters we described our first foray into hospitality and the very first 'motorhome' we had. The 23ft-long Dodge Superior with its little kitchenette, tiny bedroom, roll-out awning and hot and cold running mice was our home, transport, storage and catering facility, not to mention management office. Even in the heady days of the late 1970s we knew that this was perhaps erring on the small side, but we coped with it – well, just about. We could drive it (when it hadn't broken down), erect it ourselves and keep our small team fed and watered from it, so it sufficed.

Times have changed in Formula 1. Budgets have rocketed and motorhomes have become a statement in the form of lavish structures, as well as serving a function, despite the fact that they are used at fewer races each year as the events move out of Europe and become global. The face of the paddock has altered beyond recognition as an 'arms race' in hospitality facilities has developed, particularly between Red Bull, McLaren and Ferrari. The concept of a married couple driving around Europe in a vehicle, feeding the team and providing hospitality has become an anachronism, passing almost unnoticed in the whirlwind of development and technology that is today's Formula 1.

The size of the change can be illustrated by some simple statistics on the logistics of getting the Red Bull 'Energy Station' ready to operate at a Grand Prix:

- It takes 48 trucks to carry the various pieces of the structure to the racetrack.
- When the trucks arrive it takes two of the biggest mobile cranes in Europe to lift everything into place.

- It takes 50 riggers to assemble the building.
- The riggers need two 'cherry pickers' to work safely at height.
- A dedicated hospitality facility is shipped in to feed the 50 riggers while they work.
- Two 150km/h generators are in use, producing enough power for 25 households to be watching TV while boiling a kettle.
- The structure takes three days to build and commission.
- For Monaco, the structure, complete with a rooftop swimming pool, is built either in Italy or Antibes, and floated around the coast to dock in Monaco harbour.

Apparently size matters in lots of teams now. They have become slicker, bigger and more professional, but in the process the whole thing has become impersonal. We used to become embedded in the drivers' lives, but I don't think that happens quite so much now as drivers are surrounded by personal trainers, dieticians, PR people and the like. Most teams don't have 'Mum and Dad' figures to look out for them anymore, and now I'm not sure if anyone knows who it is that makes the tea.

Authors'
Acknowledgements

Stuart and I have worked together in motorsport 24 hours a day for over 32 years, and we are still happily married – which some people might find incredible! So my sincere thanks to him, as without him there would have been no opportunity to 'make tea' in Formula 1. I am also grateful for his support while writing this book.

I want to give a 'Very Big Thank You' to Bernard Ferguson for writing this book with me. We spent many hours together writing and reminiscing, we had fun and laughter, so I hope he hasn't regretted his decision to help! Also thanks to his wife Sue for her patience whilst he was burning the midnight oil.

Thanks are due to Peter Briggs and John Surtees for having enough faith in 1978 to offer us our first contract. It led to a job that encompassed our love of motorsport and travel, and lasted for many fulfilling years.

Thanks also to our friends from earlier years who supported us by taking an interest in our new life. Many thanks, too, to the team members, fellow motorhomers, photographers, journalists, PR people and drivers who helped make the job enjoyable – forgive me for not mentioning you all by name. And thank you to all our staff who worked with us during our three decades in motorsport – you all made our job easier.

We have been fortunate to visit many countries and to have had many wonderful experiences, meeting people from all walks of life and making many lasting friendships, particularly with fellow motorhomers, photographer and journalist James and Mary Jo Campion, and – from the very early days – Theresa Kirby, Janette Galbraith and Annie Bradshaw.

Di Spires

Thanks to Stuart Banks of Stuart Banks Engineering for his visualisation of the infamous 'Lung Tester', and to Sue Ferguson who worked so hard on editing my grammar and correcting my 'spooling mistrucks'!

Bernard Ferguson

ABOUT THE AUTHORS

DI SPIRES, with her husband Stuart, worked in motorsport for 30 years running a succession of team motorhomes, including those of Lotus in the Senna era and Benetton in the Schumacher years. Before that she was a civil servant at the Department of Employment with a role in industrial relations, which involved time at British Leyland's Longbridge plant dealing with the likes of Derek 'Red Robbo' Robinson.

BERNARD FERGUSON left his native Lancashire in the late 1960s, drawn to the Midlands by the lure of the motor industry. Following spells with Rootes, Chrysler, Peugeot and the infamous DeLorean organisation, he joined Cosworth where he worked for 23 years before retiring from his position of Director of Motorsport. He also served as the engine manufacturers' representative on the Formula One Commission.

INDEX

INDEX